APEC
as an
institution

The **Institute of Southeast Asian Studies (ISEAS)** was established as an autonomous organization in 1968. It is a regional research centre for scholars and other specialists concerned with modern Southeast Asia, particularly the many-faceted problems of stability and security, economic development, and political and social change.

The Institute's research programmes are the Regional Economic Studies (RES, including ASEAN and APEC), Regional Strategic and Political Studies (RSPS), and Regional Social and Cultural Studies (RSCS).

The Institute is governed by a Board of Trustees comprising nominees from the Singapore Government, the National University of Singapore, the various Chambers of Commerce, and professional and civic organizations. A ten-man Executive Committee oversees day-to-day operations; it is chaired by the Director, the Institute's chief academic and administrative officer.

APEC

as an institution

Multilateral Governance in the Asia-Pacific

Edited by
Richard E. Feinberg

Institute of Southeast Asian Studies
Singapore

A Project of the APEC International Assessment Network (APIAN)

First published in Singapore by
Institute of Southeast Asian Studies
30 Heng Mui Keng Terrace
Pasir Panjang
Singapore 119614
E-mail: publish@iseas.edu.sg
Website: http://bookshop.iseas.edu.sg

ISEAS Library Cataloguing-in-Publication Data

APEC as an institution: multilateral governance in the Asia-Pacific/
edited by Richard E. Feinberg.
1. Asia Pacific Economic Cooperation.
2. Technological innovations—Asia.
3. Technological innovations—Pacific Area.
4. Asia—Commercial policy.
5. Pacific Area—Commercial policy.
6. Asia—Economic policy.
7. Pacific Area—Economic policy.
8. Asia—Strategic aspects.
9. Pacific Area—Strategic aspects.
10. Non-governmental organizations.
I. Feinberg, Richard E.
II. Institute of Southeast Asian Studies.
HF1583 A839   2003   sls2003002149

ISBN 981-230-209-3

Typeset by Superskill Graphics Pte Ltd
Printed in Singapore by Seng Lee Press Pte Ltd.

CONTENTS

THE CONTRIBUTORS

Richard E. Feinberg (Project Co-ordinator) is Director of the APEC Study Center, Graduate School of International Relations and Pacific Studies (IR/PS), University of California, San Diego, USA.

Hadi Soesastro is Executive Director of the Centre for Strategic and International Studies in Jakarta, Indonesia.

David McDuff is Research Analyst of the Asia Pacific Foundation of Canada.

Yuen Pau Woo is Vice President, Research and Chief Economist of the Asia Pacific Foundation of Canada.

Stewart Goodings is Executive Director of BCIT International, British Columbia Institute of Technology, Canada.

Joseph M. Damond is Associate Vice President of Japan and Asia Pacific, PhRMA (US).

Robert Scollay is Director of the APEC Study Centre at the University of Auckland, New Zealand.

Ippei Yamazawa is Professor and President of the Institute of Developing Economies, Japan.

Myrna S. Austria is Director of the Centre for Business and Economic Research and Development, De La Salle University, Philippines.

Medhi Krongkaew is Professor of Development Economics at the National Institute of Development and Administration (NIDA) in Bangkok, Thailand.

Nigel Haworth is Deputy Director of the APEC Study Centre at the University of Auckland, New Zealand.

Michael C. Mullen was Director of the National Centre for APEC in Seattle, Washington. He is presently an Associate at Booz Allen Hamilton, a major consulting firm in Washington.

John McKay is Director of the Australian APEC Study Centre and the Monash Asia Institute, Monash University, Australia.

GLOSSARY

ABAC	APEC Business Advisory Council
AELM	APEC Economic Leaders' Meeting
AFTA	ASEAN Free Trade Area
AGGI	Advisory Group on Gender Integration
APIAN	APEC International Assessment Network
ARF	ASEAN Regional Forum
ASCM	Agreement on Subsidies and Countervailing Measures
ATCWG	Agricultural Technology Co-operation Working Group
ATL	Accelerated Tariff Liberalization
BMC	Budget and Management Committee
BMN	Business Management Network
CAP	Collective Action Plan
CBMs	confidence-building measures
CBN	Capacity Building Network
CER	Closer Economic Relations
CGE	computable general equilibrium
CGP	Centre for Global Partnership
COW	Committee of the Whole
CSCAP	Council for Security Co-operation in the Asia-Pacific
CTI	Committee on Trade and Investment
EAP	ECOTECH Action Plan
ECOTECH	economic and technical co-operation
EDFOR	Education Forum
EDNET	Education Network
EDRC	Economic and Development Review Committee
EPG	Eminent Persons Group

ESC	Subcommittee for Economic and Technical Co-operation
ETC	ECOTECH Committee
EVSL	Early Voluntary Sectoral Liberalization
FDI	foreign direct investment
GATS	General Agreement on Trade in Services
GATT	General Agreement on Tariffs and Trade
GEI	Group on Economic Infrastructure
HCB	human capacity building
HCBCG	Human Capacity Building Co-ordination Group
HLM	High Level Meeting
HRD	human resource development
HRDWG	Human Resource Development Working Group
HURDIT	Industry Technology Network
IAP	Individual Action Plan
IEG	Investment Experts Group
ISTWG	Industrial Science and Technology Working Group
ITA	Information Technology Agreement
LCD	least common denominator
LMI	Labour Market Information Network
LSPN	Labour and Social Protection Network
MAFF	Ministry of Agriculture, Forestry and Fisheries
MAI	Multilateral Agreement on Investment
MAPA	Manila Action Plan
MFN	most-favoured-nation
MRA	Mutual Recognition Arrangement
NAFTA	North American Free Trade Agreement
NATO	North Atlantic Treaty Organization
NBIP	non-binding investment principles
NEDM	Economic Development Management Network
NIEs	newly industrializing economies
NPT	Nuclear Non-Proliferation Treaty
NTMs	non-tariff measures
OAA	Osaka Action Agenda
OAS	Organization of American States
OECD	Organization for Economic Co-operation and Development
PBEC	Pacific Basin Economic Council
PECC	Pacific Economic Co-operation Council
PSM	professional staff member
PTAs	preferential trade agreements
RTA	regional trade agreements
SEC	ECOTECH Subcommittee

SME	small and medium enterprises
SMEWG	Small and Medium Enterprises Working Group
SOM	Senior Officials' Meeting
SRTA	subregional trade agreement
TAC	Treaty of Amity and Co-operation
TILF	trade and investment liberalization and facilitation
TOR	terms of reference
TRIMs	Trade-Related Investment Measures
TRIPs	Trade-Related Aspects of Intellectual Property Rights
WTO	World Trade Organization

INTRODUCTION

This book is the second major research project of the APEC International Assessment Network (APIAN), the first being *Assessing APEC's Progress: Trade, Ecotech and Institutions* (Singapore: Institute of Southeast Asian Studies, 2001). That first effort focused principally upon the substantive agenda of the Asia-Pacific Economic Cooperation (APEC) forum, but did include an article by Vinod Aggarwal and Kun-Chin Lin on "APEC as an Institution". Aggarwal and Lin concluded that "the most significant contributions of APEC have been in agenda-setting and socialization of member economies into the acceptance of global norms and principles" (p. 178) — and that institutional weaknesses have limited APEC's ability to fulfill its more ambitious substantive goals in the areas of trade and investment liberalization and integration, economic and technical co-operation and capacity building. Drawing on questionnaires circulated to experts throughout the Asia-Pacific as well as their own research, Aggarwal and Lin found a credibility gap between APEC's formal agenda and goals and its institutional capacities to realize them.

APIAN's first policy report, *Learning From Experience* (November 2000), began to tackle APEC's institutional structure. It recognized that APEC's institutional weaknesses were not haphazard but rather were purposeful acts by those present at the creation. For reasons deeply imbedded in the history and structure of the Asia-Pacific, APEC's founding members preferred a relatively loose organizational structure that would not be able to impose its collective will upon reluctant members, but rather would respect national sovereignties. APEC was organized around the core principles of consensus, voluntarism, and unilateralism — and eschewed binding agreements with strict timetables that could be rigorously monitored by agents that would seek to enforce compliance. APEC established a weak secretariat whose functions were primarily logistical; there would be no large permanent bureaucracy that might drive APEC in ways that diverged from the preferences of some of its members.

At the same time, this first APIAN policy report noted that however "soft", APEC has evolved into an institution:

> Brick by brick, APEC has been constructing its edifice. During its first decade, APEC has created a set of norms, procedures and structures that define its essence: the goal of free trade and investment flows within a paradigm of open regionalism; capacity-building through economic and technical cooperation; agreement through consensus; action by each member at its own pace; annual Leaders Meetings and regularly scheduled Ministerials that set direction, committees of senior officials that drive the process, and an array of working groups responsible for specific programmes and projects. APEC has established its special place in the panoply of international institutions (p. 4).

The report went on to argue that while this soft institutionalism served APEC well during its infancy, as APEC enters its second decade, it should reconsider the degree of its soft institutionalism: "What may have been realistic at the outset may have become an avoidable obstacle to further achievement. What may have seemed hopelessly idealistic at the beginning may have become more feasible as members gain confidence in APEC and in each other" (p. 5).

In this spirit, APIAN chose to make APEC's institutionalization the central focus of its second research project. This book is the result of that ambition. Draft papers were first presented and debated at the Annual APEC Study Center International Consortium Meeting in Merida, Yucatan, Mexico, on 22–24 May 2002. We have defined "institution" to encompass formal structures (bricks and mortar) as well as rules and norms, "soft" informal undertakings and declarations, and periodic meetings such as working groups, ministerials, and summits. Our inspiration comes not only from a belief that a more robust institutional framework might more effectively help APEC approximate its laudable goals, but also from an appreciation of the potential of APEC's uniquely post-modern virtuality. Instead of a strong, central bureaucracy, APEC has organized its activities around semi-autonomous ministerial meetings and working groups that keep in touch intersessionally via electronic means. In line with modern theories of efficient management, this non-traditional decentralized functionalism places power in the hands of the member countries' functional bureaucracies. However, as APIAN researchers discovered, APEC's decentralized functionalism is not without its disadvantages: it inhibits strategic planning and prioritization, tends to scatter efforts across an ever expanding range of topics, makes accountability more difficult and, at least in the APEC case, weakens fund-raising capacity.

The capstone of this APIAN project, and the first chapter in this book, "Remaking APEC as an Institution", offers a series of reform proposals — in management, governance, stakeholder relations, product, and finance — that are endorsed by thirty-three experts from APEC Study Centres in sixteen APEC member economies. The intent is to give APEC the capacity to adapt more rapidly to the swirl of events, to increase its credibility among international institutions, to grow its constituencies, to better brand its products and to more effectively leverage its resources. Our proposals are meant to be realistic, in that they recognize that some of the problems confronting the Asia-Pacific are rooted in global structures or domestic politics and are beyond the reach of APEC as an institution, and that various APEC members remain wary of granting APEC *qua* APEC too much power. Our proposals do not entail large budgets or big bureaucracies; rather, we seek to build on APEC's strengths as an idea-driven, decentralized institution.

Many officials participating in APEC are cognizant of its institutional shortcomings. This consciousness gives us reason to believe that our reform proposals will find an audience within APEC, so that we can reinforce and strengthen the reformers within official circles already advocating for gradual change. Institutional reform has become a regular theme at meetings of APEC Senior Officials (SOM), and the APEC Secretariat has commissioned more than one study to examine its own internal problems. We are pleased to record that APEC's Senior Officials invited APIAN representatives to brief them on the findings and recommendations of this study on two occasions — at their meetings in Merida, Mexico, on 25 May, and in Acapulco, Mexico, on 21 August 2002. Numerous APEC officials have been quick to welcome our efforts as valuable contributions to an active internal debate. In addition, the officially sanctioned APEC Business Advisory Council (ABAC) requested a briefing on this study at their meeting in Los Cabos, Mexico, just prior to the October 2002 Leaders' Meeting.

This book is organized into six major sections. Part I contains the APIAN Policy Report III, "Remaking APEC as an Institution," that was first circulated at SOM III 2002 in Acapulco. A collaborative effort, the Report's findings and recommendations are based on the research done for the chapters that make up the rest of the volume, and express the consensus of the authors and other signatories to the Report. Part II offers an overview of the origins and evolution of APEC, and a comparative study of APEC and another international institution, the Organization for Economic Co-operation and Development (OECD). Part III delves into the inner workings of APEC, focusing on the APEC Secretariat and the Budget and Management Committee (responsible for reviewing projects that the specialized APEC forums have approved for funding). Part IV investigates APEC's core agenda — trade and investment liberalization and facilitation (TILF), and economic and technical co-operation (ECOTECH) — with specific attention to the institutional procedures whereby APEC manages these substantive matters. Part V explores APEC's interactions with civil society, including the private sector, non-governmental organizations, academia, and the public policy research community. Finally, Part VI takes a preliminary look at how APEC might expand its agenda to engage regional security concerns.

The authors are participants in APIAN, a collaborative, independent project among participating APEC Study Centres whose mission is to encourage the fulfilment of APEC objectives and commitments, and to identify ways for APEC to improve its performance. With this publication, APIAN will have completed two books and three policy reports. We wish to acknowledge the invaluable support of the Center for Global Partnership (CGP) of the Japan Foundation and the Institute on Global Conflict and Co-operation (IGCC) of the University of California. We wish to thank also the Rockerfeller Brothers' Fund for funding the publication of this book. Without the administrative expertise of Martha R. Garcia, this volume would never have made it across the finish line. We are also deeply grateful for the encouragement, efficiency, and good cheer of our colleagues at the Institute of Southeast Asian Studies (ISEAS).

Richard E. Feinberg
La Jolla, California
September 2002

SECTION I

POLICY REPORT

1

REMAKING APEC AS AN INSTITUTION
The Third APIAN Policy Report

EXECUTIVE SUMMARY

This third Policy Report of the APEC International Assessment Network (APIAN) assesses the strengths and weaknesses of APEC as an institution and proposes reforms to enhance its efficiency and effectiveness.

We fear that APEC, despite its many accomplishments, has been losing ground. Yet, many of the reasons that drove APEC's creation remain valid today. Therefore, we urge APEC to do much more to get its own institutional house in better order.

Structures that may have been adequate in 1989 for an infant organization are now insufficient as APEC enters into its adolescence. Norms that were practical a decade ago are now damaging constraints that are preventing APEC from adjusting to new realities.

APEC's management structures have grown both too complex and too weak to meet the needs of a growing organization and requires a thorough overhaul.

APEC's decision-making rules, which require 100 per cent agreement, often producing paralysis, should be made more flexible.

APEC's outreach, which in earlier years was a source of strength, has languished, precisely when the private sector, academic experts, and other civil society actors are gaining weight in global diplomacy.

APEC's product has become scattered. APEC needs to clarify its roles in market liberalization, in economic co-operation, and in policy development.

APEC's financial structure is woefully inadequate in comparison with APEC's goals and objectives.

Without reform, APEC will lose its competitiveness *vis-à-vis* alternative multilateral forums towards which APEC constituents will shift their energies. With reform, APEC will be better positioned to fulfill its promise and to help restore dynamism and confidence to the Asia–Pacific region.

Management Reform

To strengthen APEC's management and its Secretariat, we propose these options for consideration:

- *The Executive Director should be a prominent figure that speaks for APEC, and who serves a multi-year term.*
- *Internal management of the Secretariat could be strengthened* by creating a permanent senior level position responsible for management, possibly supplemented by a new level of permanent middle manager specialists.
- *Experts should be hired on a multi-year basis to organize the critical tasks of research and evaluation.* A renowned scholar should lead an economic research division capable of mobilizing the research skills of academics and experts from the region.

The proposed marginal growth in the Secretariat would require modest additional resources. An increase in professional and administrative staff by 50 per cent would cost roughly $2 million more per year — a small fraction of the tens of millions of dollars that it costs just to host the annual Leaders' Meeting.

Governance Reform

- *We strongly endorse the pathfinder approach as proclaimed by the Leaders in their Shanghai Declaration and Accord.* As APEC moves from statements of principle to plans of action, decision-making based upon "flexible consensus" and "coalitions of the willing" will enable APEC to regain momentum.
- *APEC should immediately apply the pathfinder approach to already approved "statements of principle."* For example, the Non-binding Investment Principles could be implemented by a coalition of the willing. Similarly, the APEC Principles on Trade Facilitation could be readily transformed into an action agenda.

Stakeholder Relations Reform

In a globalizing world where power is increasingly diffused and the efficient sharing of tacit knowledge requires personal contact, the success of multilateral institutions depends importantly upon their openness to groups outside the government. We offer these recommendations for deepening APEC's roots in its own societies:

- *APEC should further clarify its guidelines for participation to offer a more positive welcome to civil society.* In the meantime, the APEC Secretariat and the Chairs of the Committee on Trade and Investment (CTI) and ECOTECH (economic and technical) Subcommittee should actively encourage APEC forums to implement the newly decentralized process for civil society participation.
- *The Secretariat should add staff capacity to serve as a point of co-ordination with the private sector and other non-governmental groups.* Such an appointment should not, however, be considered a substitute for mainstreaming civil society participation throughout APEC forums and activities.
- *APEC should develop a responsive process for evaluating recommendations from the APEC Business Advisory Council (ABAC).* APEC should include ABAC in ministerial and Senior Official Meetings in a more meaningful way that goes beyond receiving a formal briefing from the ABAC Chair.

Product Reform

APEC has developed a very broad array of laudable goals and initiatives. Yet, its resources — financial and political — fall far short of what would be required to seriously attempt to achieve these many ambitious objectives. It is time for APEC to clarify for itself and in the public mind its core missions and functions.

To consolidate APEC programmes and products, we recommend:

- *APEC should recognize more explicitly that policy development is one of its core missions.* If the global profile of the Leaders' Meeting could be paired with a programme of substantive policy research led by a strengthened Secretariat, APEC would have the ingredients for a substantial renewal of its relevance and credibility.
- *APEC should thoroughly reorganize its ECOTECH activities and establish strategic priorities that include human resource development.* Consideration should be given to making the ECOTECH Subcommittee a full

committee to enhance its authority to co-ordinate working groups and to engage non-APEC international institutions and civil society actors.

- *APEC projects should be designed as models which, if successful, should induce others to copy them many times over.* In the light of their small size, if APEC projects are to yield a measurable impact on key development indicators, they should be conceived of as demonstration projects to be replicated by other funders.

- *In trade and investment liberalization and facilitation (TILF), APEC should seize the opportunity to contribute to the Doha Millennium Round by advancing its work on the Singapore issues.* APEC has long-standing work programmes on the so-called "Singapore issues" that are on the Doha agenda: competition policy, investment, trade facilitation, and government procurement. In turn, progress in the World Trade Organization (WTO) should enable APEC to transform some of its voluntary principles into WTO-endorsed bound actions.

Financial Reform

To mobilize more resources behind APEC initiatives, and to make better use of member economies' contributions, we advance the following suggestions:

- *APEC should make more systematic efforts to leverage its projects.* To encourage project co-financing, the APEC Secretariat might house liaison officers seconded from capital-rich institutions, including the Asian Development Bank and World Bank.

- *Other APEC economies should join Japan in contributing to the APEC Central Fund.*

- *APEC must rationalize its financial structure.* A more efficient APEC institution would allow member economies to work out ways of transferring expenditures on travel and per diem for APEC meetings to expenditures for a strengthened Secretariat and for funding high-impact projects that advance priority APEC goals.

PREFACE

This is the third Policy Report of the APEC International Assessment Network (APIAN). The first two Reports, *Learning From Experience* (2000), and *APIAN Update: Shanghai, Los Cabos and Beyond* (2001) examined the two main pillars of APEC activity: the agendas for trade and investment liberalization and facilitation (TILF), and economic and technical assistance (ECOTECH). This report assesses the strengths and weaknesses of APEC as an institution and proposes reforms to enhance its efficiency and effectiveness. We define "institution" to encompass formal structures (bricks and mortar) as well as rules and norms, "soft" informal undertakings and declarations, and periodic meetings such as working groups, ministerials and summits.

To examine APEC as an institution, APIAN assembled an experienced research team that included experts at APEC Study Centres, many of whom have had direct involvement in APEC forums, and former APEC practitioners in both TILF and ECOTECH activities. The research team included: Myrna Austria, Joe Damond, Richard Feinberg, Stewart Goodings, Nigel Haworth, Chen-Sheng Ho, Medhi Krongkaew, Manuel Mindreau, David MacDuff, John McKay, Michael Mullen, Robert Scollay, Hadi Soesastro, Yuen Pau Woo, and Ippei Yamazawa. The researchers held a workshop in Merida, Mexico, on 24 May 2002, in conjunction with the annual APEC Study Centre International Consortium Meeting. The revised research papers are published in this volume.[1]

At the request of the Chair of the Senior Officials Meeting (SOM), APIAN presented the preliminary findings of this study to SOM II in Merida on 25 May 2002, and was pleased to receive generally favourable and, in some cases, detailed responses to its proposals. Participants in the oral exchange included officials from Australia, Brunei, Canada, Chile, China, Mexico, New Zealand, Japan, and the United States.

Since its formation in January 1999, APIAN has been guided by its mission statement: APIAN is a collaborative, independent project among participating APEC Study Centres to track and assess the design and execution of select APEC initiatives. APIAN's mission is to enhance knowledge among government officials and the general public with regard to APEC activities, to encourage the fulfilment of APEC objectives and commitments, and to identify ways for APEC to improve its performance.

We would like to express our appreciation to Dr Juan Jose Ramirez-Bonilla, the Chair of the Merida APEC Study Centres' meeting, for graciously hosting the APIAN workshop. We also wish to acknowledge the encouragement and support of the Centre for Global Partnership (CGP) of the Japan Foundation, and of the Institute on Global Conflict and Cooperation (IGCC) of the University of California.

Like the previous two APIAN policy reports, this report is a collaborative effort by a large number of APEC Study Centres from APEC member economies. The participating experts wholeheartedly endorse this report's overall content and tone and support its principal findings and recommendations, even as each participant may not agree fully with every phrase. The participating experts subscribe as individuals; institutional affiliations are for purposes of identification only. The list of signatories can be found in Appendix A. APIAN does not purport to speak for all APEC Study Centres, nor for the international consortium of APEC Study Centres.

INTRODUCTION: LOSING GROUND

As leaders in APEC Study Centres, we fear that APEC, despite its many accomplishments, has been losing ground. Thirteen years after its first ministerial, and ten years after its first Leaders' Meeting, APEC's capacity to adapt is lagging behind the accelerating rate of change that now characterizes the global political economy. To many observers, APEC's laudable core goal of regional free trade seems beyond reach, as the 2010 target date for the achievement of the Bogor goals looms uncomfortably close. While APEC sponsors valuable technical co-operation programmes, their impact is lessened for lack of funds. Too often, APEC meetings are consumed with procedural matters while substance is often diluted by a least-common-denominator diplomacy.

Yet, APEC survives and for good cause. Many of the reasons that drove its creation remain valid today. Strategically, APEC helps to stabilize relations among its diverse membership by providing a unique forum for regular discussions among leaders, ministers, technical experts, and corporate executives. APEC helps to keep the United States engaged in the region, assists the accommodation of China, and facilitates exchange between the wealthier and poorer nations of the region and between East Asia and the nations of North and South America. While it is difficult to measure its precise contributions, APEC has added its weight to those reformers throughout the Asia-Pacific that advocate more open markets and effective government and, especially in recent years, more focus on human-capacity building and a more equitable sharing of the fruits of globalization.

APEC's many committees and working groups facilitate the sharing of experiences and best practices, and through this diffusion of information have become part and parcel of the domestic bureaucratic process of reforms in many countries. Fostering these specialized networks of officials and experts contributes to APEC's central goal of community-building throughout the Asia-Pacific region.

Therefore, despite its problems and disappointments, we believe that APEC adds value to global governance and is worth remaking. We applaud those many APEC officials who have been striving, with some successes, to enhance its effectiveness. However, we urge APEC to do much more to get its own institutional house in better order.

Institutional Reform at the Core

To become a more effective organization, APEC must reform its internal structures and rules. (See Appendix C for APEC's organizational chart.) Structures that may have been adequate in 1989 for an infant organization are now insufficient as APEC enters into its adolescence. Norms that were practical a decade ago are now damaging constraints that are preventing APEC from adjusting to new realities.

APEC's management structures have grown both too complex and too weak to meet the needs of a growing organization and requires a thorough overhaul. APEC's decision-making rules, where the requirement of 100 per cent agreement too often produce paralysis, should be made more flexible. APEC's outreach, which in earlier years was a source of strength, has languished, precisely at a moment in history when the private sector, academic experts, and other civil society actors are gaining weight in global diplomacy. APEC's product has become scattered and often superficial. APEC needs to clarify its roles in market liberalization, in economic co-operation, and in policy development. So as to better match form and function, APEC's institutional structures should be adapted to meet the requirements of its evolving policy agenda and product output. APEC's financial structure is woefully inadequate in comparison with APEC's goals and objectives.

To address these challenges, APEC needs to design and implement its own structural adjustment programme. As with all such efforts at domestic reform, there will be some clashes of vested interests and some temporary pain. However, without reform, APEC will continue to lose competitiveness *vis-à-vis* alternative multilateral forums towards which APEC constituents will shift their energies. With reform, APEC will be better positioned to fulfill its promise and to help restore dynamism and confidence to the Asia-Pacific region.

MANAGEMENT REFORM

From the outset, APEC members chose to keep the Secretariat in Singapore small and weak. Still suspicious of the motives of other members, and uncertain of their own capacities, members did not want to create a strong bureaucracy that might be leveraged by others against their interests. Nor did members want a Secretariat with sufficient resources or influence to become an autonomous force capable of advancing its own agenda. Resource constraints were another factor, as some wealthy countries wanted to avoid yet another drain on scarce budgetary resources available for international affairs, while poor members shirked even very modest impositions. More positively, a decentralized, "virtual" APEC was seen as embodying modern theories of efficient management. Decentralized decision-making has allowed the specialized forums to be creative in their own agendas — and this bottom-up characteristic is one of APEC's strengths.

APIAN has carefully explored parallels between the Organization for Economic Co-operation and Development (OECD) and APEC. We recognize the OECD's virtues, especially in research and formation of policy networks, and believe that APEC could tailor them to the circumstances of the Asia-Pacific without creating such a large bureaucracy. At the same time, APIAN has found that the opposite pole — excessively weak management and the modest scope of the Secretariat — has contributed to a series of problems now plaguing APEC:

- APEC has limited quick-reaction capacity to identify and address new and emerging issues.
- APEC is unable to effectively monitor and evaluate its own work. The self-evaluations performed by APEC forums are generally pro forma, and the Secretariat lacks the resources and the authority to evaluate APEC programmes and projects and to provide critical feedback. Yet, credibility and accountability require independent evaluation of completed APEC projects to determine their cost-effectiveness and impact on APEC objectives.
- APEC has little institutional memory. The top two leaders at the Secretariat are in place for a maximum of two years and the professional staff members are seconded for two to three-year postings.
- APEC lacks its own in-house expertise. The approximately twenty-two professional staff members in the Secretariat are seconded from member economies and are usually generalists coming from the Foreign Affairs or Trade departments of their economies. Their time is consumed with providing logistical assistance to APEC forums and to overseeing projects. A 1995 review of the Secretariat found that it had been unable to provide substantive research and analytical support because of a lack of resources and expertise. This situation has not materially changed.
- APEC does draw upon outside expertise, most notably the high quality work of the Pacific Economic Co-operation Council (PECC).

However, APEC does not have the budget and the internal core expertise to drive an effective networking model capable of meeting its research needs.

- APEC's specialized forums typically suffer from insufficient administrative back-up — reflecting the limited resources of the Secretariat — and often find themselves bogged down in administrative details.

To strengthen APEC's management and its Secretariat, we propose these options for consideration:

- *The Executive Director should be a prominent figure who symbolizes and speaks for APEC, and who serves a multi-year term.* Such a position would provide better management co-ordination, continuity, and visibility. The rotating annual hosts of the APEC Leaders' Meeting could maintain some influence over the Secretariat through a special office created for that purpose that would be headed and staffed, in part, by persons appointed by the hosts.

- *Internal management of the Secretariat could be strengthened*, as suggested by a recent Secretariat memorandum, by creating a permanent senior level position responsible for management, possibly supplemented by a new level of permanent middle manager specialists for the corporate functions of finance, human resources, programme operations, and information. These additions would increase the efficiency of the seconded professional staff and enhance their capacity to provide administrative support to specialized APEC forums. Rigorous professional assessments will cost money but that is an inherent cost of business in a democratizing world.

- *Experts should be hired on a multi-year basis to organize the critical tasks of research and evaluation.* A renowned scholar should lead an economic research division capable of mobilizing the interests and research skills of academics and experts from the region. This networking approach to knowledge generation should draw extensively on the expertise of the APEC Study Centres established precisely for this purpose. Another well-respected, independent professional, hired on merit, should be responsible for organizing objective evaluations of APEC programmes and projects, relying primarily upon non-governmental, outside evaluators.

- *APEC forums could be strengthened by devolving some of their current responsibilities to an enhanced Secretariat.* APEC forums should be sufficiently productive and stimulating as to attract energetic and well-informed officials and non-governmental representatives. With better administrative backup, forums could focus more on substantive matters, thereby halting the decline in attendance among senior government officials and outside experts.

Some of the analytical work currently undertaken by the Economic Committee and the Committee on Trade and Investment (CTI) and its sub-forums could be more efficiently handled by a renewed Secretariat. Experience has shown that neither the ECOTECH Subcommittee nor the Budget and Management Committee (BMC) are capable on their own of effective project evaluation, and could instead rely upon a more independent evaluation unit.

- *The project approval process should be simplified in several ways.* The *Guidebook on APEC Projects* should be redrafted to be shorter and more accessible to prospective contractors. APEC forums might be allowed final approval of a limited number of projects below a predetermined value. In addition, the onerous disbursement process, which is the source of frequent complaints by project managers, should be reviewed.

- *The tendency of the SOM to overshadow other senior committees needs to be monitored.* The SOMs should consider delegating more genuine management authority to the Budget and Management Committee (BMC), "to put the M back into the BMC." For example, the BMC might be allowed final intersessional approval of a limited number of urgent projects. The CTI functioned best when it enjoyed the confidence of the Senior Officials. The ECOTECH Subcommittee requires more authority and resources to fulfill its assigned missions.

The proposed marginal growth in the Secretariat would require modest additional resources. For example, the current imputed cost of the Secretariat — at about twenty-two professional staff members plus the Executive and Deputy Executive Directors (now covered by the seconding member economies), and including the costs of the administrative staff (now covered by member economy allocations) and building rental (paid for by Singapore) — totals roughly $4 million per year. Logically, an increase in professional and administrative staff by 50 per cent would cost roughly $2 million more per year — a small fraction of the tens of millions of dollars that it costs just to host the annual Leaders' Meeting.

GOVERNANCE REFORM

As with many of APEC's goals and norms, the consensus rule for decision-making is open to interpretation. In the maximalist view, consensus requires the agreement of all twenty-one APEC members, and this full consensus must include agreement on substance, modalities, and timetable.

On the other hand, during the crafting of the Bogor Declaration — the closest document to a founding APEC Charter — Indonesia proposed that decisions be reached on the basis of a "broad consensus", meaning that a decision would as far as possible become a general consent, enabling countries that are ready to implement it to do so immediately while those that are less prepared will follow later on. Singapore has suggested that APEC work on the basis of a "flexible consensus" and that a "consensus does not necessarily mean unanimity".

As APEC has sought to move from general statements of ambitious intent to practical implementation, full consensus has become more difficult to obtain. Too many APEC meetings end in disappointment as a small minority of members use or misuse the consensus principle to frustrate the will of the large majority.

If the large majority of APEC members wish to move forward to advance basic APEC goals as previously determined, and if, as is generally the case, the proposed actions primarily involve domestic measures of self-help and mutual benefit to the willing members, why should a few members be allowed to veto such progress?

In the Shanghai Declaration, Leaders took the very important step of endorsing the "pathfinder approach" to attaining the Bogor goals of free and open trade and investment:

> Leaders reaffirm that those economies ready to initiate and implement a co-operative arrangement may proceed to do so, consistent with the Bogor Declaration....Use of 'pathfinder initiatives' based on a group of members piloting the implementation of the initiatives, will invigorate progress towards the Bogor Goals....Leaders also agree that these initiatives should...encourage the broadest participation by other APEC members when they are ready to join.

We are concerned that some APEC officials may be crafting a narrow interpretation of the pathfinder approach, arguing that new initiatives would still require a full consensus, even if some member economies prefer to delay implementation. We do not find this interpretation to be consistent with the letter or spirit of the Shanghai Accord. We do believe that the "pathfinder approach" is consistent with the APEC principle of voluntarism, as members remain free to decide on the timing of their own actions. Consequently:

- *We strongly endorse the pathfinder approach as proclaimed by the Leaders in their Shanghai Declaration and Accord.* As APEC moves from statements of principle to plans of action, decision-making based upon "flexible consensus" and "coalitions of the willing" will enable APEC to regain momentum. Pathfinder initiatives should be transparent and open and provide channels for all APEC members to join when they are ready.

•   *APEC should immediately apply the pathfinder approach to already approved "statements of principle."* For example, the Non-binding Investment Principles — a significant APEC achievement that showed its commitment to leadership in investment liberalization — could be implemented, in part or in full and according to an agreed timetable, by a coalition of the willing. Similarly, the APEC Principles on Trade Facilitation could be readily transformed into an action agenda.

STAKEHOLDER RELATIONS REFORM

In a globalizing world where power is increasingly diffused and the efficient sharing of tacit knowledge requires personal contact, the success of multilateral institutions depends importantly upon their openness to groups outside the government. To its credit, APEC pioneered close relations with the private sector, through the formation of the APEC Business Advisory Council (ABAC) and the annual CEO Summit. To involve academics in its work, APEC endorsed the formation of APEC Study Centres. To help it formulate its basic vision, APEC reached out to independent experts when it formed the Eminent Persons Group. APIAN research has found that strong business and civil society participation has contributed to the successful implementation of APEC initiatives.

In Brunei (2000), the Leaders asserted:

> APEC must be a process which is open and transparent and which draws on the talent and creativity of our people. We strongly encourage the continued engagement and outreach APEC has developed with our community and seek to develop partnerships with groups which share and add impetus to our goals.

In Shanghai (2001), ministers "instructed relevant APEC forums to identify and invite the participation of outside groups that can make a contribution to their work."

Good examples of such outreach and openness include the May 2000 Beijing High Level Meeting on Human Capacity Building, which included many representatives from the educational and corporate sectors, and the May 2002 APEC Dialogue on Globalization and Shared Prosperity that brought together Senior Officials, representatives from many APEC Study Centres and other independent experts, and the ongoing Women's Leaders Network.

Yet, research by APIAN participants suggests that APEC now lags behind other major multilateral organizations in accessibility to non-governmental participation. Many international agencies now routinely provide a series of formal consultative instruments and avenues of access to facilitate non-governmental interaction. Drawing on these "best practice" experiences, and on studies of APEC interactions with ABAC, APEC Study Centres and other civil society actors, we offer these recommendations for deepening APEC's roots in its own societies:

- *APEC should further clarify its guidelines for participation of non-members to offer a more positive welcome to civil society.* In the meantime, the APEC Secretariat and the Chairs of the CTI and ECOTECH Subcommittee should actively encourage APEC forums to implement the newly decentralized process for civil society participation in the spirit of the affirmative guidelines issued by leaders and ministers in Brunei and Shanghai.
- *The Secretariat should add staff capacity to serve as a point of expertise and co-ordination with the private sector and other non-governmental groups.* By doing so, APEC would conform to "best practices" observed at other multilateral agencies. Such an appointment should not, however, be considered a substitute for mainstreaming civil society participation throughout APEC forums and activities.
- *APEC should develop a structured and responsive process for evaluating recommendations from ABAC.* APEC should include ABAC in ministerial and Senior Official Meetings in a more meaningful way that goes beyond receiving a formal briefing from the ABAC Chair. To gain more outside expertise and support for its initiatives, APEC should encourage private sector participation in more working groups, such as the Investment Experts Group. For its part, ABAC needs to refine and prioritize its recommendations, and should become a wellspring for generating more public–private partnerships like the successful Shanghai Model Port Project.
- *APEC should institutionalize the example set by Mexico in Merida when it invited APEC Study Centre representatives to exchange views with Senior Officials.* Dialogues with ministers and other APEC forums should also be given careful consideration.

PRODUCT REFORM

In more than a decade of existence, APEC has developed a very broad array of laudable goals and initiatives. Yet, its resources — financial and political — fall far short of what would be required to seriously attempt to achieve these many ambitious objectives. It is time for APEC to define itself more precisely, in order to make better use of its scarce resources and to clarify for itself and in the public mind its core missions and functions.

Policy Development

Many of the best products of APEC forums consist essentially of policy development. Information exchanges, workshops, studies, and the identification of best practices and principles are among APEC's most important contributions. These policy development initiatives are welcome in a region that has lacked a multilateral institution capable of performing such a vital role in an age of rapidly shifting markets, technologies, and development strategies. If the global profile of the Leaders' Meeting could be paired with a programme of substantive policy research led by a strengthened Secretariat, APEC would have the ingredients for a substantial renewal of its relevance and credibility.

Economic and Technical Co-operation (ECOTECH)

As APIAN has underscored in its previous reports, the vast lists of ideas, goals, and projects loosely grouped under the ECOTECH umbrella need to be reviewed and reduced to a more manageable set of coherent programmes. However, APEC's very loose, decentralized structure lacks the organizational capacity to make choices and impose discipline. APEC established the ECOTECH Subcommittee (ESC) to perform such functions and now should give it a stronger role to set and enforce priorities. In so doing, the ESC should co-ordinate closely with the BMC, which is also responsible for making choices when the costs of projects approved by APEC forums exceed available funding.

APIAN continues to believe that the new ECOTECH Action Plans (EAPs) can become a valuable instrument in helping to set priorities, disseminate information on ongoing projects and best practices, and match promising projects with funding sources. The ESC might commission an independent study to evaluate and improve upon the pilot EAPs produced to date.

Trade and Investment Liberalization and Facilitation (TILF)

APIAN's previous policy reports made extensive suggestions for priority actions to advance TILF objectives, notably with regard to updating the TILF agenda, improving the Individual Action Plans (IAPs), and the review of member economies' regional trading arrangements (RTAs). We welcome the use of independent experts in the IAP peer review process as a way to encourage member economies to produce higher quality Action Plans.

APEC has long-standing work programmes on the so-called "Singapore issues" that are on the Doha agenda: competition policy, investment, trade facilitation, and government procurement. Moreover, APEC has reached a degree of consensus in each of these four areas through its adoption of the APEC Non-Binding Investment Principles, the APEC Principles to Enhance Competition and Regulatory Reform, Non-Binding Principles on Government Procurement, and the APEC Trade Facilitation Principles. The opportunity therefore exists for APEC to make substantive contributions to the World Trade Organization (WTO) round. Application of the pathfinder approach, as applied to the implementation of sections of these statements of principle, could be promptly validated in the Doha negotiations.

To clarify and consolidate APEC programmes and products, we make these additional recommendations:

- *APEC should recognize more explicitly that policy development is one of its core missions.* This Report's recommendations for strengthening the Secretariat to enhance its analytical and research capabilities are supportive of this mission. Greater engagement with independent experts, academics, APEC Study Centres, and the private sector would also reinforce APEC's ability to craft and disseminate development policies. Similarly, better articulation with other funding sources and cross-fertilization with research-rich institutions such as the Bretton Woods agencies and the OECD would be cost-effective.

- *APEC should thoroughly reorganize its ECOTECH activities and establish strategic priorities that include human resource development.* Consideration should be given to making the ECOTECH Subcommittee a full committee to enhance its authority to co-ordinate working groups and to engage non-APEC international institutions and civil society actors. The ESC should be empowered and financed to commission independent, objective assessments of the overall organization of APEC's economic and technical co-operation, the activities of the various working groups, and the outcomes of individual projects.

   The Human Resource Development (HRD) Working Group could become the paramount forum for HRD in the Asia-Pacific region if it can find adequate funding for its valuable projects, co-ordinate better with non-APEC institutions, and increase participation by civil society.

- *APEC projects should be designed as models which, if successful, would induce others to copy them many times over.* In the light of their small size, if APEC projects are to yield a measurable impact on key development indicators, they should be conceived of as demonstration projects to be scaled up and replicated by other funders. To motivate replication, potential measures could include urging project managers to have as participants potential funding sponsors of follow-on projects, and requiring projects to include Stage II follow-on activities that seek to maintain and expand project benefits.

- *In TILF, APEC should seize the opportunity to contribute to the Doha Millennium Round by advancing its work on the issues discussed in Singapore.* In turn, progress in the WTO should enable APEC to transform some of its voluntary principles into WTO-endorsed actions. We applaud the efforts by the PECC to develop an APEC agenda that responds to the challenges of the Doha Millennium Round.

  We welcome the goal that the Leaders have set in Shanghai of a 5 per cent reduction in transaction costs over five years, and believe that APEC is uniquely positioned to advance this trade facilitation agenda.

- *APEC Ministers should establish a mechanism for more formal co-ordination among APEC's central co-ordinating committees.* The chairs of the ECOTECH Subcommittee, the Committee on Trade and Investment, the Economic Committee, and the Budget and Management Committee should meet regularly so that they can better pass clear and consistent signals to other APEC forums and working groups. APEC's Executive Director should participate in these quadripartite consultations.

FINANCIAL REFORM

We recognize that the reinvigorated APEC we prescribe would require additional resources. We believe that these would be modest in comparison with the potential results, and that some of our proposals would actually save money over time. To mobilize more resources behind APEC initiatives, and to make better use of member economies' contributions, we advance these suggestions for APEC consideration:

- *APEC should make more systematic efforts to leverage its projects.* To encourage project co-financing, the APEC Secretariat could house liaison officers seconded from capital-rich institutions including the Asian Development Bank, Inter-American Development Bank, and the World Bank. The ABAC could play a role in providing private-sector representatives. APEC forums should make every effort to invite the participation of potential co-financing sources, at all stages of the project cycle.

- *Other APEC economies should join Japan in contributing to the APEC Central Fund.* Revealed preference would suggest that developed and middle-income economies (other than Japan) in APEC do not believe in APEC-funded projects, for they have refused to contribute to the APEC Central Fund beyond their *de minimus* required assessments. If the sticking point is the questionable quality and value-added of APEC projects, the reforms proposed in this Policy Report could correct these perceived shortcomings.
- *APEC must rationalize its financial structure.* Those economies whose annual gross domestic product totals some $18 trillion contribute less than $4 million to the APEC budget. Much more is spent in sending officials to attend APEC meetings. A more efficient APEC institution — as proposed throughout this Policy Report — would allow member economies to work out ways of transferring expenditures on travel and per diem for APEC meetings to expenditures for a strengthened Secretariat and for funding high-impact projects that advance the main goals of APEC.

In making these recommendations, we understand that some of the problems confronting the Asia-Pacific are deeply embedded in global structures or domestic politics and are beyond the reach of APEC as an institution. Nevertheless, we remain convinced that APEC can make a difference. We have proposed reforms in management, governance, stakeholder relations, product and finance in order to give APEC the capacity to adapt more rapidly to the swirl of events, to increase its credibility among international institutions, to grow its constituencies, to better brand its products, and to more effectively leverage its resources. Our proposals do not entail large budgets or bureaucratization; rather, we seek to build on APEC's strengths as an idea-driven, decentralized institution. Our goal and the ultimate purpose of APEC remain constant: to spread prosperity and to build community throughout the Asia-Pacific.

Notes

1. ISEAS also published the research associated with the first APIAN Policy Report: Richard Feinberg and Ye Zhao, eds., *Assessing APEC's Progress:Trade, ECOTECH and Institutions* (Singapore: ISEAS, 2001).

APPENDIX A

SIGNATORIES

Signatories are listed in alphabetical order by member economy, with institutional affiliation provided for identification purposes only.

Australia
John McKay
Director
Australian APEC Study Centre
Monash Asia Institute
Monash University

Canada
Yuen Pau Woo
Vice President, Research, and Chief Economist
Asia-Pacific Foundation of Canada

Stewart Goodings
Executive Director
BCIT International
British Columbia Institute of Technology (BCIT)

David MacDuff
Research Analyst
Asia-Pacific Foundation of Canada

Chile
Manfred Wilhemy
Executive Director
Chile-Pacific Foundation

Hernan Gutierrez B.
Director
Asia-Pacific Studies
Institute of International Studies
University of Chile

People's Republic of China
Cai Penghong
Secretary General
APEC Research Centre
Shanghai Academy of Social Sciences

Hong Kong, China
Thomas M. H. Chan
Head
APEC Study Centre
China Business Centre
Hong Kong Polytechnic University

Indonesia
Hadi Soesastro
Executive Director
Centre for Strategic and International Studies (CSIS)

Lepi T. Tarmidi
Professor
APEC Study Centre
Institute for Economic and Social Research
University of Indonesia

Japan
Neantro Saavedra-Rivano
Professor
APEC Study Centre
Institute of Policy and Planning Sciences
University of Tsukuba

Toshihisa Toyoda
Professor
APEC Study Centre
Kobe University

Hideki Funatsu
Professor
Otaru University of Commerce

Mexico
Ernesto Rangel
Director
Centro de Estudios APEC
Universidad de Colima

New Zealand
Nigel Haworth
Deputy Director
APEC Study Centre
University of Auckland

Robert Scollay
Director
APEC Study Centre
University of Auckland

Peru
Fernando Gonzalez-Vigil
Director
APEC Study Centre
Universidad del Pacifico

Philippines
Myrna Austria
Director
Centre for Business and Economic Research and Development
De La Salle University

Singapore
Siow Yue Chia
Director
APEC Study Centre and Director
Institute of Southeast Asian Studies

South Korea
Choong Yong Ahn
President
Korea Institute for International Economic Policy (KIEP)

Sangkyom Kim
Executive Director
National Centre for APEC Studies
Korea Institute for International Economic Policy (KIEP)

Chinese Taipei
Rong-I Wu
Executive Director
Chinese Taipei APEC Study Centre, and President
Taiwan Institute of Economic Research

Chen Sheng Ho
Associate Research Fellow
Chinese Taipei APEC Study Centre
Taiwan Institute of Economic Research

Thailand
Medhi Krongkaew
Professor
School of Development Economics
National Institute of Development Administration (NIDA)

Suphat Suphachalasai
Director
Thai APEC Study Centre
Thammasat University

United States of America
Vinod Aggarwal
Director
Berkeley APEC Study Centre (BASC)
University of California
Berkeley

Richard Feinberg
Director
APEC Study Centre
Graduate School of International Relations and Pacific Studies (IR/PS)
University of California
San Diego

Raul Hinojosa-Ojeda
Director
North American Integration and Development Centre
University of California
Los Angeles

Charles Morrison
President
East-West Centre
University of Hawaii

Michael Mullen
Director
National Centre for APEC

Hugh Patrick
Co-Director
APEC Study Centre
Columbia University

Peter Petri
Dean
Graduate School of International Economics and Finance
Brandeis University

Thomas Wahl
Interim Director & Associate Professor
APEC Study Centre
Washington State University

APPENDIX B

EXECUTIVE COMMITTEE OF THE APEC INTERNATIONAL
ASSESSMENT NETWORK (APIAN)

Richard Feinberg
(Project Co-ordinator)
Graduate School of International Relations and Pacific Studies
University of California, San Diego

Myrna Austria
Centre for Business and Economic Research and Development
De La Salle University
Philippines

Choong Yong Ahn
Korea Institute for International Economic Policy
South Korea

John McKay
Monash Asia Institute
Monash University
Australia

Neantro Saavedra-Rivano
Institute of Policy and Planning Sciences
University of Tsukuba
Japan

Robert Scollay
University of Auckland
New Zealand

Manfred Wilhelmy
Chile-Pacific Foundation
Chile

Rong-I Wu
Taiwan Institute of Economic Research
Chinese Taipei

APPENDIX C
ASIA-PACIFIC ECONOMIC CO-OPERATION: STRUCTURE

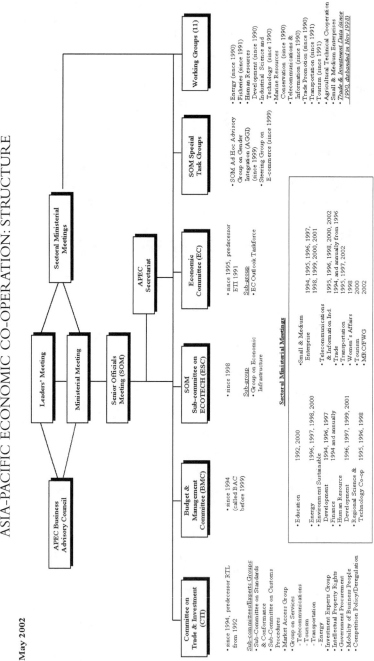

Source: http://www.apecsec.org.sg/graphics/orgsub2jpg

SECTION II

APEC'S STRATEGIC OBJECTIVES

2

APEC'S OVERALL GOALS AND OBJECTIVES, EVOLUTION, AND CURRENT STATUS

Hadi Soesastro

Introduction

Since entering its second decade, APEC has lost a great deal of the enthusiasm that accompanied its arrival. APEC reached its apex in the mid-1990s following the first Leaders' Meeting in Seattle in 1993, a period of "heightening" of APEC, in the words of Morrison (1998). At the Leaders' Meeting in 1996, APEC governments adopted the Manila Action Plan for APEC (MAPA), which was to provide further guidelines for implementing the Osaka Action Agenda (OAA) towards achieving the Bogor goals that was agreed upon in 1994. Since then, APEC appears to have lost its appeal. Among the very thin audience it has, the number of people that continue to pay serious attention to APEC seems to have dwindled rapidly. APEC is no longer the talk of the town in Asia-Pacific capitals. APEC events are no longer seen as newsworthy by the international media. Should APEC worry about this?

APEC is definitely not dead. There continue to be hundreds of APEC meetings annually, particularly at the working levels. These meetings have proliferated over the years, and are being encouraged to promote the habit of consultation and co-operation. As such, they serve a particular purpose, but the many processes at the working levels have perhaps become too absorbed in the technical details, and there seems to be a lack of clear understanding of how the different activities contribute to APEC's overall goal of *community building*.

There was also a suggestion that APEC might have been derailed from its track. Initiatives at the higher levels have also become too diffused. This was perhaps the case during the Canadian chairmanship. The agenda was seen as too ambitious while the process by which it was pursued was weak. One lesson to draw from this experience is that a broad and ambitious agenda, as proposed by Canada, can be undertaken successfully only when the co-operation process is supported by an institutional infrastructure that is capable of implementing it. This is still lacking in the APEC process. There is another important lesson. Following Manila's chairmanship a year earlier that successfully mobilized the participation of other region-wide actors (PAFTAD, PECC, PBEC and other such groups) in the process, the year under Canadian chairmanship saw the process being run exclusively by its own bureaucracy. In his study of APEC, Ravenhill (2001) has shown the important role of actors outside the bureaucracy, including the APEC Eminent Persons Group (EPG). The following meeting in Kuala Lumpur was another big disappointment. Malaysia's leader was not known to be genuinely committed to promoting APEC and thus did not provide leadership in APEC. The process was, to a large extent, saved by the dedication of the bureaucracy in charge to organize the meetings.

The New Zealand year was seen as an attempt to bring APEC back on its track. Unfortunately, it was burdened by the task of further promoting the misguided EVSL (early voluntary sectoral liberalization) programme, whose anticipated failure has only overshadowed the many achievements made during the New Zealand year. Seen from the outside, two achievements stand out. First, it has demonstrated the potentials of APEC as a regional forum for norm-setting by formulating and agreeing on a set of (non-binding) competition principles. Secondly, it has led the group to recognize that progress in APEC's trade liberalization efforts requires an effective peer review mechanism that was not yet in place.

The Brunei chairmanship in the following year took the task of championing a renewed attempt at formulating a framework for meaningful implementation of APEC's ECOTECH (economic and technical co-operation) programme. ECOTECH activities have been in a mess for a long time and efforts to rationalize the programme were not successful. As long as APEC's ECOTECH *pillar* remains weak and diffused, the APEC process will remain weak and diffused. The other pillar, namely TILF (trade and investment liberalization and facilitation), also cannot progress without a meaningful ECOTECH programme. The leaders' initiative in Brunei to promote "Human Capacity Building for the New Economy" offers a meaningful framework to revitalize and reorganize APEC's ECOTECH programme. This could lead to the development of a new ECOTECH model and modality, including the introduction of *individual action plans* (IAPs). A high-level meeting was organized as a follow up, and the meeting produced the Beijing Initiative. Unfortunately, this Initiative did not become the core around which more focused ECOTECH activities are undertaken.

The Leaders' Meeting in Shanghai produced the Shanghai Accord. In addition to recognizing the need to broaden the APEC Vision, the Accord highlights two main tasks for APEC, namely, to clarify the road-map to the Bogor meeting and to strengthen the implementation mechanism, in particular the IAP peer review process, as well as the ECOTECH and capacity-building efforts. These tasks can help revitalize APEC. The Mexican chairmanship in 2002 rightly focused its attention on these tasks. It intends to provide leadership in consolidating the APEC process.

In consolidating the APEC process, all members need to re-examine APEC's overall goals and critically review APEC's evolution, and simultaneously ask the question whether the political will that was there at APEC's inception is still present?

APEC's Overall Goal and Evolution

At its inception in November 1989 APEC was proclaimed as an "informal intergovernmental process" to promote economic co-operation in the Asia-Pacific region. This is to suggest that APEC is a consultative forum. APEC will not engage in negotiations. Participation is voluntary in nature and decisions are non-binding. However, the word "informal" has not been widely used since. The fact that it has fallen out of use reflects the growing acceptance of APEC's *de facto* institutionalization, which, despite being thin and slow, characterizes APEC's main evolution. This reflects a common political will and readiness to involve in a regional process, but there are still concerns with the preservation of sovereignty. Institutions and institutional processes are accepted only in so far as they do not infringe on members' sovereignty. It is a rather complicated task to develop effective co-operation under such circumstances. However, since this process is also driven by pragmatic considerations, some (*ad hoc*) practices such as "soft" negotiations that are inevitable in a peer review process, may be adopted. The challenge for APEC is how to balance members' "ideological" positions with the need for pragmatism. In a smaller region, the Association of Southeast Nations (ASEAN) is constantly faced with similar institutional challenges.

In January 1989, during his visit to South Korea, Australian Prime Minister Bob Hawke proposed a meeting of ministers from the region to discuss ways to establish economic co-operation at a government level. Indonesian Foreign Minister, Alatas (1994) argued that the successful inauguration of the meeting in Canberra in November 1989 could be attributed to a number of factors: the pragmatic approach on substantive areas of clear common interest among very diverse members; the sensitive approach with regard to possible operational modalities; and the careful and extensive consultations undertaken by Australia in developing and preparing the concept. It should not be overlooked, however, that the dramatic changes in the regional and international political and economic environment have led governments in the region to recognize the necessity to establish an intergovernmental forum for consultation and co-operation in economic issues.

The basic principles of Asia-Pacific economic co-operation are contained in the Summary Statement of the Chairman of the Meeting, Australian Foreign Minister Gareth Evans. They are as follows:

- The objective of enhanced co-operation is to sustain the growth and development of the region and, in this way, to contribute to the growth and development of the world economy;
- Co-operation should recognize the diversity of the region, including differing social and economic systems and current levels of development;
- Co-operation should involve a commitment to open dialogue and consensus, with equal respect for the views of all participants;
- Co-operation should be based on non-formal consultative exchanges of views among Asia-Pacific economies;
- Co-operation should focus on those economic areas where there is scope to advance common interests and achieve mutual benefits;
- Consistent with the interests of the Asia-Pacific economies, co-operation should be directed at strengthening the open multilateral trading system; it should not involve the formation of a trading bloc;
- Co-operation should aim to strengthen the gains from interdependence, both for the region and the world economy, including by encouraging the flow of goods, services, capital, and technology;
- Co-operation should complement and draw upon, rather than detract from, existing organizations in the region, including formal

intergovernmental bodies such as ASEAN, and less formal consultative bodies like the Pacific Economic Co-operation Council (PECC); and

- Participation by Asia-Pacific economies should be assessed in the light of the strength of economic linkages with the region, and may be extended in future on the basis of consensus on the part of all participants.

APEC's overall objectives and basic design were given in the above summary. The ASEAN members of APEC have had a great influence in defining APEC's overall goal and the modality of achieving those goals. This was particularly true at the time of APEC's establishment and its early years when an ASEAN caucus was in existence. Following the establishment of APEC, in early 1990 ASEAN foreign ministers met in Kuching (East Malaysia) and produced the Kuching Consensus to reiterate the principles of ASEAN participation in APEC. This was necessary because some ASEAN members, Malaysia in particular, were still very concerned about the possibility that the process would dilute ASEAN. These principles are:

- ASEAN's identity and cohesion should be preserved, and its co-operative relations with dialogue partners and third countries should not be diluted in any enhanced APEC;
- An enhanced APEC should be based on the principles of equality, equity, and mutual benefit, taking fully into account the differences in stages of economic development and socio-political systems among the countries in the region;
- APEC should not be directed towards the formation of an inward-looking economic or trading bloc but, instead, it should strengthen the open, multilateral economic and trading systems in the world;
- APEC should provide a consultative forum on economic issues and should not lead to the adoption of mandatory directives for any participant to undertake or implement;
- APEC should be aimed at strengthening the individual and collective capacity of participants for economic analysis and at facilitating more effective, mutual consultations to enable participants to identify more clearly and to promote their common interests, and to project more vigorously those interests in the larger multilateral forums; and,
- APEC should proceed gradually and pragmatically, especially in its institutionalization, without inhibiting further elaboration and future expansion.

Ravenhill (2001) was of the opinion that ASEAN's role later diminished when ASEAN members of APEC were no longer caucusing.

Although APEC's focus is in the economic field, it is believed that this co-operation will have important implications in other fields, including in the politico-strategic realm. In fact, it was also argued that politico-strategic considerations have played a role in the establishment of APEC. The end of the Cold War appeared to have had a positive influence on economic developments in the Asia–Pacific region (Soesastro 1993). As proposed by Wanandi (1990), the first important contribution of APEC is that it would help the United States to have a focus on and to maintain its presence in the region. Secondly, it could help stabilize the most important bilateral relationship in the region, namely U.S.–Japan relations. Thirdly, it could provide for a regional structure which could accommodate China's participation. Fourthly, it could offer a basis upon which the region could effectively respond to the desire on the part of Russia to have a greater role in the Asia–Pacific region. Fifthly, it could provide an effective means to counter any inward-looking tendencies on the part of the European Union. Sixthly, it could maintain the region's attractiveness even if Western and Eastern Europe might unite in the future. Seventhly, APEC could become a model for the promotion of sound and workable relations between developed and developing countries in a regional framework.

In view of the above considerations, namely, the utility of APEC, economically as well as in the politico-strategic realm, and the concerns with the nature of the process as expressed by ASEAN, and given the great diversities in the region, APEC has to give importance to confidence building measures. Confidence building measures (or CBMs) are a more familiar term in the realm of political and strategic co-operation. This is being promoted in the region through the ASEAN Regional Forum (ARF). APEC is first and foremost about community building. Community building involves and can be equated with confidence building. APEC members reached an understanding in Seattle in 1993 that the *community* they want to build is not the one written with a capital C as in the European Community. The agreement is for a "softer" or "weaker" version, namely, a family-type relationship based on what could be termed the five Ss: sense of *solidarity, supporting* one another, *strengthening* the group, *sharing* of a common destiny, and jointly *shaping* the region.

The question of shaping the region, or region building, is also an important element of community building in the Asia–Pacific. The APEC region has been drawn, rather arbitrarily, to encompass economies bordering the Pacific Ocean. There is hardly anything in common, for instance, between Chile and Vietnam. Yet, there is an interest to develop a process that encompasses the entire "region". On the side of East Asia, as suggested earlier, one of the main motivations in support of APEC is the interest to keep the United States engaged with East Asia. The United States, on its part, is also interested to participate in APEC to avoid being left out of developments in the Western Pacific. When the idea of establishing APEC was first proposed by Australian Prime Minister Bob Hawke, he left open the option of involving only the Western Pacific economies. It immediately became clear to many prospective participants in the Western Pacific, Japan in particular, that the exclusion of the United States would result in a "split" in the Pacific that could have grave strategic consequences for East Asia. It should be noted, however, that from within Japan itself there were also views suggesting that an East Asian arrangement of sorts might be necessary to manage trans-Pacific relations with the United States in the same way as the European Union (formerly the European Community) manages its trans-Atlantic relations with the United States. However, Japan could not support the establishment of an East Asian economic grouping, as proposed by Malaysian Prime Minister Mahathir, because it was seen as confrontational towards the United States. An East Asian regional structure must be developed in parallel with APEC. It is perhaps true that an East Asia that is well organized will also strengthen APEC. At the same time that an East Asian regional structure is being developed, trans-Pacific relations also need to be strengthened.

The other aspect of region building in the Asia-Pacific is the elaboration of the principle of "open regionalism". In its broadest sense, this means that the organization of the region is aimed at enhancing the region's engagement with and involvement in global affairs. In its more narrow sense, this implies that the region will not introduce measures, in trade and investment as well as in other areas of economic interactions, that discriminate against non-APEC economies. From the outset, part of APEC's main agenda has been the region's efforts to strengthen the global trading system. There is a strong belief that APEC has been instrumental in the successful conclusion of the Uruguay Round of multilateral trade negotiations.

Beginning with the APEC leaders' Vision Statement in 1993, the above principles were implemented subsequently in the Bogor Declaration of 1994 towards free and open trade and investment in the region. This was further operationalized in the Osaka Action Plan and the Osaka Action Agenda (AU) of 1995, and the Manila Action Plan for APEC (MAPA) in 1996. In the area of trade and investment liberalization, the APEC process adopted an approach known as "concerted unilateral liberalization". This is based on the realization that liberalization is beneficial to those undertaking it and thus is undertaken for one's own good. APEC as a process is aimed at encouraging and reinforcing unilateral liberalization in a concerted manner. This modality for liberalization is novel and is an important experiment as well as a test for APEC. If this modality, implemented through IAPs (Individual Action Plans) and complemented by CAPs (Collective Action Plans), cannot be made to work, it is hard to see how the APEC process can be sustained. The primary task for APEC is to make this modality work. There is no substitute to this modality, at least for some years to come.

The other task for APEC is to maintain, in broad terms, a balanced agenda. It was made clear in Bogor in 1994 why it is critical for the APEC process to pursue an agenda that gives equal importance to its three main pillars, namely, trade and investment *facilitation*, trade and investment *liberalization*, and *economic and technical co-operation*. These three pillars are now pursued in APEC together with the TILF agenda and the ECOTECH agenda. In any APEC cycle, the chair may give greater emphasis to TILF or ECOTECH or to both, but some overall balance is to be achieved and maintained. The modality for ECOTECH co-operation may be improved with the introduction of the ECOTECH Action Plan (EAP) in the area of human resources development. However, this process still needs to be monitored closely. The EAP should not end up being another collection of unrelated activities as it was the case under Part II of the Osaka Action Agenda.

There is now a clear recognition that TILF and ECOTECH are inseparable twins. Previously, this way of looking at the totality of the APEC agenda was hampered by the initial resistance of some members to include ECOTECH in the APEC agenda. Therefore, APEC chairs are well advised to give equal attention to both in any APEC cycle. An integral approach is called for (Elek and Soesastro 2000). It would strengthen the APEC process if such an agreement can be reached under the current Mexican chairmanship.

A Brief Assessment of the Process

The APEC process is characterized by, among other things, the annual cycle of its leadership. A member economy assumes the task of the APEC chair for one year, and the cycle ends with the convening of the ministerial meeting and the Leaders' Meeting (APEC Summit). The 2002 cycle is chaired by Mexico. This is not the first time that the process is led by a member from the Western Hemisphere (or Eastern Pacific). Both the United States and Canada have chaired APEC in the past. However, with Mexico chairing in 2002 and Chile in 2004, there is the expectation that emphasis will be given to strengthening trans-

Pacific co-operation. Mexico may want to bring other ideas into the process as well.

This annual cycle is one of the strengths of the APEC process. The APEC chair has a critical role in influencing the direction of APEC's development, both in terms of the content of co-operation and the nature of the process. It has a privileged position in injecting new ideas and in broadening the APEC agenda. Rather than proposing new ideas, it may, instead, opt for carrying the process forward by consolidating or by stressing on particular items in the prevailing agenda. With the rotation of the chairmanship, there is a built-in assurance that in broad terms the APEC agenda will reflect a balance of interest of its diverse members. This annual cycle, however, has its weakness as well. In view of its rather "nomadic" pattern of operation within a one-year cycle, it is not easy to establish sufficient institutional memory. Some good initiatives get lost and some others are repeatedly being reinvented.

This weakness can be overcome. The APEC chair can organize inputs to the process by drawing on the collective wisdom that has developed within non-governmental processes that have been promoting regional economic co-operation for many years, even before APEC was born.

The past has shown that APEC cannot rely solely on bureaucracy. This would produce a weak process, and as a result also a weak outcome. The APEC bureaucracy, as represented by the APEC Secretariat, is by design weak since it is not given any significant mandate. It has developed a capacity to store information and to make it available to the wider public but it cannot be assertive in relating its informed conclusions to the APEC decision-making process. The APEC bureaucracy, as represented by APEC officials in member economies, is too dispersed. Many member economies also do not have officials that devote their full time to APEC matters, and few work on APEC for more than two or three years.

The "parallel efforts" organized by non-governmental processes have retained a great deal of memory and understanding about the process of Asia-Pacific economic co-operation. Because of their concern with the APEC process, they are devoting greater attention and efforts to following the process more closely and in a much more systematic fashion. In fact, some have developed independent analytical capabilities to evaluate progress in the APEC process. Such interest and capabilities can be found in the International Steering Committee of PAFTAD (Pacific Trade and Development), the Pacific Economic Co-operation Council that has observer status in APEC, and the APEC Study Centres, as well as within the business community in the region.

The APEC process should capitalize on its inherent strength. Member economies have embarked on the process in a spirit of experimentation and the joy of a joint venture, driven by a strong sense of common destiny. In view of the region's great diversity, the future shape of the region cannot be engineered on the basis of a final blueprint. Thus, the APEC process is by its nature an evolving one. The annual cycles under a variety of leadership have shaped this APEC process. At times, the process was derailed from its track, as in the case of the introduction of the misguided EVSL (Early Voluntary Sectoral Liberalization) proposal. This could have been avoided if sufficient efforts were made at the beginning of each cycle to be clear about the essence of APEC and what it is meant to achieve. APEC is not only about trade liberalization. It is much more than that.

The APEC process has come a long way. The direct involvement of leaders in the process since 1993 has been a critical milestone for APEC. Through this involvement, some leadership has been created in APEC. The leadership in APEC, as distinct from many other regional or international arrangements, does not come from a specific country or group of countries or from a supranational institution. Rather, it has taken the form of some kind of *collective* leadership. The process moves forward on the basis of *voluntary* commitments made by all APEC leaders. The "engine" for the movement is provided by the APEC chair that proposes a new initiative and would continue to champion the implementation of that initiative in subsequent cycles. Hence, leadership in APEC is also *issue-specific*. The commitment made by a leader should be adopted by the respective economy even though that leader is no longer there. Indonesia, for instance, should continue to show leadership in achieving the Bogor goals even though Soeharto has been removed from the presidency. This continuity of commitment is often not easy to guarantee. If this is indeed the case, the respective economy would simply cease to provide that (issue-specific) leadership in APEC. It is hoped that another economy (or group of economies) would take over that leadership.

APEC has adopted consensus-building as practised in ASEAN. Consensus-building itself requires some leadership. The process towards the adoption and subsequent elaboration of the Bogor Declaration provides an important and interesting case study in consensus-building in APEC. The Bogor Declaration towards the APEC goal of free and open trade and investment in the region did not clearly specify the modality by which the goal will be achieved. A number of options were proposed but none was formally discussed in APEC meetings. Obviously, differences exist among APEC members. The APEC EPG proposed a modality that involves the creation of a free trade area, namely, negotiated liberalization among APEC members that can be extended to non-members only on a mutually reciprocal basis. The concern that the Bogor Declaration implicitly endorsed the EPG modality prompted Malaysia to issue a six-point reservation and Thailand to issue its seven-point observation on the Bogor Declaration (see Soesastro [1997], for the Malaysian and Thai submissions). Despite the expressed reservations, leaders were of the view that the differences could be overcome.

On the issue of the binding or non-binding nature of the agreement, including the 2010/2020 target dates, even Prime Ministers Keating of Australia (*The Times,* 4 November 1994), and Goh Chok Tong of Singapore (*Straits Times*, 17 November 1994) explicitly referred to the non-binding nature of the timetables. Fred Bergsten, chairman of the EPG, also stated that the Bogor Declaration should be seen primarily as a political commitment (*Asiaweek*, 25 November 1994). Views were expressed that the value of political commitments was that it could provide the momentum to trade liberalization and that once a country makes a political commitment it has to try to implement it. There was the view as well that even if the agreement was non-binding, countries could be "persuaded" to honour it either during bilateral talks or discussions within the group (see Soesastro [1997], for an elaborate discussion on these views). These ideas appear to have become the basis for the introduction of the peer review mechanism as an integral part of the agreement to adopt the concerted unilateral action modality in APEC's trade liberalization programme.

Mahathir also strongly insisted that decisions within APEC must be based on consensus. There was the view that decisions in APEC must be unanimously approved. This consensus decision-making procedure is being questioned because agreements may become more difficult to reach as APEC embarks on increasingly ambitious programmes. An important question for APEC, raised in 1994 and likely to arise again in the future, is whether the principle of "all members minus X" or some kind of "coalition of the willing" should and could be introduced in APEC. President Soeharto of Indonesia, who crafted the Bogor Declaration, proposed that decisions be reached on the basis of a "broad consensus", meaning that a decision would as much as possible become a general consent, enabling countries that are ready to implement it to do so immediately while those that are less prepared will follow later (*Jakarta Post*, 12 November 1994). Prime Minister Goh of Singapore suggested that APEC should work on the basis of a "flexible consensus" and that a "consensus does not necessarily mean unanimity" (*Straits Times*, 17 November 1994). These different views of APEC leaders were expressed to the media, and were not addressed in the Leaders' Meeting itself. It is

also not clear whether they have been taken up at other levels in the
APEC process. Be that as it may, and given Mahathir's objections to the
process by which the Bogor Declaration was arrived at, Malaysia has not
been the laggard in implementing the Osaka Action Agenda through its
IAPs in the area of trade and investment liberalization.

The APEC process began with a meeting of ministers, aided by
meetings of senior officials. Having brought the leaders into the process
allows for bolder decisions to be made. However, their involvement also
carries some risk. Leaders may be more concerned about deliverables or
even announceables instead of strengthening the processes of co-operation.
Fortunately, APEC summits also provide an opportunity for bilateral
summits. These bilateral summits are often of such great importance that
it would help reduce the pressures on the APEC summit itself to produce
spectacular deliverables. Another risk is that the process may become too
much of a "top-down" process. It should be kept in mind that community
building and economic co-operation in the Asia-Pacific region, as distinct
from the initial top-down Asia Europe Meeting (ASEM) process, began
with a bottom-up process by non-governmental actors long before
governments were ready to do so. Therefore, the continued involvement
of these various non-governmental groups can help strengthen the
APEC process.

Another significant feature of the APEC process that tends to be
overlooked is the involvement of developing and developed, as well as
small and large countries, in the process. This is the fact that developing
and smaller countries can have an equally important role in the process.
There was the concern that the APEC process would be dominated by
the larger economies, such as the United States and Japan. This has not
been the case.

Finally, it needs to be stated that the APEC process has progressed
despite the thinness of its institutions. This thin institutional arrangement
is by design. Being a voluntary and loose process, member economies are
extremely cautious in developing institutions that could result in the
transfer of the locus of decision-making from individual governments to
a regional institution. However, if APEC were to be invented today,
perhaps its architects would propose ways to make the process more
efficient by a greater readiness to develop certain institutions, such as
providing a proper home for ECOTECH activities. The current structure
of Working Groups is far from sufficient.

In addition, APEC needs to address the serious deficiency it has
because so much institutional memory is lost. This relates to the overall
structure of APEC as well as the nature of the APEC Secretariat. If the
overall structure of a *voluntary* APEC, as it is now, is retained, the APEC

Secretariat should perhaps be transformed into an OECD-type organization albeit much less elaborate. Above all, APEC should have structures that force the organization to think strategically.

Tasks Ahead

The APEC 2002 cycle and beyond should be a sustained and effective regional response to global challenges, as well as a time of regional consolidation, including the consolidation of the APEC process itself. The main global and regional challenges facing APEC include how to deal with (or manage) globalization, and managing the various sub-regional and bilateral free trade agreements (FTAs).

Dealing with globalization should become APEC's main agenda in view of the backlash against globalization. The APEC Leaders' Declaration of November 2000 in Brunei Darussalam has outlined a number of policy directions under the heading, "managing globalization". In this realm, APEC's tasks should include:

1. confidence-building measures (CBMs) within APEC:
    a) APEC's concept of "concerted unilateral liberalization" has become all the more relevant and appropriate as a CBM. This modality needs to be strengthened continuously.
    b) APEC's ECOTECH agenda also needs to be strengthened by focusing on co-operation in policy development, institutional development, and capacity building.

2. APEC's intellectual leadership in managing globalization:
    a) APEC should set up a high-level (*ad hoc*) group to outline new strategies, principles, and policy directions guiding existing and new global, multilateral, and international regimes, including the strengthening of the World Trade Organization (WTO).
    b) This initiative should not be confined to an inter-governmental one.

3. An APEC outreach initiative:
    a) APEC should hold regular exchanges with civil society at the national and regional levels.
    b) APEC should invite and include regional/international civil society organizations in developing the above strategies.

Another important agenda for APEC is *managing sub-regional and bilateral FTAs*. While the initiators of these initiatives profess to abide by the principles of open regionalism, the dynamics of the negotiation process do not guarantee that the outcome accords with the APEC architecture. In addition, sub-regional and bilateral initiatives are not free of potentials to create tensions in the wider region. Therefore:

- APEC should establish a high-level group to monitor and "scrutinize" the process, based on some "open clubs" principles that APEC needs to formulate.
- These principles should go beyond WTO consistency.

Finally, APEC leaders should be encouraged to ponder on *APEC's longer term institutional development*. The idea of transforming the APEC Secretariat into an APEC OECD has been mentioned before. This idea should be examined within the overall development of APEC, specifically in relation to the question of whether APEC should move away from being a *voluntary* APEC (*V*-APEC) to a *binding* APEC (*B*-APEC).

The first question to ponder is whether a *V*-APEC or a *B*-APEC is simply a stage in a process of confidence and community building. A further question is whether it is possible to be in an in-between situation, for instance, to accept the political commitments of leaders as symbolically binding. Some in-between organizational principles would include "coalitions of the willing" (flexible consensus), and the conduct of "soft" negotiations.

Perhaps a more fundamental question is whether a *B*-APEC is indeed what APEC should become, and if so, how to get there. In the past, there was the discussion of how to transform the APEC NBIP (non-binding investment principles) into a binding one, either for the region or globally. This discussion opened up an array of important questions for APEC. What is the purpose of the NBIP? Is it meant, in the first place, to influence domestic policy formulation? Should it be made binding only for members that voluntarily sign it? Is it a code for APEC as a means to consolidate the region? Is it a first step towards developing a multilateral code that is binding at the international level?

While these issues remain to be settled, the more immediate task for APEC is to make *V*-APEC function more effectively. This task of *consolidating the APEC process* involves redefining and streamlining APEC's priorities, programmes and management, which should include, among other things, the following:

1. In the TILF agenda:
    a) Strengthening the IAP peer review process and inviting an ongoing independent assessment of the process (APEC Study Centres' APIAN and PECC).
    b) Widely publicizing the various APEC facilitation programmes.

2. In the ECOTECH agenda:
    a)   Undertaking a radical change in the process and structure by selecting two or three "umbrella" themes, such as that undertaken in Brunei Darussalam (Action Agenda for the New Economy).
    b)   Assigning leaders for each such "umbrella" theme.
    c)   Introduce the concept of EAP (ECOTECH Action Plan) in a coherent manner under each "umbrella" theme.
    d)   Focusing on policy development, institution and capacity building.

It would be useful, however, for APEC to spell out more explicitly and perhaps codify the principles of *V*-APEC and outline the architecture of *V*-APEC. Some principles of *V*-APEC could include the following:

1. APEC actions are actions of APEC members undertaken within a commonly agreed framework.
2. APEC co-operation is based on a modality that rests on:
    a)   *voluntarily* subjecting oneself to (APEC's) "peer pressure" so as to help reinforce one's own action plan;
    b)   *voluntarily* placing one's action plan into (APEC's) collective agenda to benefit from synergy.
3. APEC (even a *V*-APEC) can constrain the behaviour of members in forming FTAs that could undermine APEC's agenda.
4. *V*-APEC must permit the adoption of "flexible consensus".
5. *V*-APEC should be driven by champions/heroes.

In terms of APEC's architecture, the following comments can be made:

1. TILF and ECOTECH should be seen as ways to organize activities, and should not be seen as competing agendas. In fact, they are inseparable twins.
2. IAPs (Individual Action Plans) are the *core* of APEC actions, which are the actions of APEC members.
3. The main mechanism in APEC is an effective "peer pressure" and "peer review", while the institutions in APEC should focus on creating synergy.
4. APEC should relate and co-operate with "second track" activities to keep the momentum going, to channel the aspirations of the people, and increase relevance.

Concluding Notes

A *B*-APEC is an option for the long-term. If proposed today, it can be adopted only by a smaller APEC, which, however, is not what APEC is about. The early proposals for regional economic co-operation in the Pacific had limited membership, only among developed countries (Kojima's PAFTA) or core and associate members (Drysdale's OPTAD). They have been overtaken by the need to encompass a wider geographic region. Region building is an important element of APEC. The greatest challenge here is the development and strengthening of trans-Pacific relations.

APEC has clearly recognized the difficulties of moving the process that involves twenty-one economies of such great diversity. It has wisely introduced a moratorium of its membership. For some time to come, APEC should not expand its membership. Even the task of consolidating the process of *V*-APEC would be made more difficult with more members. A *V*-APEC must allow for the adoption of flexible consensus and the operation of coalitions of the willing. A consolidated *V*-APEC will have to rationalize its action agenda and programmes. Activities should be conducted at two levels. The working level is where exchanges, studies and explorations can take place. The operational level is where co-operation initiatives and activities are to be undertaken. Here is where programmes are to be implemented through IAPs and CAPs, and where a peer review mechanism should be introduced.

APEC should not be overwhelmed by new initiatives every year. The one-year cycles under different chairs create a strain on the organization. In that sense, it is too short. The APEC chair must begin the cycle, or in fact prior to assuming the chairmanship, with an effort to shop around the many Working Groups or other activities within APEC as well as "second track" activities to see what potential area(s) of co-operation can be elevated to become a new, additional, or overarching theme for APEC. Once selected and elevated to an initiative by the leaders, it should be translated into programmes that lend itself well to implementation through IAPs and CAPs.

A *V*-APEC is by nature a loose one, but continuous efforts at consolidation are likely to produce greater effectiveness. It needs to be recognized, as Aggrawal (1993) already showed some years ago, that the APEC regime will be a weak one. It is weak because of the region's diversity and because it is market driven. But why should this be a problem, if it can facilitate community building in this diverse, and exciting, Asia-Pacific region?

References

Aggarwal, Vinod K. "Building International Institutions in Asia-Pacific". *Asian Survey* 33, No. 11 (November 1993): 1029–42.
Alatas, Ali. "Basic Principles, Objectives and Modalities of APEC". In *Indonesian Perspectives on APEC and Regional Co-operation in Asia Pacific*, edited by Hadi

Soesastro, pp. 23–29. Jakarta: Centre for Strategic and International Studies, 1994.

Elek, Andrew, and Hadi Soesastro. "ECOTECH at the Heart of APEC: Capacity Building in the Asia Pacific". In *Asia Pacific Economic Co-operation (APEC) — Challenges and Tasks for the Twenty-first Century*, edited by Ippei Yamazawa, pp. 218–54. London: Routledge, 2000.

Morrison, Charles E. "APEC: The Evolution of an Institution". In *Asia-Pacific Crossroads — Regime Creation and the Future of APEC*, edited by Vinod K. Aggarwal and Charles E. Morrison, pp. 1–22. New York: St. Martin's Press, 1998.

Ravenhill, John. *APEC and the Construction of Pacific Rim Regionalism*. Cambridge: Cambridge University Press, 2001.

Soesastro, Hadi. "Implications of the Post-Cold War Politico-Security Environment on the Pacific Economy". In *Pacific Dynamism and the International Economic System*, edited by C. Fred Bergsten and Marcus Noland, pp. 365–88. Washington, D.C.: Institute for International Economics, 1993.

Soesastro, Hadi. "The Institutional Framework for APEC: An ASEAN Perspective". In *APEC Challenges and Opportunities*, edited by Chia Siow Yue, pp. 36–53. Singapore: Institute of Southeast Asian Studies, 1994.

————. "Designing Mechanisms for Trade and Investment Liberalization in the Asia-Pacific". In *The New Asia-Pacific Order*, edited by Chan Heng Chee, pp. 220–45. Singapore: Institute of Southeast Asian Studies, 1997.

Wanandi, Jusuf. "Asia Pacific Economic Co-operation: Ideas about Substance". Mimeographed. M26/1990. Jakarta: Centre for Strategic and International Studies (CSIS), 1990. Abridged version: "APEC and Other Regional Organizations". In *Indonesian Perspectives on APEC and Regional Co-operation in Asia Pacific*, pp. 30–36. Jakarta: CSIS, 1994.

3

APEC AS A PACIFIC OECD REVISITED

DAVID MACDUFF AND YUEN PAU WOO

The idea of a trans-Pacific institution created along the lines of the Paris-based Organization for Economic Co-operation and Development (OECD) is almost as old as the OECD itself. The Pacific Trade and Development Conferences, which bring together economists from around the Asia-Pacific, discussed proposals for a trans-Pacific intergovernmental forum from the time of the first meeting in 1968.[1] This idea took form in Peter Drysdale's proposed "Organization for Pacific Trade and Development",[2] which drew on some elements of the OECD while underscoring that the European model was only partly applicable to the Pacific.[3] In 1978, U.S. Senator John Glenn, as chairman of the Senate's Subcommittee on Asia and the Pacific, commissioned a paper entitled "Evaluation of a Proposed Asian-Pacific Regional Economic Organization." On the eve of APEC's creation in 1989, Australian Prime Minister Bob Hawke also proposed an institution which would "develop a capacity for analysis and consultation on economic and social issues, not as an academic exercise, but to help inform policy development by our respective governments." The so-called Hawke Initiative made direct reference to the OECD as a model, albeit recognizing that the Paris-based organization operated within a very different context.[4]

The founding members of APEC did not, however, subscribe to Hawke's vision, and the trans-Pacific forum that was created instead adopted a distinctly anti-institutional character. By 1994, with the announcement of the Bogor targets, the focus in APEC was clearly on "free and open trade" (by 2010 for developed member economies, with an additional ten years for developing member economies to achieve the same). The means for achieving the Bogor targets were "open regionalism" and "concerted unilateral liberalization" — a process of voluntary tariff reduction through enlightened dialogue among APEC members, and the extension of these market-opening measures to non-members without a call for reciprocal actions.[5] In 2002, at the half-way mark to the first Bogor milestone, APEC's trade liberalization agenda was sidelined by the rise of bilateral free-trade agreements among APEC members, proposals for Asia-only regional integration, continued momentum towards a Free Trade Area of the Americas (which would include five APEC members), and the launch of a new multilateral trade round. Even though APEC has priorities other than trade and investment liberalization (and takes pains to emphasize these other priorities, notably trade facilitation and economic/technical co-operation), it would not be unfair to characterize the liberalization agenda as APEC's *raison d'être* during most of its existence. This emphasis on liberalization was accompanied by a belief among many APEC officials and scholars that the enlightened voluntarism behind "concerted unilateral liberalization" and "open regionalism" precluded a need for much institutional infrastructure. It is no surprise, therefore, that for much of APEC's history and especially the period from Bogor (1994) to the failure of the Early Voluntary Sectoral Liberalisation (EVSL) initiative in 1998, the idea of APEC as a Pacific OECD — indeed, the very mention of OECD in official APEC circles — was considered heresy. In this context, the recent interest of APEC officials in institutional reform and strengthening — for example, at the level of the APEC Secretariat[6] — should be seen as part of a deeper unease about APEC's main purposes and perhaps as an unspoken quest for a new *raison d'être*. Accordingly, while this chapter asks an old question about the relevance of a Pacific OECD, it poses that question in the new context of a twelve-year-old trans-Pacific organization that is itself reflecting upon its institutional arrangements. Specifically, the chapter will look at aspects of the OECD model that may be adopted by APEC to reinvigorate its economic co-operation mandate. It will also suggest practical measures for advancing the idea of a Pacific OECD. As the chapter will point out, there are numerous aspects of the OECD's work that are not relevant to APEC and perhaps not desirable as well.[7] The use of the OECD as a benchmark should not be seen as institutional mimicry or as a case of organizational envy, but rather as a reference point for APEC to map its own unique path. If 2002 marks the start of a new literature on APEC as an institution, the likelihood is that this literature will be defined less by reference to other institutions, such as the OECD, but increasingly on its own terms.

The modest literature on APEC as a Pacific OECD is mainly found in academic and government debate, with occasional media attention.[8] In 1990, just after APEC was launched, Edward English discussed the emerging institutional environment in the Pacific and raised the possibility of an OECD-like body.[9] In 1995, Japan's year for chairing APEC, its Ambassador to the International Organizations in Vienna, Nobutoshi Akao, wrote an article favouring the gradual adoption of the OECD treaty-based paradigm.[10] In 1998, Sylvia Ostry offered a somewhat sceptical evaluation of the idea, noting political obstacles, and suggesting that a modestly revised status quo might be preferable.[11] During the 2001 Australian federal elections, the trade spokesman for the Labour Party, Peter Cook, proposed a Pacific OECD to both deepen his country's linkages with Asia, and grapple with obstacles to development in the region.[12] In the same year, Hadi Soesastro discussed the possibility of an OECD-like institution to give shape to the ongoing process of East Asian integration, viewing it as a desirable but unlikely outcome.[13]

At a more general level, scholars of Asia–Pacific affairs have expressed interest in the idea of "epistemic communities" of experts that converge around shared knowledge and norms, which would be a core feature of a Pacific OECD.[14] The inadequate state of information dissemination and sharing among Asia–Pacific economies has been viewed for some time as an obstacle to further co-ordination and integration. For instance, in a critical appraisal of APEC's prospects in 1995, Richard Higgott observed that, "The absence of quality information concerning the domestic economic policies and strategies of member states is a source of uncertainty and misunderstanding in the Asia-Pacific region, a potential source of future aggravation and, importantly, one that is not beyond resolution. If the commitments espoused at the inaugural and subsequent APEC meetings, in the nature of the work programs and in the hyperbole of the Seattle summit [in 1993] have any meaning, then the provision of better information is a priority of the organisation."[15]

Michael Wesley suggests that APEC made a transition from the "inductive approach" to Asia-Pacific integration (a focus on dialogue) to the "deductive approach" (producing media-friendly "deliverables" on liberalization), resulting in what he labels as a "pledge then deliver" mentality.[16] To the extent that this characterization points to the need for more emphasis on co-ordinated information sharing and dialogue, it is in line with the idea of a Pacific OECD. A more precise critique, however, would be that APEC never went much beyond a superficial expression of the "inductive approach" even as it developed a tendency to promise deliverables on a regular basis. A large part of APEC activity year after year remains the "inductive" practice of dialogue and information exchange, but this exchange takes place without the benefit of institutional support and continuity, especially in the area of research.

Comparing the OECD and APEC

Historical and Political Dynamics

The formation of the Organization for European Economic Co-operation (OEEC), the forerunner to the OECD, and whose nomenclature closely resembles Asia-Pacific Economic Co-operation, was an integral component of the European Recovery Programme, and must be viewed in the context of the start of the Cold War. Following the failure to reach agreement with the Soviet Union on the shape of the post-World War II order, in 1947 U.S. Secretary of State George Marshall expressed American willingness to assist Europe in its reconstruction, based on a co-ordinated plan to be formulated by the Europeans. The Committee of European Economic Co-operation (CEEC), composed of sixteen countries, prepared a report and subsequently liaised with the U.S. Office of the Special Representative (OSR) to co-ordinate the details of the recovery plan. The CEEC also examined the possibility of establishing a permanent organization, leading to the Convention for European Economic Co-operation, the founding document of the OEEC, in April 1948. The eighteen members were: Austria, Belgium, Denmark, France, Greece, Iceland, Ireland, Italy, Luxembourg, Netherlands, Norway, Portugal, Sweden, Switzerland, Turkey, United Kingdom, and Western Germany (originally represented by both the combined American and British occupation zones [the Bizone] and the French occupation zone). The United States and Canada obtained associate membership in 1950.

The key purpose of the OEEC was to lock in market-based economies in the face of Stalinism by co-ordinating the European recovery and keeping the United States informed on its progress. More specifically, the OEEC's objectives included the study of free trade areas and customs unions (Article 5), freer movement of persons (Article 8), and the promotion of lower tariffs and non-tariff barriers (Article 6). Even so, the OEEC soon ran into difficulties in reaching agreement among its members on the European Recovery Programme and the allocation of Marshall Aid funds.[17] The OEEC was sidelined in the early 1950s with the end of Marshall Aid and with the strengthening of the

North Atlantic Treaty Organization (NATO), as security issues became even more prominent after the start of the Korean War. It took on some specialized functions, such as the European Nuclear Energy Agency, but by 1957, with European reconstruction largely in place and the establishment of the European Community, the OEEC lacked a unique purpose. There is a parallel with Asia-Pacific regional institutions at the start of the twenty-first century, when new initiatives such as the ASEAN Plus Three grouping are prompting existing groups such as APEC to re-examine their roles.

Accordingly, the Organization for Economic Co-operation and Development replaced the OEEC in 1960. Its convention established very broad parameters for the institution. Article 1 highlights three objectives: obtaining the "highest sustainable economic growth and employment and a rising standard of living in member countries"; "contributing to the sound economic expansion in member as well as non-member countries in the process of economic development"; and fostering "the expansion of world trade on a multilateral, non-discriminatory basis in accordance with international obligations."[18] Article 2 further commits parties individually and collectively to the efficient use of economic resources; development of science and technology, including research and vocational training; policies to achieve economic growth together with internal and external financial stability; reduction and abolition of barriers to trade in goods and services, and the extension of capital mobility; and assisting with economic development, especially through capital flows, as well as technical support and export opportunities.

The twenty original signatories included Austria, Belgium, Canada, Denmark, France, West Germany, Greece, Iceland, Ireland, Italy, Luxembourg, the Netherlands, Norway, Portugal, Spain, Sweden, Switzerland, Turkey, the United Kingdom, and the United States. Subsequent members, by year of ratification, include: Japan (1964); Finland (1969); Australia (1971); New Zealand (1973); Mexico (1994); Czech Republic (1995); Hungary, Poland and South Korea (1996); and Slovak Republic (2000). These parties broadened the scope of the OECD from an entity focused on rich countries in Europe to one with participants from four continents with a wide range of income levels.

The most obvious difference in the circumstances around the creation of the OEEC and a putative Pacific OECD is in the geopolitical structure. The OEEC was part of a larger effort to counterbalance an external power, the Soviet Union. American engagement in Europe was, in the apt phrase of Geir Lundestad, an "empire by invitation", in which the Europeans requested U.S. involvement in the continent, quite distinct

from the forceful imposition of communism in the East.[19] In contrast, a
Pacific OECD based on APEC membership would include the United
States and China, the latter being what George W. Bush has termed a
"strategic competitor" (although the war on terrorism may have
temporarily attenuated this view).

When considered in its present form, the OECD has become an
institution defined not by region, but by ideology, although somewhat
masked by the "neutral" technical analyses it produces. It is composed of
like-minded countries committed to market economics *and* pluralistic
democracy. APEC, on the other hand, is only committed to market
economics — and with many different varieties. Hence, in contrast to
the OECD, APEC members belong to a (rather loosely-defined) region,
but represent a wide variety of ideological/political models, from one-
party states to multi-party systems.

Structure

The OECD Convention provides for a Council to be composed of all
members, meeting in sessions of ministers or permanent representatives,
and serving as the source of all OECD acts (Article 7). The Council is led
by a Chairman and two Vice-Chairmen (Article 9). Additionally, a
Secretary-General is appointed for a five-year term by the Council,
together with an unspecified number of deputies, and is accountable to
the Council (Article 10). The Secretary-General chairs meetings of the
Permanent Representatives (that is, ambassadors).

The Convention does not specify the administrative structure of the
OECD, which employs about 1,900 international civil servants. The
March 2001 Organization Chart[20] is divided into four units: General
Secretariat, Communications, Semi-Autonomous Bodies, and Executive
Directorate. For the purposes of this chapter, the Executive Directorate
is of special interest, given its focus on the substantive activities of the
institution. The Executive Directorate consists of the following: the
Economics Department; Statistics Directorate; Environment Directorate;
Development Co-operation Directorate; Public Management Service;
Trade Directorate; Directorate for Financial, Fiscal, and Enterprise Affairs;
Directorate for Science, Technology, and Industry; Directorate for
Education, Employment, Labour, and Social Affairs; Directorate for Food,
Agriculture, and Fisheries; and Territorial Development Service.

The OECD also has institutionalized outreach capabilities, through
the Business and Industry Advisory Committee (BIAC),[21] and the
Trade Union Advisory Committee (TUAC),[22] operational since 1962.
These reflect the long-term input of both of these groups since the

founding of the OEEC, as well as Europe's historically corporatist economic system.

The structure of the OECD, in both its legal and bureaucratic forms, stands in marked contrast to APEC. Beginning as a ministerial meeting, APEC lacks a formal founding document, although its core mission of realizing the Bogor goals and its operating principles of flexibility, voluntarism, and consensus are widely understood. Ostry characterizes the institutional framework of APEC as a "virtual secretariat" composed of think-tanks, INGOs, and member governments, conveying the impression of a vast network comparable at least in size with the OECD Secretariat. In reality, however, the "virtual secretariat" of APEC stakeholders is a disparate group that provides useful input on particular issues, but which generally does not provide for the specificity and continuity of focus that are fundamental to institutional development. Indeed, the "bricks and mortar" APEC Secretariat in Singapore, with fewer than thirty professional staff, is minuscule compared with the OECD. The limited resources at the APEC Secretariat restrict the ability of staff to perform much more than research support, project management, and public relations. The position of Executive Director rotates with the chair of APEC, resulting in a yearly turnover of the top Secretariat position. There are no specific member-economy missions to APEC as there are to the OECD. The closest parallels to the Permanent Representatives located in Paris are APEC's Senior Officials, who meet three times a year to help prepare the forum's agenda in advance of the Leaders' Meeting. These arrangements fall far short of a permanent managerial and priority-setting forum along the lines of the OECD. In terms of outreach, the equivalent to the OECD's Business and Industry Advisory Committee is the APEC Business Advisory Council, established in 1995. There is no labour counterpart in APEC to the Trade Union Advisory Committee of the OECD.

One clear structural advantage that APEC has over the OECD is the annual Leaders' Meeting, which was inaugurated in Seattle in 1993. The OECD has an annual Council meeting at the *ministerial* level, but not among heads of government. The annual G-8 meetings, involving leaders of key OECD economies, are widely seen as a surrogate for a similar top-level event at the OECD. In spite of perceived weaknesses in APEC's substantive work programme, the Leaders' Meetings command a level of attention that the OECD's annual ministerial meetings cannot hope to achieve. If the global profile of the Leaders' Meetings can be paired with a programme of substantive policy research led by a strengthened Secretariat, APEC would have the ingredients for a substantial renewal of its relevance and credibility.[23]

Functions

The OECD takes pains to emphasize that it is not in the business of lending money, distinguishing itself from international financial institutions such as the International Monetary Fund (IMF) and the World Bank, or regional lending institutions such as the Asian Development Bank.

The OECD Convention sets broad parameters for how the institution should achieve its objectives. Article 3 rather vaguely calls for members to keep each other informed, "consult together on a continuing basis, carry out studies and participate in agreed projects." Nonetheless, one can distill five specific functions of the contemporary OECD: (1) research, (2) cross-cutting dialogue, (3) creation of norms, (4) negotiations, (5) peer review, and (6) collaboration with regional and international organizations. A brief survey of these functions is presented below, followed by a discussion on corresponding activities in APEC. Generally speaking, APEC has some role in each of these areas, but not in the same depth as the OECD.

Research. The substantive scope of the OECD, as Ostry points out, is the broadest of any post-war institution.[24] The OECD's website lists thirty-three areas of work, namely, ageing society; agriculture, food and fisheries; biotechnology; competition and regulatory reform; corporate governance; corruption; development; education; electronic commerce; emerging and transition economies; employment; energy; enterprise, industry and services; environment, finance, and investment; food safety; future studies; growth; health; information and communication technologies; insurance and pensions; international migration; macroeconomics; money laundering; public governance and management; science and innovation; social issues; statistics; sustainable development; taxation; territorial economy; trade; and transport.

The OECD's most widely-known publications are its bi-annual forecasts of output, prices, employment, and current account balances for its members, together with policy recommendations, prepared by its Economics Directorate. Summaries of the overall projections for the "OECD area", as well as briefs on individual countries and statistical annexes are available on the organization's website. In addition, the reports contain special chapters on diverse policy issues, providing a first sample of more in-depth OECD research projects.

In contrast, the APEC Secretariat covers only a small portion of the OECD's agenda, and performs at best a supporting role for research activities undertaken by member economies, consultants, and other researchers. Even to the extent that APEC's working groups and committees have touched on most of the OECD's policy themes, the relatively *ad hoc* and voluntary nature of APEC fora would suggest that APEC's coverage of these themes has been more cursory than in the OECD. In terms of the core economic mandates of the two organizations, there are some rough parallels. The *APEC Economic Outlook*, produced by the APEC Economic Committee, serves a similar function to the OECD's bi-annual reports. However, given the fluid nature of the Economic Committee's leadership and members, the consistency and quality of the annual economic report cannot be taken for granted. Even accounting for its more recent vintage, the *APEC Economic Outlook* does not command the same degree of respect and attention as its OECD equivalent.

Cross-cutting Dialogue.   A central feature of the OECD process is the annual ministerial summit. These summits place importance on what might be termed cross-cutting research and dialogue — for example, studies on sustainable development and the sources of economic growth.[25] At the 2001 meeting, a joint session of ministers of finance/economics and environment was held to examine the interrelationships between these two areas of policy-making.

Since 2000, the OECD's Public Affairs and Communications directorate has organized an annual conference to engage a wider audience of business, labour, and non-governmental organizations (NGOs). The title of the OECD 2002 Forum, "Getting the Fundamentals Right: Security, Equity, Education and Growth" epitomizes the institution's broad coverage of policy themes, in this case incorporating the post-11 September environment into more traditional areas of its research programme.

APEC's role in cross-cutting dialogue, both in its formal annual processes and its broader connections with NGOs, has some similarities with the OECD. The Shanghai Leaders' Meeting connected security with APEC's traditional economic agenda, including issues of financial control and transportation safety. Additionally, APEC's High-Level Meeting on Capacity Building, held in Beijing in May 2001, was an important advance in achieving a dialogue on the connections between the new economy and education and training. The Dialogue on Globalization and Shared Prosperity, held in Merida, Mexico, in May 2002, also looked at cross-cutting issues of economic change and civil society engagement.

Creation of Norms (Soft Law).   The formation of flexible consensus is an important task of a body dedicated to dialogue and information sharing. One example of this non-binding "soft law" is the OECD guidelines for multinational enterprises, first adopted in 1976.[26] After a review in 2000, the fifth in its lifetime, provisions on consumer rights, fighting corruption, and eliminating child labour were added. All OECD governments, plus Argentina, Brazil, and Chile supported the guidelines.

The creation of norms is even more important in APEC, because of its informal nature. APEC has succeeded in establishing both "process" and "results" norms. Examples of the former include consensus, flexibility, and voluntarism, while the idea of free trade and investment, exemplified in the Bogor goals, is an example of the latter. Paul Davidson has argued that these norms represent a form of "soft law" which helps to guide APEC members in their relations with one another.[27] Other examples of these norms include APEC's non-binding investment principles, trade facilitation principles, and non-binding principles on government procurement.

Conducting Negotiations. The OECD also serves as a forum for the negotiation of legally-binding multilateral agreements. One example is the OECD Convention on Combating Bribery of Foreign Public Officials in International Business Transactions, which entered into force in 1999.[28] The Convention requires signatories to make it a crime under their own law for anyone to offer, promise, or give "undue pecuniary or other advantage" to a foreign public official. The Convention leaves the investigation and prosecution to the specific rules of each country, and provides monitoring and follow-up through its Working Group on Bribery and International Business Transactions.

A less successful example of the OECD's efforts in brokering negotiated agreements is the Multilateral Agreement on Investment (MAI). The objective of the MAI was to build on previous OECD guidelines on investment and conclude a comprehensive agreement on non-discrimination, including protection and dispute settlement provisions. The OECD, rather than the World Trade Organization (WTO), was chosen as the venue for the negotiations because it was felt that as a smaller body agreement could be achieved more rapidly. After four years of preparatory work and another three years of negotiations, the MAI foundered in 1998 on the objections of civil society groups around the world and the withdrawal of support from key governments (France, in particular). As William Dymond has observed, "The MAI negotiations were a sobering experience for the OECD as an institution. Its traditional strengths of policy analysis and development and its operational style served it poorly when confronted with the challenge of negotiating a complex treaty text involving binding and enforceable commitments .... Patient repair are [sic] required to the reputation of the OECD in order to refocus its work in its areas of greatest strength and to commit it to eschewing all further negotiating initiatives."[29]

There are interesting parallels between the MAI and APEC's Early Voluntary Sectoral Liberalization (EVSL) scheme. Both failures can be attributed, at least in part, to an attempt on the part of the respective organizations to extend their reach beyond institutional capabilities. Indeed, it seems that in the future both APEC and the OECD will serve as what Ostry calls "parallel substantive" organizations *vis-à-vis* the WTO, supporting the advancement of a rules-based international economic order through dialogue and "soft law", rather than serving as negotiating bodies to reach specific, binding agreements.

Peer Review. Peer review through the OECD's Economic and Development Review Committee (EDRC) is as old as the institution itself. Under this system, a group of impartial examiners makes an assessment of each member country's economic performance, pointing out its present situation, key challenges, and possible solutions. It is also tasked with explicitly addressing recommendations made in previous years and actions taken towards achieving them, providing a degree of continuity. The time between reviews is not to exceed eighteen months.

The peer review process begins with the OECD Secretariat sending a draft questionnaire covering both macroeconomic and structural dimensions of economic performance before meeting with each member country's mission. "Questions for Examination" are then prepared, following closely the draft survey's assessments and recommendations, and provides the basis for the formal examination — a highly structured one-day discussion aimed at assisting the Secretariat in redrafting the Economic Survey in light of the committee's deliberations.

APEC's peer review is unique in that it focuses not on the overall economic performance of member economies but on the Individual Action Plans (IAPs). The selection of economies subject to peer review is strictly on a voluntary basis. In October 2001, APEC leaders agreed to a more rigorous peer review process using independent experts. Under the new process, the review will be based on comments from member economies, sub-fora, and the APEC Business Advisory Council (ABAC); responses to a formal questionnaire directed at the economy under review; and face-to-face interviews with government officials. The independent expert's report will then be presented at a formal peer review session held in conjunction with the APEC Senior Officials Meeting.

Collaboration with Non-Members, Regional and International Organizations. The OECD established a Centre for Co-operation with Non-Members in 1998 and currently has active relationships with seventy non-members. Although the OECD is a membership-based organization, its connections with outside parties might be seen as a variant of APEC's "open regionalism", designed to spread some of the benefits of its activities to the wider world. This co-operation ranges from one-time studies on specific topics to multi-year projects.

Of special interest here are co-operation initiatives between APEC and the OECD. In autumn 2000, the two bodies agreed to a conference and three workshops on regulatory reform, following the 1999 APEC Principles to Enhance Competition and Regulatory Reform and the 1997 OECD Principles for Regulatory Reform. The first two meetings were held in Singapore in 2000 and Beijing in 2001, with subsequent meetings in Merida, Mexico, in April 2002, and Seoul in October 2002. The agendas included broad overviews about the results of comparative efforts, deregulation, and discussions on how to implement regulatory reform proposals, ensure transparency, and communicate with stakeholders.

The Debate on a Pacific OECD: Assessing the Arguments

The preceding comparison of the OECD and APEC reveals a number of differences that only in part boil down to the size of the respective secretariats. Historical and political factors, in particular, have been raised as obstacles to APEC becoming a Pacific OECD. Ostry, for instance, has cited "system differences" based on geopolitical competition between China and the United States. She also noted at the time of writing her chapter, that China was not a member of the WTO, which is no longer the case. This points to a larger objection, which suggests that the APEC economies are too divergent in levels of growth and development as well as in their approach to market economics to take on the OECD model.

This position ignores the fact that, as Dinan has shown, the OEEC economies also varied widely, and that it was still transformed into a research organization in the shape of the OECD.[30] Indeed, there is a good case for an organization devoted to information-sharing and dialogue among diverse economies, to reduce misunderstanding. Moreover, establishing a more robust system of information-sharing on economic issues could help to reinforce what China and the United States have in common, a strong and growing trade relationship, and to deflect attention from their geopolitical differences. An effort to adopt some elements of the OECD sooner, rather than later, would be appropriate, given Sino-American *rapprochement* in the wake of 11 September.

A more intangible obstacle to the creation of a Pacific OECD is the Asia-Pacific region's loss of lustre following the 1997 financial crisis. In outlining the history of efforts to create an OPTAD, Drysdale has made clear that one of the underlying forces was the belief that economic power had shifted from the Atlantic to the Pacific. The political will to establish a new type of trans-Pacific institution may be lacking on both sides of the Pacific — especially in the Americas where hemispheric free trade is a priority, but also among Asian members who are concerned about being left out by a putative Free Trade Area of the Americas and would therefore give priority to Asia-only regionalism and/or bilateral agreements with North American partners.

Another argument questioning the formation of a Pacific OECD suggests that the present structure may be good enough. As mentioned above, Ostry has talked about APEC's "virtual secretariat" of think-tanks, working groups, INGOs, and member governments: "Could these rotating and migrating intergovernmental groups be substitutes for the OECD location-based continuity-based meeting infrastructure? Perhaps."[31] Recent experience, however, has demonstrated that this "virtual secretariat" has not been sufficient to ensure follow up pledges in Leaders' Statements, as indicated by the re-appearance of the goal of "implementation" in the priorities of the lead economy year upon year.

The traditional argument against strengthening the APEC Secretariat is based on an aversion to unnecessary bureaucracy and concerns about the costs to member governments. To the extent, however, that a strengthening of the professional secretariat staff would reduce the need for member governments to deploy officials to more than 300 APEC meetings a year, it is not clear that the overall costs to APEC members would increase. The APEC Secretariat budget of US$3 million per year is, after all, a very small percentage of total spending by member economies on APEC activities. There is a case for re-allocating some of this spending from national budgets to a strengthened central secretariat.

Practical Steps Towards APEC as a Pacific OECD

This chapter closes with some practical suggestions to advance the idea of a Pacific OECD. These suggestions involve changes in both the conceptual underpinnings of APEC and the way in which APEC operates as an institution. In the sense that "form has to follow function," one set of changes without the other will not succeed. On the contrary, a change in the conceptual underpinnings of APEC without commensurate changes in the institutional structure, or vice versa, will only serve to create greater dissonance and frustration within the organization and among member economies.

- *Articulation of APEC's Unique Role in Regional Policy Development*
  Even though there is no explicit, official statement of APEC's function as a regional forum for policy development, the work of most APEC fora, in fact, amounts to policy development through

information exchange, workshops, studies, and identification of best practices/principles. A clear articulation of this function would provide a focus to APEC activities that is consistent with the ultimate goal of free and open trade. Indeed, by defining APEC's policy development activities as serving the goal of free and open trade, the onus on APEC shifts from that of delivering trade liberalization as such (which it is ill-equipped to do) to a more realistic agenda of delivering policy prognoses and prescriptions that are supportive of the liberalization agenda. This conceptual shift would be tantamount to the idea of a Pacific OECD and would open the door to more substantive reforms in institutional structure and funding.

An updated conception of APEC as a regional policy forum would raise questions about the role of economic and technical co-operation (ECOTECH) — traditionally a major pillar of APEC's work. Even though APEC has disavowed any role as a source of development funding for members, there is a lingering sense among some APEC officials and analysts that ECOTECH is about delivering technical assistance projects. While there is no necessary conflict between policy development and the delivery of technical assistance projects, an unclear relationship between the two has the potential to undermine APEC's institutional development.

In practice, APEC as an institution does not deliver any meaningful quantum of technical assistance or development funding, but it provides a venue for member economies and third-party funders, such as the World Bank and the Asian Development Bank, to do so. To the extent that APEC is evolving into a regional policy development forum, this distinction is an important one to emphasize. One trajectory for APEC's evolving structure is to conceive of policy development as the basis for which technical assistance activities can be designed and delivered by member economies and multilateral development banks.[33] The ECOTECH agenda, in turn, would have two aspects: firstly, provision of modest technical assistance (from collective APEC resources) to developing economy members for the purpose of enabling them to participate fully in the policy development process, and secondly as a vehicle for member economies to pledge and report on development co-operation activities that emerge from or are related to the broader APEC agenda. This clear delineation between policy development and ECOTECH would not only reinforce the case for a Pacific OECD but would represent an important and beneficial departure from the Paris-based model.

- *Permanent Professional Staff Positions at the APEC Secretariat*
Re-conceptualization of APEC along the lines of a Pacific OECD
would raise questions about the role and structure of the Secretariat.
The need for some professional staff and institutional continuity at
the APEC Secretariat — already a widely held view in APEC circles
— would be further strengthened by such re-conceptualization.
Starting with the Executive Director position, staff positions should
have a minimum tenure of three years, with the option of renewal.
The professionalization of staff should start with research positions,
consistent with a greater emphasis at the Secretariat on regional
policy development. The head of research and analysis, in particular,
should be a senior person hired on merit.

These changes would necessitate a modest expansion of the
Secretariat, both in the number of employees and in its budget.
While the prospect of increased financial contributions will create
resistance among member economies, the effective transfer of
responsibilities to the Secretariat should over time lead to reductions
in expenditures at the working group and committee levels. A
gradualist approach to Secretariat expansion would allow member
economies to work out ways of transferring expenditures on APEC
meetings to expenditures for a strengthened Secretariat.

- *Devolution of Selected APEC Fora Activities to the Secretariat*
Another implication of re-conceptualizing APEC as a regional
policy development body is in the role of its working groups *vis-à-
vis* a strengthened Secretariat. Under the existing system, APEC
working groups are effectively proxies for a regional Secretariat
involved in policy development activities. These working groups,
however, are severely limited in their ability to produce substantive
policy outputs because of their fluid membership, frequent rotation
of leadership, and uncertain meeting schedules.

The gradual devolution of selected APEC fora activities to the
Secretariat would provide for greater depth and continuity in these
activities, and can be seen as a pilot project or "pathfinder" for
APEC's institutional development. An excellent first choice for
devolution would be APEC's Economic Committee (EC) because
of the regularity in its work programme (especially the preparation
of the annual Economic Outlook) and the potential for the Economic
Committee over time to branch out into other areas of comparative
policy research and analysis. Another candidate for early devolution
is the Committee on Trade and Investment (CTI), given the centrality
of the trade and investment agenda in APEC and the important

function that CTI plays in the co-ordination of numerous sub-committee activities.

Finally, the road to a Pacific OECD should include greater linkages between APEC and the OECD. The purpose of these linkages is to expand institutional collaboration in new areas and should go beyond the co-hosting of meetings to the conduct of joint policy research. A more formalized approach to co-operation might be modelled on the recently-signed OECD-UNCTAD agreement. This co-operative approach would provide APEC with a basis, over time, to identify areas where it can build a substantive work programme that is unique to the needs of the Asia-Pacific region. There would be mutual learning in areas such as peer review, where APEC and the OECD pursue similar goals but through different approaches and instruments. Likewise, there is scope for co-operation in the preparation of economic outlook and other analytical products, as well as the avoidance of overlapping areas of work. Not least, co-operation with the OECD will serve to clarify for APEC members the necessary conceptual and operational changes that are needed in moving towards a Pacific OECD, as well as the pitfalls to avoid. If a Pacific OECD is to emerge, it will be defined as much by its "Pacific" roots as by the Paris prototype.

Notes

1. Kiyoshi Kojiman, "Japan's Interest in Pacific Trade Expansion", and Peter Drysdale, "Pacific Economic Integration: An Australian View". In *Pacific Trade and Development*, edited by Kiyoshi Kojima (Tokyo: Japan Economic Research Center, 1968).
2. Peter Drysdale, "The Proposal for an Organization for Pacific Trade and Development Revisited", *Asian Survey* 3, No. 12 (December 1983): 1293–304.
3. Peter Drysdale, *International Economic Pluralism: Economic Policy in East Asia and the Pacific* (New York: Columbia University Press, 1988), pp. 204–25.
4. Department of the Prime Minister and Cabinet, "Regional Cooperation: Challenges for Korea and Australia" (Speech by Prime Minister Bob Hawke to a Luncheon of Korean business associations, Seoul, South Korea, 31 January 1989).
5. Yuen Pau Woo, *APEC After Ten Years: What's Left of 'Open Regionalism?'* (New York: Oceana Publications, 1999).
6. For a recent discussion, see "Summary Conclusions of the First APEC Senior Officials' Meeting [SOM] for the Fourteenth Annual APEC Ministerial Meeting," Mexico City, 28–29 February 2002, p. 16.
7. Nicholas Bray, "Europe 50 Years After the Marshall Plan — Unhappy Birthday: OECD is Grappling with Identity Crisis as Group Turns 50," *Wall Street Journal Europe*, 26 May 1997.

8. Anthony Rowley, "Parisian model: OECD may set pattern for future APEC structure", *Far Eastern Economic Review*, 16 November 1989, pp. 12–13.
9. Edward English, "An OECD of the Pacific? A Canadian Perspective," Working Paper #1, Asia Pacific Research and Resource Centre (Ottawa: Carleton University, 1990).
10. Nobutioshi Akao, "Strategy for APEC: A Japanese View", *Japan Review of International Affairs* 9, No. 3 (Summer 1995): 169–77.
11. Sylvia Ostry, "APEC and Regime Creation in the Asia-Pacific: The OECD Model?" in *Asia-Pacific Crossroads: Regime Creation and the Future of APEC*, edited by Vinod K. Aggarwal and Charles E. Morrison (New York: St. Martin's Press, 1998), pp. 317–50.
12. Jack Taylor, "Australia must push for OECD-style APEC: Shadow Trade Minister", Agence France-Presse, 26 August 2001.
13. Hadi Soesastro, "Asia at the Nexus: APEC and ASEM," *Panorama* 4 (2001): 15–30.
14. The most important statement of the idea of epistemic communities can be found in Peter Haas, "Introduction: Epistemic Communities and International Policy Coordination", *International Organization* 46, No. 1 (Winter 1992): 1–35.
15. Richard Higgott, "APEC: A Sceptical View", in *Pacific Cooperation: Building Economic and Security Regimes in the Asia-Pacific Region*, edited by Andrew Mack and John Ravenhill (Boulder: Westview Press, 1995), pp. 71–72. See also Ostry, op. cit., p. 319.
16. Michael Wesley, "APEC's Mid-Life Crisis? The Rise and Fall of Early Voluntary Sectoral Liberalization", *Pacific Affairs* 74 (Summer 2001): 185–204.
17. Desmond Dinan, *Ever Closer Union?* (Boulder, Colorado: Lynne Reinner Publishers, 1994), pp. 18–19.
18. OECD, "Convention of the Organisation for Economic Co-operation and Development," 14 December 1960, at http://www.oecd.org/EN/document/0,,EN-document-0-nodirectorate-no-6-5610-0,FF.html
19. Geir Lundestad, "Empire by Invitation? The United States and Western Europe, 1945–1952", *Journal of Peace Research* 23, No. 3 (1986): 263–77.
20. OECD, *OECD Annual Report*, pp. 114–15.
21. Business and Industry Advisory Committee to the OECD: http://www.biac.org
22. Trade Union Advisory Committee to the OECD: http://www.tuac.org
23. Yuen Pau Woo, "Globalisation and Comprehensive Security" (Paper presented at the 14th Asia Pacific Roundtable, Kuala Lumpur, 3–7 June 2000).
24. Ostry, op. cit., p. 328.
25. OECD, "Meeting of OECD Council at the Ministerial Level: A Synthesis," 16–17 May 2001, at http://www.oecd.org/pdf/M00005000/M00005122.pdf
26. OECD, "The OECD Guidelines for Multinational Enterprises", Revision 2000, at http://www.oecd.org/pdf/M000015000/M00015419.pdf
27. Paul Davidson, "The Development of an APEC Framework for Regulating International Economic Relations and its Compatibility with the Legal

Framework of the WTO" (Paper presented to the APEC Study Centre Consortium Conference, Tianjin, China, 17–20 May 2001).

28. OECD, "OECD Convention on Combatting Bribery of Foreign Public Officials in International Business Transactions", November 1997, at http://www.oecd.org/oecd/pages/document/displaywithoutnav/0,3376,EN-document-notheme-1-no-no-7198-0,00.html

29. William Dymond, "The MAI: A Sad and Melancholy Tale", in *Canada Among Nations 1999: A Big League Player?*, edited by Fen Osler Hampson, Martin Rudner and Michael Hart (Toronto: Oxford University Press, 1999), p. 50.

30. Dinan, op. cit., p. 19.

31. Ostry, op. cit., p. 348.

32. The APEC Economic Integration Programme, funded by the Canadian International Development Agency, is an example of a technical assistance project inspired by the work of the APEC WTO Capacity Building forum but funded entirely by a member economy.

SECTION III

MANAGEMENT REFORMS

4

THE APEC SECRETARIAT
A Management Perspective

STEWART GOODINGS

Introduction

This chapter is designed to stimulate discussion and informed debate about the organizational structure and role of the APEC Secretariat. The chapter reviews the evolution of the Secretariat, its current situation, its weaknesses, as well as options for improvement. Finally, it makes some recommendations to strengthen the effectiveness of the Secretariat.

Background

The APEC Secretariat was established in Singapore in 1992 with the intention of creating a support mechanism that reflected the informal, consensus-based nature of the APEC process. Thus, it was decided to keep the Secretariat small, based on secondments from host economies. It was not expected to emulate the much larger permanent staffs of other multilateral organizations such as the OECD. The Secretariat was mandated to provide four core functions:

- Advisory, operational, logistic, and technical services to member economies and to APEC fora.
- Financial oversight, control, and evaluation of projects funded from the APEC Operational and TILF (trade and investment liberalization and facilitation) accounts.
- Information and public affairs support to promote APEC's role and activities.
- Capacity to support research and analysis in collaboration with APEC Study Centres and the Pacific Economic Co-operation Council (PECC).

During the past decade, there has been a substantial enlargement of the APEC agenda, with more committees and fora, more sectoral ministerial meetings, and more projects than was the case in the early days of the organization. The issue now is whether the current resources and structure and operational procedures of the Secretariat are adequate to cope with both this increased workload and the greater expectations of member economies.

Current Situation

At present, the APEC Secretariat is led by an Executive Director seconded from the member economy which is hosting the annual APEC process. There is a deputy Executive Director, seconded from the member economy which will host the APEC process in the subsequent year. The deputy is in effect "learning the ropes" for the following year during which he will have full responsibility for leading APEC when his economy is the host.

There are approximately twenty-three officials seconded from member economies on two to three-year postings, and an equivalent number of locally engaged administrative support staff. The programme staff are usually generalists coming from the Foreign Affairs or Trade departments of their economies. Each one is assigned to provide programme and technical assistance to the Lead Shepherd or Chair of one or more committees or fora. In addition, there are programme staff assigned to look after certain corporate functions such as finance, public information, evaluation, and research.

Weaknesses of the Current Situation

1. There is a serious lack of continuity in the Secretariat. The top two leaders are in place for a maximum of two years. Their primary duty is to their respective member economies to ensure that the annual

hosting process works smoothly. They spend much of their time travelling to member economies preparing for the annual Ministerial and Leaders' meetings. Thus, their opportunities for focusing on the management of the Secretariat and building stable procedures and practices are severely limited. As for the programme staff, the rotation is constant, with seconded staff leaving to return to their homes, and new ones arriving, often with no overlap in timing. An office where the most experienced employee is a "veteran" of three or perhaps four years is unlikely to have much of an institutional memory or commitment to long-term thinking.

2.   There is no provision for specialists in the Secretariat. Whomever the member economies send to Singapore must then be assigned to work on committees and functional areas based on the expertise each brings to the assignment. While the Secretariat does try to recruit the specialized skills needed from member economies, this does not always work, and often there is a gap between what is needed and what is available. This hampers the ability of the Secretariat to address particular problems, such as the well documented need to do a better job of evaluating APEC projects, or of reaching out more effectively to non-governmental and community groups.

3.   The Secretariat lacks several basic managerial practices. For example, there are few regular staff or management meetings, there is no procedures manual, there is no performance appraisal or measurement system, and there is no system of professional development. As a consequence, decisions tend to be taken without full consultation, staff "get by" but lack the opportunity to learn while in Singapore, and improvements are gained on an *ad hoc* basis without integrating them into the ongoing life of the Secretariat.

4.   There is very limited capacity to address new and emerging issues in APEC. For example, leadership of the committees and fora in APEC has not been spread widely among member economies. While detailed data have not yet been collected, anecdotal evidence suggests that a relatively small number of economies have borne the main burden of chairing committees, running projects, and hosting meetings. Some member economies may be able to take on greater leadership if they have additional support from the Secretariat, but at present, this is not possible. It would be unfortunate if leadership in APEC became divided between the "haves" and the "have-nots".

5.   It is difficult for the Secretariat to keep up with the increasing work-load of the organization. It is one thing to organize regular committee meetings and handle the ongoing administrative requirements. It is quite another thing to reflect on the organization's

experiences, to monitor and measure the achievements and identify the lessons learned, and to anticipate the upcoming needs. To use a sporting analogy, the staff are sprinting to stand still. With APEC moving confidently into its second decade, the organization's permanent office should be matching APEC's evolution and assuming a more sophisticated and constructive role in support of leaders' directions.

Options for Improvement

1. One possibility would be to create a new senior position with primary responsibility for management of the Secretariat, either by appointing a Secretary-General as the top policy and programme person, with a 5–7 year appointment, or by hiring a General Manager who would not have "policy" responsibilities, but would have the role of managing the operational aspects of the Secretariat. In both cases, each year's annual host would continue to appoint a senior representative to be based in the Secretariat with the primary duty to ensure the smooth functioning of the annual series of APEC meetings. The Secretary-General or General Manager would hold regular staff and management meetings, would handle all human resource questions, and would be the organization's main link with other organizations.

2. A new level of middle manager specialists could be hired to lead certain key functional areas in the Secretariat, for example, finance, human resources, public information, research, and programme operations. These Director-level managers would give leadership to their respective areas, and would be responsible to the Secretary-General, or General Manager for all matters within their sphere of control. They would be recruited as permanent staff, with five-year contracts, with options for renewal. Seconded programme staff from member economies would be assigned to teams led by these Directors.

3. New procedures could be put in place to raise the level of professionalism of the Secretariat. For example, a detailed human resource management system could be developed that would include proper job descriptions for all positions, a performance appraisal system, a training and development policy, an employment equity and employee assistance programme, and so forth. In addition, it would be helpful to have a complete management information system that would provide all staff with immediate access to historical materials, current budget and administrative information, and current decision-making needs.

4. The Budget and Management Committee (BMC) could play a more effective role as liaison between the Secretariat and the Senior Officials' Meeting (SOM). If the BMC created a small management advisory committee to link up on a regular basis with the Secretary-General or General Manager, this might lead to a more normal "legislative/executive" relationship and might avoid the seemingly constant but fruitless studies and reviews of the Secretariat's operation, which have characterized APEC so far.

Recommendations

In making a number of recommendations to strengthen the Secretariat, this chapter acknowledges that the Secretariat has performed quite successfully during the first decade of APEC's existence. It should also be recognized that APEC members probably do not wish to see the Secretariat become "another OECD", in other words, there is no desire to grow the permanent staff in a significant way. APEC is an organization *pas comme les autres* and members take justifiable pride in having a small-sized secretariat with a reasonable budget. Despite these caveats, evidence suggests that some thoughtful and modest initiatives could be taken that would serve member economies and the leaders well without changing the essential character of either the organization or the Secretariat. These suggestions are designed to help APEC move more efficiently into the next phase of its evolution, and to deal with an increasing work-load.

1. Create a permanent senior level position responsible for the management of the Secretariat.
2. Create six permanent Director-level positions to manage the corporate functions of finance, human resources, research, evaluation, public information, and programme operations.
3. Develop internal management policies in the areas of personnel and information management.
4. Set up a BMC advisory committee for ongoing liaison with the senior staff person in the Secretariat.

Conclusion

This review of the APEC Secretariat suggests that with some modest improvements, significant change could be expected in the level of support provided to the APEC agenda. There would be additional costs, but they would not be exorbitant. With these enhancements, better service would be provided to the leaders and committees of APEC, and an assignment at the Secretariat would become a more satisfying professional experience.

5

PROJECT SELECTION AND EVALUATION
APEC's Budget and Management Committee and the Secretariat

RICHARD E. FEINBERG

This practical chapter describes the APEC project approval and evaluation process, and the roles of the Budget and Management Committee (BMC) and the APEC Secretariat in the project cycle. It explores weaknesses in these procedures and institutions and concludes with various policy recommendations to enhance the efficiency and transparency of APEC decision-making and to bolster project quality and impact.

Background: The APEC-Funded Project Cycle

Most APEC-funded projects consist of workshops and conferences, short-term capacity-building training sessions, construction of databases, surveys, and policy-oriented research and publications. APEC is not in the business of financing large-scale, brick and mortar projects. A significant percentage of APEC funding is allocated to participant travel and per diem and to consultant fees. Few APEC projects receive more than US$300,000, and most receive considerably less. Yet, projects are vitally important to many APEC fora, embodying their objectives and making concrete their agendas.

There are two sources of project funding (which together make up the "APEC Central Fund"): the Operational Account, which is funded from APEC member economy annual contributions; and the Trade and Investment Liberalization and Facilitation or TILF Special Account, which to date has received funding only from Japan. Each year, the Operational Account allocates about US$2 million and the TILF Special Account up to 500 million yen, or an annual total of US$5–6 million in project funding.

The project approval process, similar in most respects for both accounts, is as follows:

1. The proposed project manager ("overseer") and APEC member economy sponsor or sponsors initiate discussion within an appropriate APEC forum (for example, a Committee or Working Group, or with increasing frequency within the Senior Officials' Meeting or SOM). Most project overseers are themselves government officials, although occasionally an academic or independent expert with close ties to his/her government can play that role.

2. Project documentation is cumbersome and project overseers may work closely with the professional staff member (PSM) at the APEC Secretariat assigned to that subject or forum. Nevertheless, project submissions often do not fully conform to the detailed format requirements laid out in the official *Guidebook on APEC Projects* (available on the APEC Secretariat website). These discrepancies may be due to the many obligatory clearances, the time pressures imposed by the various deadlines in the project cycle, and the permutations of the requirements themselves.

3. The project sponsors circulate a draft proposal, and through an iterative process refine the proposal to reach a consensus among participants in the forum. Consensus is defined as 100 per cent acceptance — for example, any APEC member economy can veto a project. In APEC fashion, formal votes are not taken, and vetoing can occur indirectly, through delaying tactics. Approved project documents require the signatures of the forum's Chair or Lead Shepherd.

4. The Operational Account limits each APEC forum to 15 per cent of the current year's total budget, or roughly US$300,000. This

ceiling is APEC's main mechanism for distributing members' annual dues across the array of initiatives. However, the TILF Special Account has no such ceiling.

5. Forums are requested to rank the order of their projects. When the total number of forum-approved projects exceeds the budgets of the Operational or TILF Accounts, as occurred for the first time in 2001, the BMC will largely rely upon forum rankings to "send back" (reject or defer) projects to the originating forums.

6. If a forum falls within the jurisdiction of the Committee on Trade and Investment (CTI), that Committee will review all proposals from its sub-forums and rank them. The ECOTECH Subcommittee, however, enjoys no such authority.

7. Project sponsors frequently circulate projects informally to the SOMs and (with increasing frequency in recent cycles) will include in the project proposal wording such as "SOMs have enthusiastically endorsed" the proposal.

8. Projects endorsed by relevant APEC forums are reviewed and approved by the Budget and Management Committee (BMC), at its February/March meeting for "urgent" projects and its July/August meeting (APEC is currently reviewing its definition of "urgent"). The BMC convenes at the APEC Secretariat in Singapore, because the Secretariat staff plays a central role in project preparation and financial control. The BMC consists of officials from the twenty-one APEC member economies, generally at the deputy SOM or office director level, often from foreign ministries, and in a few cases with representatives from local embassies. If, as in most years, the amounts requested are less than the available funds, the BMC will approve all or almost all projects, perhaps deferring a few projects pending further clarifications. The BMC will question whether some proposed line items meet APEC guidelines, but rarely will second guess the worthiness of the project itself, deferring to the judgments of the specialized APEC forums.

9. The BMC-approved budget, which includes lists of the approved projects, proceeds for pro forma concurrence by the SOM and Ministers. For the regular, non-urgent projects, this means at the SOM III in September and at the ministers' meeting associated with the Leaders Meeting in October/November.

10. Funds are available from the Operational Account in January of the following year. In conformity with the Japanese budget cycle, funds from the TILF Special Account are not available until the following April/May, although subject to prior approval of the BMC, urgent projects may commence in January.

11. The entire approval cycle generally requires 7–12 months for the Operational Account and up to 17 months for the TILF Special Account. That is measured from the moment of approval by the initiating forum (to move through the BMC, SOMs and Ministers to the availability of funds); in addition, the discussion process within the sixteen or so APEC forums — where the effective decisions are generally taken — can itself take many months.
12. Funding is for a single year. Any multi-year projects must submit fresh requests in subsequent years.
13. The project overseers themselves are responsible for evaluating their own projects upon completion. The relevant APEC forums are charged with assessing these evaluations and forwarding them to the BMC. The BMC has established "small groups" that, via electronic correspondence, review these self-evaluations and convey any comments it might have to the appropriate forums.

Criteria for Project Selection

The *Guidebook on APEC Projects* lists these criteria for project selection (abstracted from Annex B, as revised in July 2000):

1. *APEC Values*. Projects should:
    a) be a direct response to the priorities of the Leaders and Ministers as set out in their declarations;
    b) be approved by a committee or working group, consistent with its policy statements;
    c) have the active participation of a large number of APEC members;
    d) encourage participation from the business/private sector and non-governmental institutions and women;
    e) add specific APEC value;
    f) support the role of women in achieving sustainable development; and
    g) and for ECOTECH projects, be highly focused and results oriented, and have explicit objectives, milestones, and performance criteria.

2. *Project Design*. Projects should:
    a) identify the kinds of institutions in member economies intended to benefit from the results;
    b) have a timetable for the accomplishment of each project component, with associated outputs; and
    c) indicate possible contributions to related projects in APEC or elsewhere.

3. *Dissemination of Results.* Projects should:
   a) have a budgeted plan for the publication and dissemination of results; and
   b) indicate the target audience.

This is a strong list of criteria, in many respects consistent with those advocated in previous APIAN studies. Less clear is the ranking of criteria, and whether some criteria are themselves sufficient reasons for approval — for example, endorsement in a statement by Leaders or Ministers (a critical issue in that it affects the degree to which the project process is bottom-up or top-down). Also unclear is the manner in which various forums apply these criteria, as the BMC and SOM typically do not second-guess the forums. Comparisons across issues and forums — for example, how to compare an anti-terrorism project with a health initiative, or a training session with a research study — are avoided.

Five Issues for Consideration

1. *The project approval process is lengthy, complex, and time-consuming, particularly when measured against the modest size of the grants.* The onerous disbursement process, which requires continual documentation and operates on a reimbursement basis, is also the source of frequent complaint by project managers. These complexities delay progress, reduce the net benefit from expenditures, and reportedly discourage some potential project managers from applying altogether.

   The APEC Secretariat is currently charged with revising and updating the *Guidebook on APEC Projects*, in co-ordination with the BMC. It could be encouraged to undertake a thorough revision with the aim of simplifying the entire process, including not only format but also the approval process itself.

   Whether the SOM and Ministers need to clear the BMC-approved budget and projects, with the resulting delays, should be reconsidered. The BMC, after all, are government officials who work directly for the SOMs and could be empowered with final approval, just as in the international financial institutions, for example, executive directors are empowered to approve budgets and projects without waiting for ministerial-level sign-off. In effect, the SOMs should delegate more genuine management authority to the BMC, "to put the M back in the BMC."

   Another potential reform would be to allow the APEC forum final approval of a limited number of projects under a predetermined amount (well beyond the current ceiling of US$20,000); this is not as radical a departure as it may seem, since effective approval typically occurs at the forum level and the BMC and SOM/Ministers' approvals are largely pro forma.

2. *The project process is for the most part the purview of government officials seeking funding for government-driven projects.* The private sector and independent citizens often participate in projects, but it is very difficult for them to originate projects or to self-navigate the approval process. (With its long-standing ties to the APEC process, PECC is a partial exception to the rule.) While the *Guidebook on APEC Projects* is posted on the APEC website, in fact, for most citizens of APEC economies, the project approval process is hardly transparent. This exclusivity sharply limits the ability of APEC to engage the creativity and participation of most of its peoples. It undercuts APEC's ability to reach out to the broader community, to build a wider constituency, and to improve its public image. It also reduces the number of project submissions and, therefore, in all probability the overall quality of APEC projects.

    How can the project approval process be opened up? One option would be for APEC to set aside a certain amount of funds that could be approved by a commission of independent experts, in the manner of many government-funded programmes that support the sciences and arts. Perhaps the BMC might retain the right of final review. If such a commission were created, APEC should provide for resources to widely disseminate its existence and procedures, so as to generate sufficient numbers of quality projects from a widening array of project sponsors.

3. *The ultimate impact of most APEC projects is probably small.* There are many excellent APEC-funded projects that respond to APEC mandates and advance important development objectives. Yet, most APEC projects are very small, even taking into account the total size of the project, including co-financing. Moreover, most projects have little or no follow-up.

    In the light of their size, if there is to be measurable value-added, APEC-funded projects need to be conceived as model or demonstration projects to be scaled up or replicated many times over. To accomplish this, potential measures include requiring all projects to have as participants potential funders of follow-on projects, from the private sector, international financial institutions, and bilateral donors, in the hope that if the project succeeds they will catalyze replications and larger-scale endeavours; and requiring all projects to include Stage II follow-on activities, to maintain and expand project benefits.

The APEC Secretariat might house liaison officers of these various sources of co-finance, seconded from the various capital-rich institutions. The APEC Business Advisory Committee (ABAC) might play a role in providing private-sector representatives.

The Asian Development Bank (ADS) is the obvious regional body to co-finance and leverage APEC projects. Institutionally, the ADB is under the guidance of finance ministries, and has willingly co-financed most of the APEC-funded projects proposed by the Ministers of Finance. Yet, the ADB has not engaged equally with other APEC forums, reflecting the reluctance of its finance ministry masters to follow the lead of a process largely under the control of foreign ministries. Only the Leaders can overcome this bureaucratic logjam and mandate a wider and deeper ADB engagement with APEC.

There is also the question of APEC member contributions to the Operational and TILF accounts. Revealed preference would suggest that most APEC developed economies (other than Japan) do not believe in APEC-funded projects, for they refuse to contribute beyond their *de minimus* required assessments. Despite the talk about overcoming traditional North–South roles, the developing economy members of APEC are reluctant to contribute additional resources. Perhaps it is a question of collective action: member economies do not want to contribute unless all will do so. If that is the case, APEC as a body should review its financial structure. If the sticking point is the questionable quality and value-added of APEC-funded projects, perhaps other reforms suggested here may correct these perceived shortcomings.

The extraordinary March 2002 Monterrey conference on development finance, where the United States and many other donor nations pledged significant increases in foreign assistance, offers a wonderful opportunity for APEC to claim a small portion of those additional resources. It would be entirely fitting for Mexico, which so successfully hosted the Monterrey summit, to take the lead in linking the Los Cabos Leaders' Meeting with decisions taken at this earlier event.

4.   *It is unreasonable to expect self-evaluation by project overseers to be objective.* While BMC efforts to improve its evaluative procedures are to be welcomed, they have focused primarily on process matters rather

than on evaluating the fundamental purposes and results of the projects. Robust project evaluation is critical to assure APEC economies that their monies are being well spent, and to provide feedback for the improvement of future projects and the dissemination of best practices.

Credibility and accountability require independent, expert evaluation of completed APEC projects. It is not surprising that governments shy away from potential criticism, but that is not a sufficient excuse for the lack of accountability that typifies APEC expenditure of what after all is public, taxpayer money. Rigorous, professional assessments will cost money but that is an inherent cost of business in a democratizing world. It is time for APEC to seek outside independent evaluations. APEC Study Centres are one potential source of such expert counsel.

As one deliverable from this new project audit, APEC could publish a booklet of "best practice" projects, to advertise APEC success stories and to encourage their replication.

5.   *The APEC Secretariat in Singapore provides valuable administrative support to APEC forums and to project managers — but it could do more.* The Secretariat advises project managers on administrative and financial rules, such as what costs are allowable. Previous APIAN reports have suggested that a "stronger Secretariat that has more in-house capacity to monitor implementation of APEC initiatives can help APEC to better evaluate, rationalize, and coordinate both TILF and ECOTECH." A 1995 review of the Secretariat found that it had been unable to provide substantive research and analytical support for lack of resources and expertise. This situation has not materially changed. Once again, the APEC Secretariat has submitted suggestions to the SOMs (2002/SOM1/032) that would improve its abilities to analyse APEC programmes and evaluate APEC projects. Among its proposals are for member economies to assign more specialized functionaries that fit the Secretariat's forum-focused positions — in particular, specialists suitable for assignment to the designated specialist positions; that have trade policy experience to be responsible for OAA Part I (CTI); and that has broad sectoral or development assistance experience to be responsible for OAA Part II (ECOTECH). Other project evaluation specialists would work for the BMC and ECOTECH Subcommittee.

Some of the reforms suggested above might also require enhanced capacity at the Secretariat. For example, it would fall to the Secretariat staff to select and manage independent project evaluators, to co-ordinate the work of an expert commission charged with the approval of certain projects, and to work with forums to advertise successful projects and to pursue their replication.

To improve co-ordination and continuity within the Secretariat, the addition of a multi-year general manager or chief operating officer has been suggested. This falls short, however, of the earlier APIAN proposal that the Executive Director himself be made multi-year, to provide not only better management co-ordination and continuity but also to present the world with a Voice of APEC. The rotating annual hosts of the APEC Leaders' Meeting could maintain some influence over the Secretariat through a special office created for that purpose that would be headed and staffed, in part, by persons appointed by the hosts. In addition, to more realistically equate personnel with Secretariat responsibilities, APIAN had also suggested a modest enlargement in the number of professional staff.

The proposed marginal growth in the Secretariat would require modest additional resources. For example, the current imputed cost of the Secretariat — at about 22 PSMs plus the Executive and Deputy Executive Directors (covered by the seconding member economies), and including the costs of the administrative staff (covered by member economy allocations), and building rent (paid by Singapore) — totals roughly US$4 million per year. Logically, an increase in professional and administrative staff by 50 per cent would cost roughly US$2 million more per year — a small fraction of the tens of millions of dollars that it costs just to host the annual Leaders' Meetings.

Thanks to the generosity of Singapore, the Secretariat has taken possession of a brand new building in late 2002. This landmark event offers an excellent opportunity for APEC to take stock and to consider reforms to enable its Secretariat to fulfill those functions that the APEC process, now well into its second decade, urgently requires.

SECTION IV

TRADE, INVESTMENT AND ECOTECH

6

THE APEC DECISION-MAKING PROCESS FOR TRADE POLICY ISSUES
The Experience and Lessons of 1994–2001

JOSEPH M. DAMOND

Introduction

This chapter examines the APEC decision-making process, with particular focus on how it has worked in recent years with respect to trade issues. In studying the decision-making process, I will assess it with respect to three questions: first, where do new initiatives come from, and how are they advanced in the APEC process; secondly, how is consensus reached with respect to these initiatives, and what does that consensus mean; and thirdly, how, and how well, are decisions implemented. The analysis begins with a brief exposition of APEC decision-making institutions, and their relationship, at least in principle, to one another in a typical annual APEC cycle. I then proceed to examine how these institutions have actually functioned to generate new initiatives, build consensus around them, and implement them. On the basis of this analysis, I draw some conclusions and recommendations about the process.

The analysis of these questions draws largely from my personal experience as the U.S. representative to the Committee on Trade and Investment (CTI) in 1997–99, which also involved being one of a small team of staff to the United States Trade Representative (USTR) on APEC issues, and my experience as Chair of the Committee on Trade and Investment (CTI) in 2000 and 2001, which gave me a particularly good vantage point to be involved in and observe the staff and Senior Officials process.

In addition, I will draw on my knowledge of the decision-making process just prior to my personal involvement in APEC, during 1994–96. Since these years were particularly successful in producing significant decisions, they can help explain the institutional factors behind APEC's success. At the same time, they provide a useful contrast to the years 1997–99, which were dominated by the Early Voluntary Sectoral Liberalization scheme, or EVSL. The EVSL itself was one of APEC's most ambitious efforts, an attempt to build upon the heady successes of the preceding years. However, elements that made APEC successful in those years proved lacking during the EVSL period, as will be demonstrated. Moreover, the EVSL experience itself has cast a long shadow over decision-making since 1999, and affected the way work proceeded in 2000–2002. In describing the decision-making process during these three periods — pre-EVSL (1994–96), EVSL (1997–99) and post-EVSL (2000–2002) — I will pay particular attention to the key APEC institutions involved in decision-making, and explore the degree to which the functionality of these institutions affected the decision-making process.

On balance, it appears that much steam has gone out of the APEC trade policy-making process in recent years, potentially undermining APEC's credibility and relevance in this area. APEC can regain the momentum that it attained in the mid-1990s, but it will require sustained interest and effort at the Leaders' and Ministerial level, which includes ensuring that their Senior Officials and other trade officials faithfully implement the vision set forth at each year's meeting.

APEC Decision-Making Institutions and the Annual Cycle

The APEC trade policy process operates on four main levels. In ascending order, they are: the Committee on Trade and Investment and its sub-fora; the Senior Officials' Meeting (SOM); Ministers (principally the Trade Ministerial meeting in mid-year and the Joint Ministerial (Trade and Foreign Ministers) meeting at year's end; and the APEC Economic Leaders' Meeting (AELM).

In any APEC year (that is, during the annual tenure of an APEC host economy), the Senior Officials process is central to the development of new initiatives. New initiatives are usually unveiled at the Senior Officials level, including trade-related initiatives. APEC members prefer to raise new ideas at the SOM instead of the CTI to gain visibility, to ensure that they are taken seriously as political as opposed to merely technical proposals. However, the SOM generally avoids technically fleshing out such proposals (it lacks the expertise, and in any event is not an experts group). The CTI, its sub-fora, or some grouping of CTI level officials would typically be asked to perform such work, which then flows back to the SOM for consideration. In conducting its work, the CTI will often call on the APEC Secretariat to help compile and organize the various proposals that emerge from member economies for carrying the work forward. The Secretariat is rarely, if ever, asked to proffer its own ideas, although it may sometimes do so informally.

Typically, there are two CTI and two SOM meetings prior to the mid-year Trade Ministerial meetings. These meetings normally begin by determining how to implement the decisions made by Ministers/Leaders at the end of the previous year. The SOM, assisted by the Secretariat, will compile such decisions from the Ministerial and Leaders' texts, and assign their implementation to the relevant APEC forum. Trade and investment liberalization and facilitation issues will thus be delegated to the CTI for action. However, the oversight and management of such "TILF (trade and investment liberalization and facilitation)" issues occupies a significant part of the SOM's own work, and it will often discuss and direct CTI work as it proceeds. Significantly, the SOM itself includes senior *trade* (as opposed to foreign ministry) officials; sometimes, this is in the person of a member's SOM leader (for example, Australia, New Zealand, Korea); in cases where the SOM leader is from a foreign ministry, the "plus one" is typically a trade ministry official (such as from the USTR in the United States). Notably, this senior trade official, whether he is the SOM leader or the "plus one", is a more senior official than the CTI representative for that economy.

At the same time, the SOM is determining how to implement the previous year's decisions, and the host is also working to determine the directions in which to take APEC in the current year. In the past several years, the host economy initiated this process by announcing one or more broad "themes" for its year, which signalled to other APEC members the direction it hoped new initiatives would take. For example, in 1999, New Zealand made clear that "Strengthening the Functioning of Markets" was to be a key theme, and worked with other members to develop specific initiatives that fit this rubric.

For a number of years, a critical forum in which new initiatives have been tested is the Senior Officials "retreat", which takes place away from the site of the formal SOM meeting, usually the day before that meeting begins. These relaxed, informal meetings, which include only the "SOM plus one" from each economy, are an opportunity to build relationships and float new ideas in a non-confrontational setting. The CTI Chair is invited to these meetings, but typically plays a support or staff role; the process is led by the SOM.

This informal SOM process begins an informal dialogue that is usually continued by the SOM Chair after the meetings. The SOM Chair travels frequently to APEC capitals between meetings, often visiting key members more than once during the course of the year. These contacts ensure that the Minister chairing the Trade Ministerial meeting has good intelligence on both the type of initiatives that are likely to be pushed at the meeting, and the likely "real" positions (as opposed to postures, or negotiating positions) of the member economies. This in turn allows options to be tailored within a reasonable range of the prevailing consensus, with the aim, at least in post-EVSL years (as will be seen below), of avoiding major contention at the Ministerial meetings.

Just before the Trade Ministerial, Senior Officials usually convene an "informal SOM", to work out final details on the proposals under consideration. The informal SOM includes minimal staff, and is the last chance to hammer out agreement on all but the most important policy decisions, allowing Ministers to concentrate their efforts on the big questions.

Trade Ministers themselves are afforded ample opportunity to meet informally at their mid-year meeting, often at a dinner on the day the formal meeting begins. Ministers clearly prefer to do their real "negotiating" at these sessions, involving minimal staff. Staff, of course, led by the host economy or SOM Chair, are expected to draft the results of the Ministerial statement, though many Ministers are directly involved in key parts of the text itself.

In the second part of the year, after the Trade Ministerial meeting, there is a third SOM, which usually involve additional travel by the SOM Chair to key member countries, and ultimately, the Joint Ministerial and Leaders' Meetings. Often, as might be expected, the truly big decisions of the year are taken very late in the process. The most significant decisions may even be deliberated by the Leaders, as the Bogor goals and the Information Technology Agreement (ITA) were. Typically, however, Ministers work to spare the Leaders the complicated task of using their precious meeting time on group negotiation, and work out key decisions

— even Leaders' decisions — in advance of the AELM. Such was the case in both 1997 and 1998 with respect to the EVSL initiative, which was settled by Trade Ministers before the Leaders even met.

For better or worse, these APEC institutions and the cycle of meetings have tended to reify with time. Below is a discussion on how key APEC decisions came to be practised during the past decade, which appears to demonstrate that, for one thing, the process was more fluid in the earlier years, and became more "institutionalized" with time.

APEC's Heyday: 1994–96

APEC Leaders have been gathering now for a decade. The initial APEC Leaders' Meeting at Blake Island in 1993 initiated a period of intense activity and high ambition for the organization. It is generally recognized that the most impressive manifestation of this period of ferment occurred in Indonesia in 1994, where APEC Leaders announced the "Bogor vision."

The commitment of APEC Leaders to the Bogor goals — free and open trade in the region by 2010/2020 — is to this day APEC's best known and most important decision. A confluence of favourable factors, both substantive and procedural, facilitated the Bogor initiative:

- Following from Blake Island, there was strong and active leadership from the United States, and commitment to a strong APEC outcome at the highest levels. American APEC negotiators were thus empowered to push for ambitious results in 1994, backed by support at political levels.

- There was an active and effective informal consultative process at the Senior Officials level that included key APEC members, such as the United States, Australia, New Zealand, and importantly, Indonesia, that year's APEC host. Moreover, the host was willing to conduct considerable and extensive informal consultations at the Senior Officials level to vet the idea of a clear goal by a certain date with all other APEC members. In short, the initiative was the subject of an orchestrated and active, though informal, diplomacy campaign, which could adapt the specifics of the proposal to the feedback received.

- The Bogor idea was given intellectual legitimacy, and could be floated in a more public manner by the Eminent Persons Group (EPG). Significantly, it could be characterized and assessed as a "neutral" initiative (since the EPG consisted of members from all APEC economies) on its own merits, and avoid the political baggage of being associated with one or a small group of APEC members.

- Finally, Soeharto, the APEC Leader host that year, had (at that time) the political prestige, will and experience to drive the initiative home, in a way that a developed economy host would have had problems with.

In 1995, APEC momentum, in the form of the Osaka Action Agenda (OAA), continued, again because the host economy was well placed (note, for example, that Japan has subsequently proven to be a stumbling block on many APEC trade liberalization initiatives), and because of a close-knit and effective senior officials process that vetted ideas informally, actively, and inclusively (that is, through extensive travel to capitals, and not simply at SOM meetings). The OAA itself, a unique beast by international trade agreement standards, thus reflected a balance of extensive and substantive (if at times vague) goals together with an implementation mechanism that relied on peer pressure and co-operation rather than on legally enforceable obligations. This was less rigorous than some in the developed economies had hoped for, but nonetheless a step forward in a region that is economically diverse, and in an institution as young as APEC. The important point is that the unique structure of the OAA was moulded to fit the political realities of the time, while at the same time pushing the process forward in a concrete manner. It achieved this by virtue of the active but informal consultative process of idea and feedback.

Another noteworthy point is that within this general atmosphere of close consultation at the Senior Officials level, the newly founded Committee on Trade and Investment could do the important technical work of fleshing out important details of the OAA. Trade officials on the CTI had a clear idea that the OAA exercise was a critical priority, which established an environment conducive to hammering out a meaningful product. However, there should be no doubt that the cogency of the final product in this case flowed from the strong shared sense among key delegations at the Senior Officials and Ministerial levels of the need for a credible document. Left solely to its own devices, it is certain that the CTI process would have produced a much less coherent and ambitious document than the OAA which resulted.

That said, the OAA avoided addressing the chief trade policy question raised by the Bogor vision: would APEC become a free trade area, where liberalization was only extended to other members, or would open and free trade in the region somehow be extended outside the region. Officials and Ministers knew from the beginning that eventually this question would need to be broached, but they also knew that nothing like a consensus could be formed in the short run. The OAA thus represented a clever means of moving the process forward without facing the central issue posed by the Bogor decision. The OAA made the most of a difficult policy choice, but its failure to address the issue squarely would soon have consequences. In fact, while on balance the OAA represents a logical progression from the vision set at Bogor, some have concluded[1] that the OAA itself was too substantively weak to produce strong liberalization results, and thus sowed the seeds for later problems.

A perhaps little noticed result of the good co-operation in developing the OAA is that its section on tariffs laid the groundwork for real work on sectoral liberalization. The Manila Action Plan for APEC (MAPA) in 1997, in fact, established sectoral liberalization as a result of the OAA process.[2] (This contrasts sharply with the post-EVSL environment, in which some delegations were opposed to using the term "sectoral" even in the most anodyne contexts.)

The year 1996 produced two significant results in APEC, which together signalled the continued maturation of the institution in the trade area. Parenthetically, I do not include the MAPA, the supposed centrepiece of that year's meeting as one of these results, for its substance was tepid at best (though, as noted above, it did initiate the idea of sectoral liberalization), as will be discussed below. The two truly remarkable outcomes were, first, the strong statement in favour of concluding an Information Technology Agreement in the World Trade Organization (WTO), which was introduced only in August 1996 at the Senior Officials level. The second was the fateful decision to build upon APEC's success in acting as a trade caucus on the ITA, by moving forward the sectoral liberalization process, first specified in the OAA, to 1997.

The process for advancing the ITA initiative itself is worth noting. The proposal to use APEC to promote the longstanding goal of concluding the ITA — for which the European Union (EU) was the most significant "target" member, came from the United States, and as noted, late in the year. The United States had calculated that APEC members, which produce the major part of information technology (IT) equipment in the world, had a fundamental common commercial interest in the ITA. Moreover, a growing awareness of the importance of IT to economic efficiency and growth more generally buttressed the idea that levying duties on such equipment (skilfully packaged as an input, not an "end product") was economically counterproductive. The United States initiative came late, but received traction because of its compelling logic for the region, and also because members, and the host especially, began to become worried about relying on the MAPA as the year's chief outcome.

The process succeeded because, first, the United States conducted an intensive lobbying campaign within APEC that included active involvement at the Ministerial (that is, USTR) level. Secondly, this campaign was buttressed by an equally intensive lobbying campaign by the U.S. private sector, which had significant investments in a number of key APEC members from whom support would be critical. In other words, U.S. companies were willing to "put their money where their mouths were" by lobbying foreign governments on the benefits of the ITA for them (perhaps surprisingly, trade officials in these countries were often unaware of the potential benefits). Thirdly, as in Bogor and Osaka, the host country adopted the initiative as a key outcome, and was willing to campaign itself (not relying solely on the United States). Finally, in this case, the President of the United States himself was willing to use his own considerable personal leverage and persuasive powers to convince his colleagues to adopt a strong statement, the result of which was a stronger statement from the Leaders on ITA than the Ministers had been able to conclude.[3]

From a policy perspective, it is significant to note that using APEC as a trade caucus to achieve multilateral liberalization in the WTO is one conceivable means of moving towards the adoption of the Bogor goals, and thus resolving the conundrum of whether Bogor requires an eventual regional free trade agreement (FTA). It is for this reason that some APEC members placed so much stock in the EVSL exercise, which adopted and extended this "multilateral caucus" approach, in the following two years.

What about the MAPA itself? In fact, much staff time, especially at the CTI level, was spent developing Collective Action Plans (CAPs) and Individual Action Plans (IAPs) in 1996. However, as APEC moved for the first time from plan to implementation, its limitations became clearer. In the short run, the extent to which any APEC member was willing to "voluntarily" liberalize its IAP was limited, beyond measures that had already been planned. This is not to say that nothing was produced in the first round of IAPs, but that the results did not appear worthy of the APEC Leaders, especially in view of the build-up of 1993–95. The lack of clarity in determining whether APEC was a nascent FTA or a catalyst for global liberalization clearly contributed to the reluctance of most APEC members to make meaningful "contributions" to their IAPs — why give away a negotiating coin?

Secondly, the CAPs, while worthy, did not constitute liberalization in and of themselves, and thus would be discounted by the media and the private sectors. In short, most of the CTI (and sub-fora) staff time in 1996 was spent on projects that, while worthwhile from a longer-term perspective, were already not considered especially valuable at the

Ministerial and Leaders' levels. The lack of close, direct, and sustained attention by the Ministers to the quality of the MAPA essentially assured its mediocre result. It appears that at some point in the year the Ministers drew the conclusion that only a limited amount of real liberalization was feasible politically through the MAPA, and thus shifted their focus to more promising and media-attractive results. Thus, the real "action" in 1996, that is, the ITA and the acceleration of the EVSL project, essentially bypassed any CTI involvement. This outcome was not in itself bad for APEC, but the de-emphasis of MAPA by the Ministers constituted a worrisome lack of follow-through on the previous year's scheme.

Forcing the Point: The Rise and Fall of EVSL

Nonetheless, the CTI was tasked in 1997 with implementing the 1996 decision to find other possible sectors for early liberalization. It was clear from the start that any exercise of defining and reaching consensus on possible sectors for liberalization would require large amounts of technical staff work. Thus, even though the initiative also demanded and drew intensive involvement by Senior Officials and Ministers, the CTI became integral to the EVSL process. Yet, the CTI's involvement began somewhat awkwardly in 1997, with a complicated and bureaucratic proposal by the CTI Chair at its first meeting in January to move the process from the bottom up — through the CTI and its sub-fora. In the event, this proved not to be a particularly cogent idea because: a) forcing consensus from bottom levels had never been very effective in APEC (especially at the technical levels of CTI sub-fora), as the staff were generally not empowered to put serious policy options on the table.

Moreover, staff on the CTI and especially its sub-fora were often from ministries rather than those driving APEC at the policy level, and lacked the bureaucratic stake in a positive outcome. The lack of bureaucratic co-ordination and co-operation within many APEC members made this situation difficult to rectify (a problem which continues to this day). Finally, the CTI and sub-fora structure was simply unsuited to a sectoral project, as sub-fora were structured on functional (for example, customs, standards) and not sectoral lines. Perhaps more to the point, the CTI Chair's proposal, although well intentioned, simply was not in line with what the Ministers, or at least the proponents of sectoral liberalization, had in mind: it was too slow, and there was not enough involvement at the policy level to move sectors forward.

In other words, the process of nominating sectors for liberalization was inherently a *political* one, not a technical one, and thus required political level input and involvement (even if actual negotiations were conducted by lower level officials, as is the case in the WTO) to work. It became clear that a "bottoms–up" process was not suited to a project of this political magnitude. Many APEC members recognized these problems with the CTI Chair's scheme from the outset in 1997, and suggested instead that the APEC members themselves could simply propose which sectors should be candidates for liberalization (which would of course have the approval of the policy level officials in the nominating economy). However, as this appeared to bypass APEC's own institutions, the CTI Chair was not amenable, and insisted on a subcommittee process that would not even produce candidates until the following year. Because there were APEC members amenable to the slow cumbersome process, especially at the lower "bureaucratic" levels, there was no way for APEC members favouring a more effective process to reverse the CTI Chair's scheme at the Senior Officials level in January 1997.

The "friends of sectoral liberalization", however, could bide their time, and attempt to get the Ministers to put in place a more sensible process when they met in Montreal in May 1997. In fact, the decision to do so came at a Ministerial dinner in Montreal at which no staff were even present. The Ministers decided upon a much simpler process for mooting new sectors — asking economies to simply nominate and justify sectors of interest to them. In addition, they agreed that the "ITA approach" would be the model for proceeding — that is, APEC members would work to create a critical mass of support worldwide for new sectors and turn its sectoral initiative into a global agreement in the WTO.[4]

Once the Ministers agreed upon the nomination process and the ITA model approach, the decision was left for Senior Officials and the CTI to implement in the second half of 1997. The SOM immediately delegated to the CTI the task of developing a nomination and deliberation process for potential sectors for liberalization. Senior officials continued to discuss overall procedural parameters (for example, how would sectors be selected from those nominated), but the work of nominating, justifying, and fleshing out sectoral proposals was performed by the trade experts of the CTI. Significantly, however, the EVSL process took place outside the formal CTI structure; CTI members and staff were very involved, to be sure, but to carry out the EVSL task, informal task forces were established, which were overseen by the Canadian host in 1997. The CTI's initial missteps in addressing the problem in early 1997 had led most to conclude that it was not equipped to address a politically urgent and sensitive matter such as sectoral liberalization. In essence, the APEC

Committee with specific purview for trade initiatives was formally sidelined from implementing the process. The CTI Chair, working with the Secretariat, was engaged primarily to consolidate and circulate proposals, as well as tabulate their relative degree of support, according to a scheme determined at the SOM level.

Moreover, while they developed and discussed a wealth of data and the economic justifications for the sectors nominated, officials at the CTI level were not in any position to reach consensus on the sensitive question of which sectors should be selected for early liberalization. The Senior Officials discussed intensively which package of sectors might be politically acceptable, but were also not anywhere close to consensus. None of this should in any way be viewed as a shortcoming of the APEC process, as the selection of EVSL sectors was again a fundamentally political decision that could only be taken by Ministers (or possibly, even Leaders).

The way that the final decision was arrived at was exceedingly novel, however, and in several ways set the stage for problems to come. The CTI, working with the Secretariat, and in consultation with key economies, developed a scheme for the economies to rank the various sectoral proposals. The rankings were compiled and distributed by the Secretariat. Such a compilation was meant to provide delegations with a sense of which sectors had the most support, and about which consensus could perhaps most easily be formed.

Indeed, the tabulated rankings led to further intensive negotiation, as the nominating economies worked to alter their proposals in order to persuade others to improve their rankings of them. Nonetheless, nothing like consensus existed in September 1997, even as this intensive process continued. Following the third Senior Officials Meeting in late August 1997 (at St. Johns) many delegations in fact doubted whether agreement on any of the sectors could be reached; the more optimistic hoped for at most a handful (3–5).

The process for reaching decision effectively short-circuited the laborious process of building up consensus from the staff level, and likely came as a shock to many delegations. After SOM III, a list actually ranking sectors by level of support was circulated. This table revealed that even the most strongly supported sectors were opposed by several major member economies. Two to three weeks before the meeting in Vancouver, a non-labelled paper was circulated by Canada proposing that *all* of the sectors with more than 50 per cent support be selected! This approach, of course, did some damage to the idea of consensus, but it began to take root. Not surprisingly, the most vehement objections came from Japan,

which had voiced strong opposition from the beginning to any proposal
under the purview of its Ministry of Agriculture, Forestry and Fisheries
(MAFF), which had not budged in the least during the deliberation
process.

In Vancouver, when it was clear that Japan took similarly inflexible
positions with respect to true commitments to liberalize the agricultural
sectors, the problem was effectively "solved" by some deft Canadian
drafting that was interpreted by Japan as addressing its concerns —
namely, the idea of "voluntarism."[5] In short, a trade-off was made
between the number of sectors selected (the fifteen selected accounted
for a sizeable proportion of world trade) and the "fine print" which
defined what such selection actually meant. In any event, the Ministers
put off the difficult work of specifying the parameters of liberalization
(product scope, end dates, and end tariff rates) to the following year.

Significantly, however, Japan left Vancouver apparently having a
different perception of the meaning of "voluntarism" than many other
economies. A number of other economies, including the United States,
focused on the fact that the decision was based on the concept of "critical
mass" (as agreed at Montreal), as well as the need for a "balanced and
mutually beneficial package". This was the approach applied to the ITA,
and meant that while all economies did not necessarily need to participate,
the participation by any country was conditioned upon a sizeable
percentage of world trade being covered in the final package. In practical
terms, as with the ITA, this meant that all major trading partners needed
to participate in all key sectors. Brunei, perhaps even Thailand, could opt
out of a sector or two, but Japan's absence from any sector would surely
mean that no other country could support liberalization in that sector.
Japan, as it happened, focused on the literal meaning of voluntarism —
it would not be required to participate in any sector which it deemed
politically difficult. Ministry of Trade and Industry (MITI) negotiators
had needed to use this argument to sell the package to MAFF negotiators,
who remained implacably opposed to any mention of agricultural sectors
in the package.

In the end, Vancouver represented a papered-over consensus. One
explanation for this was that there was simply no alternative short of
outright failure. Unlike the hard bargains that resulted from WTO
rounds, the EVSL exercise lacked sufficient political or economic trade-
offs to members like Japan for them to wholeheartedly accept the plan
as adopted.[6] One might argue the substantive merits of Japan's approach,
but it is difficult to conclude that it made irrational decisions within the
context of its political system.

Implementing the 1997 EVSL Decision

In 1998, as the CTI sectoral experts went about specifying the parameters of each of the selected sectors, the difference in interpretations came home to roost. Notwithstanding the fact that Ministers and Leaders had made an explicit political commitment to work towards liberalization in the sectors,[7] Japanese agricultural negotiators, who had no intention of participating in sectors under their purview, nonetheless hedged their bets (it was always possible that external pressure could result in their view being overruled), doing everything in their power to block the agricultural sectoral initiatives of any substance. That is, they vetoed any agreement on the products covered (any items for which Japanese tariffs were not already zero, and would thus have to be reduced), on the end dates for liberalization, or on the end rates.

However, Japanese intransigence ran straight into the face of the task explicitly set for Trade Ministers for their meeting in Kuching, Malaysia — to "complete the work on these proposals through finalizing the scope of coverage, flexible phasing, measures covered, and implementation schedule, including choice of measures and instruments for implementation based on existing proposals in each of these sectors."[8] Thus, in the weeks and days preceding the Kuching meeting, Japan steadily began to lose the debate on the purely "technical" questions of defining the scope, end dates, and end tariff rates for each sector, shifting the debate instead to how much "flexibility" would be allowed with respect to these parameters. This was, of course, an issue of importance to many members. Most flexibility proposals, even from the most sensitive developing countries, talked primarily about the need for longer time-frames for flexibility, or the possibility of not adopting the final end rate tariff (which, in most cases, was a "zero" rate), or at most, not to cut tariffs on all items specified. Japan, virtually alone, insisted on the flexibility to opt out of *all* tariff cutting in a sector entirely. In the view of most, if Japan's stand prevailed, it would effectively unravel the entire EVSL initiative from the outset, as each country opted out of its most sensitive sectors.

In the end, the fact that Malaysia was hosting the Trade Ministerial proved to be pivotal to producing a positive decision. Malaysian Trade Minister Rafidah Aziz was the most experienced Trade Minister in Asia, known for her forceful character, and like all hosting ministers, desired that the Kuching meeting be perceived as a success. Moreover, Malaysia's status as a developing economy gave it added credibility in the drive to get Japan to adopt meaningful liberalization commitments. Significantly, Japan was totally isolated, for the remaining north Asian countries, all similarly sensitive on agriculture, were effectively "neutralized": the newly installed Kim Dae Jung government in Korea had moved from equal intransigence on EVSL to a pro-liberalization policy; Chinese Taipei, at best ambivalent about liberalization, laboured also to play a constructive role, under strong diplomatic pressure from the United States; and finally, China, focused on its WTO accession negotiation, decided to take a neutral to constructive stance, so as not to alienate its main WTO negotiating partner, the United States. China, in particular, could count on the fact that any meaningful expectations for liberalization would be posed in the WTO, not in APEC, and so worried little about the EVSL outcome.

Japan's lonely situation allowed Minister Rafidah to pose a simple choice to its isolated Ministers: adopt the consensus view, or be responsible for the failure of the Kuching meeting. Faced with the prospect of such humiliation among its neighbors, Japanese Ministers grudgingly acquiesced to the "consensus" agreement on sectoral scope at Kuching in May 1998, as well as a fairly contained definition on "flexibility" (though even here, the existence of a key footnote provided sufficient leeway for them to be able to justify continued intransigence). That said, the Kuching Ministerial was probably the most overtly contentious in APEC history, and Japan's essentially coerced acceptance of the consensus foreshadowed problems ahead.

In fact, notwithstanding the formally satisfactory results of Kuching (the success in achieving the key objectives of specific parameters while limiting the scope of flexibility), Japanese negotiators were, unsurprisingly, no more co-operative in the second half of 1998, when efforts began to determine just how each APEC member would comply with these specific EVSL goals. Moreover, as APEC members began to submit specific plans for liberalization, it soon became clear that several developing members sought very large exemptions ("flexibility") from the goals set at Kuching.

Efforts to flesh out specific "voluntary" liberalization plans after the Kuching meeting demonstrated just how fragile its consensus decisions were. Japan continued to be the most vocal and active proponent of maximum flexibility and "voluntarism" in complying with the Kuching targets. However, with hindsight, it became clear that Japan's vociferous objections masked serious difficulties in a number of other members, particularly within ASEAN. ASEAN Ministers had, of course, joined in the Kuching consensus, unlike Japan, without serious contention. In view of the middling to poor offers of liberalization that most ASEAN members made after Kuching, many reached the conclusion that ASEAN acquiescence was more a matter of ensuring a Malaysian success, rather than any sincere commitment to liberalization. This is not to say that

ASEAN Senior Officials did not work hard after the Kuching meeting to put together credible liberalization packages; rather, it appeared that strong political support was often lacking, thus restricting these efforts.

As the date of the November Kuala Lumpur Ministerial and Leaders' Meetings approached, it became clear that a fully specified package of tariff cuts from APEC members could not be completed. Too many members simply had not completed the technical and political efforts necessary to fulfill this aim. Efforts thus shifted to defining "flexibility formulas" in each sector — specific parameters for the maximum number of items in each sector which could be exempted from the agreed upon parameters and liberalized on a more gradual, longer term basis. Proponents of EVSL guessed that in the end, some limited product exemptions would also be allowed, but held the line at any outright exceptions to the Kuching goals. At a meeting of EVSL experts (mostly CTI level officials, but with some key senior trade officials participating) a final attempt was made in Kuala Lumpur to agree upon such formulas just prior to the Ministerial Meeting. The attempt failed. Several developing members, including China, joined Japan in opposing the specific formulas proposed, saying that they were too stringent, and it soon became clear that no agreement was possible without watering them down tremendously, and thus undermining the entire EVSL project.

Thus, it proved impossible, at Kuala Lumpur, to unveil a specific schedule of tariff cuts from APEC members, or formulas that would at least limit exceptions to the already agreed general parameters. To some members, including the United States, defining such cuts was not viewed as essential in any case. The Ministers had agreed the year before that the EVSL should follow the ITA model. To the United States, at least, this ITA model meant that specific tariff liberalization negotiations should take place at the WTO in Geneva, where they could be legally bound.[9] The EVSL in this view was meant to generate a political commitment from APEC members to tariff cuts in specific sectors, followed by technical work to define the sectors (a step that went beyond ITA, where the product scope had been defined in Geneva), and then negotiations in the WTO on the specific tariff cuts.[10]

Viewed from this perspective, the decision to "punt" the EVSL initiative from APEC to the WTO was not the failure of APEC decision-making that some perceived it to be. U.S. officials from the beginning had argued for just such an outcome. However, other proponents of the EVSL viewed it differently: Australia and New Zealand, for example, had hoped that tariff cuts would emerge directly from the Malaysian Leaders' Meeting. It became clear that much of the outside world saw it the same way. U.S. protestations to the contrary were viewed by much of the media as just a spin. Moreover, the relief on the part of many developing member participants — not just Japan — was palpable, another manifestation that the consensus achieved in Vancouver and Kuching was thin.

The Legacy of the EVSL

The Kuala Lumpur meeting was thus viewed by some as APEC's first real stumble, after five solid years of achievement at Leaders' Meetings. Yet it can be argued that the decision to move the EVSL initiative into the WTO was really quite solid — on paper. Not only were the specific parameters for liberalization recommended for introduction in Geneva, but the Ministers agreed to push the process by "working constructively to achieve critical mass in the WTO necessary for concluding agreement in all 9 sectors."[11] The Ministers also pledged to improve their own participation in each of the initiatives and "endeavoring to conclude agreement in the WTO in 1999."[12]

The Kuala Lumpur statement could also be viewed as a trade policy success in view of the fact that using APEC as a catalyst for multilateral trade liberalization was one of the few coherent means of giving effect to the Bogor goals apart from forming an APEC FTA, which most members were clearly not prepared to contemplate. (A third possible approach — relying solely on "voluntary" actions in the IAPs, appeared increasingly fanciful to most, especially with a new WTO Round on the horizon).

As New Zealand began its host year in 1999, a quick effort was made to maintain the momentum of work on EVSL sectors, now renamed "Accelerated Tariff Liberalization (ATL)" in the WTO. Teams of experts were dispatched to EU capitals to explain the initiative and to bring the EU on board. Just as quickly, however, the weakness of the APEC consensus was revealed: Japan also initiated contact with the EU, and made clear that it had no intention to implement the ATL, notwithstanding the language its Leader had just used in committing Japan to work towards adoption in good faith.

Moreover, by the mid-year Trade Ministerial in Auckland, the prospect of any additional serious work on the six remaining EVSL sectors ("the Back Six") was nil. Even the proponents of the EVSL lacked the will, or perhaps more accurately, recognized the futility of trying to achieve APEC consensus to move tariff initiatives on sectors as sensitive as food, oilseeds, and automobiles. Very weak language was agreed well ahead of the Ministerial Meeting, so as to avoid a repeat of the contentions in Kuching, and tariff initiatives in these sectors were not discussed again, either in APEC or in the WTO.[13]

New Zealand, in fact, had determined that after the bruising year in Malaysia, it was time for bridge-mending in APEC. The New Zealand Trade Minister, Lockwood Smith, expended his efforts on rebuilding comity among the Ministers, and for pushing a very sensible, if unexciting, plan for "Strengthening the Functioning of Markets." The price for achieving consensus in this year was the sudden loss of APEC's ambition to drive either regional or global trade liberalization, the hallmark of its earlier years. True, lip service was paid to these goals, but in the months just prior to the Seattle meeting, it was deemed, with some justification, unwise to foster a divisive debate within APEC on regional liberalization in pursuit of these aims.

In fact, the looming WTO Trade Ministerial affected the overall complexion of APEC's trade-related work in 1999. The WTO Ministerial became the chief priority for virtually every Trade Minister in that year. The primacy of WTO objectives strongly limited the amount of attention and political capital that the Ministers were willing to expend on strictly APEC-related trade goals (and again raising the issue of how committed many of them were to these goals). The Ministers desired to avoid a repeat of the contentious process in 1998, which could spill over into the more important Seattle WTO Ministerial process, the aim of which was to launch a new trade round. Moreover, the strongest possible language in support of a WTO Round itself became the focus of both meetings of APEC Trade Ministers. That said, the United States, with strong support from Australia and the New Zealand host, pressed for, and succeeded in attaining quite strong and specific ATL language at the June Auckland Ministerial Meeting.[14]

However, despite the positive language on ATL emerging from the Auckland meeting in June, and a similarly strong text from the September 1999 Joint Ministerial Meeting,[15] in reality, no consensus existed. Once APEC delegations arrived in Seattle, there was no concerted effort to promote the ATL. It was not the highest priority even for the APEC members who most strongly supported it, and others, such as Japan, worked actively against it. The Seattle meeting was therefore inconclusive, but if issues in other areas had coalesced, it is virtually certain that support for the ATL would not have been part of the Seattle package. Moreover, and just as importantly, despite the fairly strong language in support of a new trade round (in principle) in the Auckland Ministerial statements, APEC was effectively split down the middle on the most contentious issues — agriculture and anti-dumping — and was not a factor as a grouping in Seattle. This proved another blow to the credibility of APEC decision-making.

The more mundane, if still important CTI and SOM work on other trade issues also began to experience problems in 1999, as a result of the fall-out of the EVSL. New Zealand's efforts to develop a coherent set of initiatives tailored to APEC strengths — the "Strengthening the Function of Markets" initiative, as well as a plan to strengthen the IAP process — were well conceived. They, nonetheless, marked a significant step down from the sweep and ambition of APEC initiatives in the mid-1990s.

In addition, the 1999 initiatives were watered down in substance, as many APEC members — most notably Japan and Malaysia — became seized with the importance of stressing the "voluntarism" of every new initiative. Not only was the means by which APEC members would *carry out* new initiatives to be "voluntary" — the original meaning of the term — but a sizeable plurality of members began to insist that the *substance* of the initiatives themselves, for example, the "Principles to Enhance Competition and Regulatory Reform", was also "voluntary" — that is, not binding even in principle. Despite that fact, many members worked on weakening the substance of the rules themselves. While it would be an exaggeration to say that the principles were lacking in merit, in comparison with earlier years, or with a WTO process, they still in some ways reflected the worst of all worlds — relatively weak (and vague) "rules", weakly binding, with weak mechanisms of implementation.

The APEC decision-making process, in short, had succumbed to a least common denominator (LCD) approach in reaching consensus, in contrast to its earlier years where strong leadership and dedication at high levels had succeeded in bringing the more skeptical along. Several factors had helped to produce this outcome. The EVSL experience had clearly generated a rancour in the organization that the Ministers and Leaders wished to prevent from recurring. The goal of tranquillity came to trump other goals. This was especially important, given the priority, before and after the Seattle meeting, that Trade Ministers placed in getting a WTO Round launched. Divisiveness within APEC, it was reasoned, would only make attaining consensus on WTO issues more difficult. Moreover, increased attention on the WTO meant that fewer staff resources and policy attention were being paid to APEC. Finally, the Asian financial crisis came to reverberate in the region by 1999–2000 in a trade policy sense: many APEC members became more internally focused, and generally less ambitious about the prospects for regional liberalization.

The result of these factors was that the APEC decision-making process began to break down in an important respect: technical experts would raise objections to initiatives such as the Competition Principles, and the objections were addressed and resolved at the technical level primarily, with little emendation made at the Senior Officials (much less

Ministerial) level to make them more acceptable from a broader policy perspective. Decisions in effect were being made from the bottom-up, something that the Senior Officials had stepped in to prevent in the past (for example, with respect to the OAA).

The "LCD approach" began to apply on big matters as well as small. When New Zealand initiated an arguably innocuous (in the sense that it was not binding) review of IAPs in 1999, the reaction from a plurality of economies was that the review could not make normative judgments about the quality of individual members' IAPs, as this would violate the spirit of "voluntarism". It was agreed that only broad statements about the quality of IAPs overall, without mentioning specific economies, could be made. The other aspect of the IAP review was just as substantively weak: a "self-review" conducted by each member, which could hardly be expected to bring great weaknesses to light. The fact that avoiding any substantive analysis of the quality of individual IAPs largely undercut the mechanism by which they were intended to work — peer pressure, or in the words used in Osaka, "comparability" — was noted by virtually no one at either the CTI or SOM level. The Ministers themselves could hardly be bothered to discuss the issue at all. In short, despite the considerable effort and prestige that the Ministers and Leaders had invested in establishing the Osaka Action Agenda and the IAP process in 1995–96, by 1999, they evinced little interest in ensuring that the IAPs were credible.

More concerted attempts to improve the IAP process[16] — which had reverted to becoming the chief avenue of APEC liberalization (little serious discussion on the broader issue of FTA versus WTO catalyst took place) — produced better results in 2000–2001, often by dint of technical advances. Specifically, it became possible to create a much improved and more transparent "e-IAP" on the APEC website. Nonetheless, even the establishment of the "e-IAP" ran into trouble as some members tried to limit its functionality, by making it hard to compare electronically one IAP with another. Others argued that the very reason that IAPs were created was to foster a healthy competition among APEC members, but in the minds of some, even the modicum of transparency implied by electronic IAP comparisons compromised "voluntarism". In the end, after much effort, it was agreed that electronic comparisons would be allowed (as long as they were not called comparisons). Officials who remembered the spirit and enthusiasm that surrounded the OAA in 1995 and the establishment of IAPs were discouraged that APEC disputes had come to revolve around issues so essentially trivial.

Yet, momentum did pick up in 2001, as APEC officials were able to agree, after much consultation, on a scheme for an improved "IAP peer review process", an agreement to broaden and update (if modestly) the terms of the Osaka Action Agenda, and for a plan to improve trade facilitation measures in the form of the "Shanghai Accord". Chinese leadership (the fact that it was China, a large and influential developing economy, was critical), as well as good co-operation among key APEC members at the Senior Officials level, including the United States, Australia and Japan, made these advances possible.

Two other initiatives valued by the private sector picked up steam in these years: the APEC automobiles dialogue and chemicals dialogue, both private/public sector discussions of issues affecting these highly traded sectors. Both initiatives had originated not from APEC Ministers or Leaders but from industrial groups in the region who desired policy dialogues on issues affecting trade in these sectors. Not coincidentally, both sectors had been among the fifteen selected for EVSL; once it became apparent that tariff cuts were not to take place, the automobile and chemicals sectors skilfully turned the discussion on the "non-tariff measures (NTMs)" affecting their industries (NTM issues had always been a part of EVSL) into proposals for policy dialogues involving both industry and government representatives. Both initiatives were advanced only because of the efforts of the private sectors involved to convince members that it was in their self-interest (and not "threatening") to engage in such discussions. Notably, such policy dialogues are unique APEC animals: they do not exist in the WTO. That said, it remains to be seen how much they actually accomplish.

These outcomes were much less ambitious than the hallmark decisions of the mid-1990s, but at least these more modest targets were feasible, and had a reasonable chance of being achieved. Many APEC members believed that the EVSL/ATL experience demonstrated that there were clear limits to what APEC could achieve in the trade policy realm, and that it was necessary to adjust APEC's work accordingly. Thus, one sees in 2000 and 2001 an increasing emphasis on initiatives outside the traditional trade policy realm (see, for example, the Shanghai Accord). In view of the perceived realities, the APEC decision-making process itself is perhaps not to be faulted for this shift. The new reality, however, does raise questions about APEC's ability to achieve the lofty and worthy goals that the Leaders set in Bogor.

Recommendations

The chief question for the future of APEC is whether there is enough will at the political level to set more ambitious goals, and just as importantly, to follow through and accomplish them. The answers surely relate to a complexity of trade policy factors in the region that are not the subject of this chapter. However, in the event that APEC decision-makers, or at least many of them, seek to move the APEC trade agenda to a higher level, they may want to consider the following lessons, which can be reasonably drawn from the past decade's experience:

- Leaders and Ministers have to determine APEC's vision and direction. Sustained, multi-year commitment to a specific set of trade policy objectives at this level is a necessary precondition to success. This, in turn, will involve the expenditure of leadership and capital from a subset of key Leaders and/or Ministers.
  - Committed Ministers in turn need to advocate APEC trade policy issues more in the course of their *bilateral* business with other APEC members. This is often not the case currently, especially for some of the larger members.
  - A corollary issue raised by this recommendation is the question of where such specific trade policy initiatives should originate. They can have their genesis anywhere (private sector, academia, eminent persons), but need to be adopted by the APEC host, and shared by a hard core of like-minded members at the highest levels from early in the APEC year, in order to have a reasonable chance of success.
  - As was done in APEC's earlier years, a core caucus of key APEC members — including perhaps the United States, Australia, Japan, a developing ASEAN member, China and a Latin member could form at a senior policy level (Deputy Minister perhaps) to steer the APEC liberalization process. It is certainly possible that such a broad-based group will not produce practical results, but on the other hand, the current process is already hampered by the lack of a common vision across the APEC spectrum, so there is little to lose.

- To shape and achieve consensus around new initiatives, robust consultation at the political *and* Senior Officials level is required from early in the year. Again, the tone is set by the host, with a cadre of influential members. If the host has only a weak idea at year's beginning what its trade policy aim is, the outcome is more likely to be incoherent or lacking adequate commitment by other members. If the host is "large", and has vision from an early point in the year, it has a reasonable chance of attaining meaningful results. If the host is a smaller member, it needs to convince a core of larger members on both sides of the Pacific to "internalize" its vision from an early stage, if it is to meet with reasonable success.

    — A host can also seek to "validate" its vision or aims by attaining the support and buy-in from prominent parties outside government, including the private sectors and academia. These outside parties could and should also be used better as inputs or resources in developing the vision. Again, the earlier such parties are approached, the more useful to the process they are likely to be.

• To forge political consensus around ambitious new initiatives, the tactic of coming in late and at high levels by the host (used to achieve the Bogor goals, ITA, and EVSL at the Vancouver meeting) typically has the flaw that the resulting "consensus" is thin. There is, in short, no substitute for genuine deliberation and understanding. In cases where weak consensus exists, follow up on implementation is predictably poor, in particular because APEC decisions are "voluntary" and non-binding.

• Means need to be found to *sustain* focus on APEC's core trade policy tasks, in particular the achievement of the Bogor goals. Each host wishes to put its own stamp on the APEC process (for example, "Strengthening the Functioning of Markets in 1999", and the "Shanghai Accord" of 2001). This fact has produced results over time that are often less than coherent and consistent. The Leaders and Ministers should consider setting a multi-year "vision" or multi-year "plan of implementation" with clear trade policy goals *and* clear metrics. Experience has shown that these will not be easy to achieve. Failure to do so, however, will probably mean the continued proliferation of annual initiatives which not only lack coherence but also strain staff resources.

• Substantively, either the IAP process needs to be made to work better, by ensuring a more transparent, objective and measurable means for IAP assessment, or it will increasingly be seen as not credible and irrelevant.

    — If the IAP process is allowed to fail in this way, the whole APEC liberalization process will be brought into question. If so, then it would be best if APEC Leaders acknowledged that "concerted unilateralism" is not working, and strive to find other means of attaining the Bogor goals.

• The CTI process has been weakened over time, as the focus in trade policy initiative since the ITA has moved increasingly towards the SOM. The original vision of the CTI as the engine driving APEC trade liberalization can only work if, firstly, the SOM and the

Ministers themselves delegate more of this function to the CTI, instead of burdening the SOM, whose agenda of issues outside the trade area appears to be growing year by year; and secondly, it can ensure capable, more senior representation at the CTI level and its sub-fora, without which the technical process would produce weak results.

— In addition, the CTI could more effectively use its power to approve projects proposed by the CTI sub-fora to exert control over their operations and to ensure adherence to the goals set by the Ministers and Leaders. In this way, the CTI can add real value to the process.

- APEC could consider a larger policy role for the Secretariat in terms of generating specific ideas for its trade policy direction, but that does not appear feasible at this point. Members almost unanimously do not desire this, and arguably, if they were ready to implement new policy initiatives, could do it themselves.
- Most members are too distanced from their own private sectors. The private sector would generally approve of stronger institutions and decisions (ABAC makes this clear virtually every year), but "LCD" decisions reflect the views of cautious and turf-conscious government bureaucracies. Consultation with and the involvement of the private sector needs to be improved as an input into the process. APEC Ministers have stated their intention to achieve this result in past years, but it has not been achieved at the CTI/SOM level.

Notes

1. The author thanks Fred Bergsten for this observation.
2. See the Manila Action Plan for APEC; in its tariffs section, it is meant to implement the OAA guidelines in this area. It states, "Members also agree to submit to APEC Ministers in 1999 a list of priority sectors developed through consensus among members and in consultation with business, in which progressive reduction of tariffs and non-tariff measures may have a positive impact on trade and economic growth or for which there is regional industry support for early liberalization in APEC."
3. In the Joint Ministers Statement (23 November 1996), the Ministers merely "endorsed the efforts at WTO to conclude an information technology agreement and urged all other members of the WTO to work toward that end." Leaders were much stronger and more specific than their Subic Bay Statement (25 November 1996) when they decided to "call for the conclusion of an information technology agreement by the WTO Ministerial Conference that would substantially eliminate tariffs by the year 2000, recognizing the need for flexibility as the negotiations in Geneva proceed."

4. The Montreal Trade Ministerial Meeting's Statement of the Chair (10 May 1997): "Ministers instructed officials...to have full regard for...critical mass, by developing initiatives supported by significant groups of APEC members, taking into account the different levels of economic development and diverse circumstances of APEC member economies and, where appropriate, providing a foundation of participation beyond our region, and where appropriate, for incorporation into the WTO." The "where appropriate" formulation primarily referred to the fact that liberalization of non-tariff measures (NTMs) might not be amenable to a WTO approach. The EVSL from the beginning covered NTMs as well as tariffs.

5. The text of the EVSL Annex to the Joint Ministers' Statement of Vancouver (22 November 1997) is a masterpiece of ambiguity: "Recognizing the need for a balanced and mutually beneficial package, and recalling that the process of early liberalization is conducted on the basis of the APEC principle of voluntarism, whereby each economy remains free to determine the sectoral initiatives in which it will participate, we therefore call for the development of appropriate agreements or arrangements ...based on existing proposals in the following sectors..." Proponents of the EVSL focused on the need for the package to be "balanced and mutually beneficial" as well as its call for "agreements" (that is, more than the unilateral lists of products that members were willing to liberalize), requiring Japan's participation. Japan, of course, relied on the definition of "voluntarism" literally.

6. The key word here is "sufficient", as the package did have benefits for Japan. Japanese exporters in the chemicals, medical equipment, and scientific instruments, and other industrial areas would have benefited greatly from tariff cuts in the developing APEC members. This gain was apparently insufficient to offset the pain suffered by agricultural sectors.

7. The Ministers' Joint Statement of Vancouver (22 November 1997) contains a number of general statements asserting a commitment to liberalize these sectors — for example, "The launch of this process signals APEC members' clear commitment to promote economic growth based on a substantial programme of trade liberalization in the region" (EVSL Annex to the Minister's Joint Statement).

8. EVSL Annex to the Ministers' Joint Statement, Vancouver, 22 November 1997

9. In fact, U.S. trade law forbade the United States from cutting its tariffs in any context other than bindings in the WTO.

10. Importantly to the United States, this latter step would involve the EU, which should not be allowed to "free ride" the APEC initiative.

11. Joint Ministerial Meeting Statement, Kuala Lumpur, 15 November 1998, paragraph 15 (ii).

12. Ibid., paragraph 15 (i).

13. "Ministers of participating economies therefore resolved that the tariff elements of the remaining six EVSL sectors should be negotiated in the WTO *during the course of the negotiations on agriculture already mandated in the WTO*..." (Statement of the Chair, Auckland Trade Ministers' Meeting,

30 June 1999.) In short, these sectors would be addressed in the next WTO trade round, and could no longer be considered "early liberalization."

14. "Pursuant to their agreement in Kuala Lumpur on the front nine EVSL sectors, Ministers of participating economies emphasised the importance of the Accelerated Tariff Liberalisation (ATL) initiative in providing impetus to the wider negotiation on industrial (non-agricultural) tariffs which they agreed should be launched at Seattle. They welcomed progress in the initiative since November, including the support it had received from a number of non-APEC WTO members and instructed officials to continue to promote the initiative, endeavouring to conclude agreement in the WTO in 1999. They also agreed that participating economies should engage again with WTO members in July on their reaction to the initiative and on how it will tie into the launch, conduct, and outcome of any new WTO negotiations." (Auckland Trade Ministers'Meeting, Statement of the Chair, paragraph 15, 30 June 1999)

15. See paragraph 26 of the Auckland Joint Ministerial Statement (10 September 1999), which includes the sentence, "[Ministers] further agreed that participating economies should continue to engage with WTO members with the objective of realizing the ATL package on the basis of critical mass, based on APEC's EVSL initiative agreed by Ministers in Kuala Lumpur, by the end of next year."

16. That is, the process by which each APEC member voluntarily reports each year the actions it will take to implement the Bogor goals in each of the areas specified in the Osaka Action Agenda.

7

TOWARDS AN ASSESSMENT OF APEC TRADE LIBERALIZATION AND FACILITATION

IPPEI YAMAZAWA AND ROBERT SCOLLAY

APEC's Trade Liberalization and Facilitation Objectives

APEC's trade and investment agenda began to take shape in 1993, with the release of the first report of the Eminent Persons' Group (APEC/EPG 1993), followed by the articulation at the 1993 APEC Economic Leaders' Meeting (APEC/LM 1993) in Seattle of the vision of the Asia-Pacific as a region of free trade and investment. This was followed at the 1994 APEC Economic Leaders' Meeting (AELM) by the landmark Bogor Declaration (APEC/LM 1993), in which APEC's members committed themselves to the establishment of free trade and investment in the Asia-Pacific region. The Bogor Declaration states that the goal is to be achieved by 2010 in the case of the developed members of APEC, and by 2020 in the case of the developing members. No definition of "developed" or "developing" economy status was provided then nor has one been provided since, so that the choice of target applicable to each individual APEC member is effectively a matter of self-selection. There has likewise been no definition of the precise meaning of "free trade and investment", leaving the way open for debate whether free trade means "zero tariffs" or the reduction of tariffs to a range of very low values, such as 0–5 per cent.[1]

The Bogor Declaration envisaged that action towards the achievement of the free trade and investment targets should begin immediately. This was a significant departure from the caution expressed only a short time earlier in the second EPG report, which had recommended that implementation should begin in 2000. The Pacific Business Forum, on the other hand, had recommended that action should begin immediately, and it was this approach that was adopted in the Bogor Declaration. This confident approach reflected the high expectations which were held for APEC at that time, and which were maintained during the subsequent three years as APEC moved quickly forward to establish first the Osaka Action Plan (OAA) in 1995 (APEC/MM 1995) and then the Manila Action Plan for APEC (MAPA) in 1996 (APEC/MM 1996), before embarking on the ambitious Early Voluntary Sector Liberalization (EVSL) initiative in 1997.

A notable original feature of the APEC agenda was that free trade and investment in the region was to be achieved through a voluntary process based on "open regionalism". The voluntary approach, and the associated non-binding nature of the commitments envisaged within APEC, was adopted in deference to the strong preferences of the East Asian members of APEC, particularly the ASEAN economies. APEC's version of the concept of "open regionalism" was understood as the gradual reduction of trade barriers by APEC members on a non-discriminatory basis, so that APEC was explicitly intended from the first not to be a conventional preferential trade agreement. This reflected the twin concerns felt among APEC members in the early 1990s over the apparent fragility of the multilateral trading system in the face of the stresses imposed on it by the Uruguay Round negotiations, and over the perceived threat to that system posed by the spread of preferential regional trading arrangements. By adopting a non-discriminatory approach APEC's members intended to provide both emphatic and unambiguous support for the newly-established World Trade Organization (WTO) as the cornerstone of the world trading system, and to offer an alternative to the preferential approach to regional trade liberalization.[2]

In the year following the Bogor Declaration, APEC members set about developing the framework for implementing APEC's Bogor vision, and this was formalized as the Osaka Action Agenda, adopted by APEC leaders at the end of 1995. The OAA set out nine "guiding principles"[3] for APEC's TILF (trade and investment liberalization and facilitation) agenda and established objectives in each of fifteen "action areas",[4] to be achieved by a combination of individual actions, involving liberalization initiatives by the individual member economies, and collective actions, involving the building of capacity for liberalization through the pooling of expertise and the development of shared understandings.

The distinctive APEC approach to regional liberalization clearly required a distinctive modality. A voluntary liberalization process as envisaged by APEC implies a unilateral dimension, in that individual member economies are expected to announce and implement their own liberalization and facilitation programmes without any formal requirement for reciprocity from fellow-members, and without the establishment of any agreed binding rules or disciplines beyond those already in place as a result of existing obligations. At the same time, the acceptance of a common goal of regional free trade and investment implies that the economies of the region will be moving together towards that common goal, even though each may choose and map out its own individual path. These two dimensions of the APEC approach are captured in the term "concerted unilateralism" that was coined to describe the modality for regional liberalization adopted by the APEC members. Both dimensions provide potential benefits: while it is always open to individual economies in isolation to secure for themselves the benefits of unilateral liberalization, the "concerted" aspect of APEC's approach recognizes that if the group liberalizes together each member will benefit more than if it liberalizes in isolation, and that concerns over the political sustainability of liberalization will also be reduced since the benefits will be spread more widely within each member economy.

The additional benefit expected from the "concertation" of individual economies' liberalization initiatives is that it provides a basis for the use of "peer pressure" as a mechanism to encourage each member to maintain a credible level of performance towards achieving the APEC targets. If an individual member, say, economy A, fails to perform, the potential benefits to all members are reduced. This in turn reduces the incentive for each member to perform, and therefore increases the probability that other members may choose not to perform, with a consequent loss of expected benefits for all members, including economy A. Thus, the other members have an incentive to exert "peer pressure" on Economy A to perform, and Economy A has an incentive to respond to that pressure.

Having adopted the Osaka Action Agenda and agreed on the modality of "concerted unilateralism", the next step for APEC members was to develop a detailed plan for implementing the agenda on the basis of the agreed modality. It was agreed that for each of the fifteen "action areas" of the Osaka Action Agenda there would be both Collective Action Plans (CAPs) setting out joint work programmes in each "action area", and Individual Action Plans (IAPs) in which individual APEC members would progressively record their commitments designed to ultimately achieve the OAA objectives in each area. It was envisaged that the sharing of experiences through the CAPs and the monitoring of the progress of individual members as recorded in their IAPs would help to generate momentum towards the achievement of APEC's agenda through the building of confidence and the exertion of "peer pressure". The complete set of IAPs and CAPs was developed in 1996, and packaged together in November of that year by the Philippines, the APEC hosts for the year, as the Manila Action Plan for APEC. Implementation of the IAPs and CAPs commenced formally on 1 January 1997.

The Potential Gains from Achieving the Bogor Targets

The standard methodology for analysing the potential effects of achieving APEC's objective of free trade in the Asia-Pacific region has been computable general equilibrium (CGE) analysis. Surveys by Petri (1997), APEC Economic Committee (1997) and Scollay and Gilbert (2000) report on the results of a large number of studies using this methodology. The studies surveyed for the most part utilize the GTAP database, though they differ in model structure (static or dynamic, perfectly or imperfectly competitive) and in experimental design (level of disaggregation by sector and region, closure assumptions, and the range of interventions assumed to be removed as a result of APEC liberalization).

Despite these differences, there is a high degree of consistency in the predicted results of complete APEC liberalization as reported by the studies. Although Petri (1997) found that welfare gains ranged from US$54 billion to US$519 billion, the later survey of a much larger number of studies by Scollay and Gilbert (2000) found that the results for the most part clustered within the range of US$60 to US$80 billion. Among these results, larger gains tended to be reported by the studies that use some form of dynamic simulation, or which allow for imperfect competition in some sectors. Studies which deal specifically with agricultural trade liberalization also highlight the importance of liberalization in this sector in achieving the overall welfare gains available from APEC liberalization; in every study where the gains from agricultural trade liberalization are separately identified, they account for between 50 and 70 per cent of the total gains from complete APEC liberalization.

Scollay and Gilbert (2000) also note that the majority of studies predict gains for all APEC members. In the few studies where this is not the case, small welfare losses are sometimes recorded for member economies that are already members of an existing preferential trading arrangement, particularly Canada and Mexico as members of NAFTA (North American Free Trade Agreement), and in one case also Malaysia and Indonesia as members of AFTA (ASEAN Free Trade Area). The likely interpretation in these cases is that APEC-wide liberalization erodes some of the welfare gains that these economies derive from membership in the relevant preferential arrangement. The largest gains in absolute terms not surprisingly generally accrue to the larger APEC economies. When welfare gains are expressed as a percentage of gross domestic product (GDP), however, the largest gains are generally found to accrue to the developing ASEAN economies of Southeast Asia, and among developed economies like New Zealand, especially when the liberalization includes agricultural trade. The interpretation of this pattern by Scollay and Gilbert (2000) is that projected APEC liberalization delivers the largest proportional gains to economies with the highest initial levels of protection, where the potential allocative efficiency gains from their own liberalization are greatest, and to economies whose trade is most closely integrated with fellow APEC members.

A number of studies also compare the gains from APEC non-discriminatory liberalization with those from the establishment of a preferential free trade area among APEC members. Petri (1997) and APEC Economic Committee (1997) concluded that the studies covered in their surveys showed decisively that higher welfare gains are available from non-discriminatory compared with preferential liberalization by APEC members. The later survey by Scollay and Gilbert (2000), however, covering a larger number of studies, was unable to reach such a clear-cut conclusion, finding a number of studies in which the gains from preferential liberalization exceeded those from non-discriminatory liberalization, as well as vice versa.

Several studies also compare the results from "unconditional" non-discriminatory liberalization by APEC members, where liberalization proceeds without any expectation of reciprocity from non-members, and "conditional" non-discriminatory liberalization, where APEC members liberalise only if non-members reciprocate. Not surprisingly, the welfare gains reported for "conditional" non-discriminatory liberalization are consistently higher than for the "unconditional" variant. The study results, however, also throw some light on the objections typically raised to the "unconditional" approach, based on a perception that this would allow the rest of the world to "free ride" on APEC liberalization. The studies indicate little basis for this concern. The effects of APEC "unconditional" non-discriminatory liberalization on non-members of APEC are invariably minor in proportional terms, and fairly evenly split between positive and negative effects.

The APEC Approach to Regional Trade Liberalization

The maintenance of momentum by APEC in moving from the Bogor Declaration to the Osaka Action Agenda and then to the Manila Action Plan raised expectations on the level and speed of liberalization that could be expected from APEC. Inevitably, questions arose on the extent of the contribution that the APEC process itself could be expected to make towards the achievement of APEC's own objectives, and how that contribution might be measured.

An early assessment by PECC et al. (1996) concluded that the existing liberalization trends within APEC economies, based on multilateral commitments and unilateral initiatives, were on the whole broadly consistent with the achievements of APEC's Bogor targets. The conclusion was therefore drawn that "APEC rides on, and mainly reinforces, the liberalization wave sweeping the Asia Pacific region rather than being the leading force" (PECC et al., 1996). APEC's primary function, in other words, was to act as a "support club of liberalizers in the region".

An alternative view was that in order to justify APEC's existence, the APEC process would need to yield tangible results that demonstrably "added value", primarily in the form of "WTO-plus" commitments by members that went beyond their Uruguay Round obligations. Yamazawa and Urata (2000) and IAP Study Group (1997,1998) contain reports on the results of a study organized by the Japan committee of the PECC which tried, in the face of significant information gaps, to quantify the "added value" of the APEC process. The study attempted to quantify individual member's achievements and commitment for liberalization made in their IAPs against their Bogor target (full mark 100). It was no surprise that the developed country members obtained higher marks than the developing country members. However, additional commitments beyond the Uruguay Round commitments were generally low, so that their liberalization efforts in IAPs were characterized as "UR plus small alpha". However, in facilitation areas, APEC members generally obtained higher marks. According to the assessment of Yamazawa and Urata, the comparatively good progress in trade facilitation was due partly to the fact that efforts in these areas were supported by effective CAPs. The CAPs serve the important function of assisting in developing understanding of the relevant issues in each area and of the actions needed to make progress towards the OAA objectives, as well as building the capacity for the implementation of those actions. The precise degree of progress in advancing collective action in the various areas of the OAA has depended to a large extent on the degree of initiative exercised by convenors in charge of various APEC subcommittees and expert groups.

The PECC returned to the assessment of IAPs in 1999, with an independent review of the APEC IAPs, reported in PECC (1999). This review concluded that the APEC member economies were continuing to make reasonable progress towards the attainment of APEC objectives in a number of areas of the OAA, although a need for improved performance was identified in a number of other areas. In the areas where progress was less satisfactory, the PECC review found that a lack of clarity in defining objectives and modalities was often part of the problem, suggesting a need for some revision of the OAA in these areas. Like the Yamazawa and Urata study, the PECC review found that the most satisfactory progress was often evident in areas where the IAPs were supported by effective CAPs.

There were a number of criticisms of the format of the early IAPs. The degree of transparency in the IAPs varied considerably, and they were generally structured to list commitments made while omitting mention of significant remaining impediments to trade and investment. These deficiencies, together with a lack of consistency in the formats used by the APEC members, made it difficult to compare progress across economies and therefore weakened the scope for exertion of "peer pressure". They also made it difficult to communicate clearly to business and other stakeholders the extent of progress being made by APEC member economies towards the objectives set out in the OAA. It was recognized that this in turn was contributing to a growing scepticism about the value and effectiveness of APEC. By the end of the 1990s, there was widespread recognition that improvements in the format of the IAPs were essential if they were to provide meaningful support for APEC's function as a "support club of liberalizers in the region", let alone if they were to be used more proactively as instruments of liberalization.

APEC members have responded with a number of initiatives designed to improve the transparency of the IAPs and their effectiveness as a communication tool and as indicators of progress towards APEC's goals. Initiatives to improve and standardize the format of the IAPs culminated in the development of the e-IAPs, designed to provide observers with ready access to any specific information they might require about the content of each IAP. Since 1998, a process of "peer review" of the IAPs has been operating in conjunction with Senior Officials' Meetings (SOMs). Each year, a number of APEC economies volunteer to submit themselves to the "peer review" process. The results of the "peer review" process are not, however, disclosed to outsiders. An important innovation in 2002 was that for the first time provision was made for the inclusion of assistance by independent experts in the "peer review" process.

The EVSL Experiment

A combination of optimism towards the prospects of liberalization within APEC and frustration at the slow progress reflected in the early IAPs led APEC members to introduce the Early Voluntary Sectoral Liberalization initiative in an effort to accelerate APEC liberalization through the adoption of a sectoral approach.

Some groundwork for a sectoral approach had already been laid in the OAA, where the CAP on tariffs (and non-tariff measures) states that:

> APEC members will identify industries in which the progressive reduction of tariffs (and non-tariff measures) may have positive impacts on trade and on economic growth in the Asia-Pacific region or for which there is regional industry support for early liberalization (Osaka Action Agenda, 1995, Section C, page 6–7).

A further impetus towards sectoral liberalization was provided in 1996 by the apparent success of the United States' proposal for an Information Technology Agreement (ITA), under which all tariffs and non-tariff measures (NTMs) on semi-conductors and other parts and materials input to information technology equipment were to be reduced or eliminated by the year 2000. The ITA was endorsed at the 1996 APEC Leaders' Meeting and then forwarded to the WTO Ministerial Meeting in Singapore just two weeks later, where it was adopted as a binding agreement within the WTO framework, open for signature by all WTO members.[5]

Encouraged by the success of the ITA, the Canadian chair for APEC in 1997 proposed to accelerate APEC liberalization by proceeding with the EVSL initiative, whereby a group of selected sectors would be targetted for "fast-track" liberalization. A call for nominations of suitable sectors from APEC members produced a list of sixty-one sectors suggested as candidates for EVSL. Each had nominating economies and supporting economies but was not necessarily supported by all economies. By the time of the 1997 APEC Leaders' Meeting in 1997, the list had been narrowed down to fifteen designated sectors. Of these, nine (the "front nine") were selected for immediate action, with a schedule for liberalization to be agreed in 1998, and implementation to begin in 1999. The remaining six sectors (the "back six") were to be subject to an initial investigation with a view to implementation in a subsequent year.

The initial recommendation of the APEC Ministers was progressively tightened as work on the EVSL proceeded. The Ministers initially emphasized the voluntary aspect of EVSL:

> Recognizing the need for a balanced and mutually beneficial package, and recalling that the process of early liberalization is conducted on the basis of the APEC principle of voluntarism, whereby each economy remains free to determine the sectoral initiatives in which it will participate, ...we recommend that Leaders endorse members beginning immediately to complete the work on these proposals through finalizing the scope of coverage, flexible phasing, measures covered and implementation schedule, including choice of measures and instruments for implementation based on existing proposals in the... (selected) sector(s).[6]

The Leaders, however, moved beyond the Ministers' statement to emphasize the "package" element of the proposal.

> ... action should be taken with respect to early voluntary liberalization in 15 sectors, with nine to be advanced throughout 1998 with a view to implementation beginning in 1999. We find this package to be mutually beneficial and to represent a balance of interests.[7]

The schedule for EVSL envisaged that an implementation plan would be agreed upon by the Trade Ministers' Meeting in June 1998. At that meeting, however, the Trade Ministers failed to agree on the chair's proposal. The implementation plan stated as follows:

> Participation in the 9 sectors and all three measures (trade liberalization, facilitation, and ecotech) in each sector will be essential to maintain the mutual benefits and balance of interests, which Leaders had established when selecting the sectors in Vancouver.

The proposal had thus explicitly become a "package" requiring the participation of all economies in each type of measure for all nine sectors.

Japan, however, concluded that the implementation of commitments in the fisheries and forestry sectors would create unacceptable levels of political difficulty in the domestic context. It considered liberalization in these sectors to be unavoidably linked to the WTO negotiations on agriculture scheduled to commence in 2000, and adopted a firm position that these sectors could not be negotiated in APEC in advance of the WTO negotiation. The unwillingness of Japan to proceed in these two sectors led to the unravelling of the balance of interests underpinning the willingness of other APEC members to proceed with the proposed EVSL liberalization commitments, particularly when it also became evident that the United States Administration lacked the authority to implement commitments that might arise out of an eventual EVSL agreement.

At the APEC Ministerial Meeting in Kuala Lumpur in 1998, the decision was made that the tariff element of the EVSL proposals would not be implemented within APEC, but would instead be forwarded to the WTO for possible adoption on a binding basis by the full WTO membership. In the meantime, implementation of the NTM, facilitation, and ECOTECH elements of EVSL was to proceed within APEC (*Summary Conclusion of the First SOM* 1999). The inclusion of facilitation and ECOTECH elements in combination with the liberalization elements of EVSL had been a feature of the EVSL, which distinguished it from the GATT/WTO approach to liberalization. It had been envisaged that the incorporation of facilitation and ECOTECH measures could mitigate the adjustment cost of liberalization, and even enhance the benefits of liberalization. The EVSL initiative has continued in the form of surveys and sectoral seminars and workshops to advance the work on NTMs, facilitation, and ECOTECH. APEC also promotes sectoral policy dialogue comprising government and industry representatives in the auto and chemical sectors.[8] The continuation of these residual elements could not, however, disguise the blunt fact that, considered as an attempt to accelerate liberalization by APEC members, the EVSL was a failure.

There had in fact been a number of criticisms of the EVSL concept. While the EVSL had been welcomed by some trade officials as a way of introducing more rigorous liberalization commitments into the APEC process, it had been regarded by others as an unfortunate intrusion of the reciprocity-based WTO style of negotiation into a process that the members had earlier agreed would be based on voluntarism.

From the perspective of economic efficiency, Dee et al. (1998) warned against the "second-best" nature of the piecemeal approach to liberalization embodied in the sectoral approach of EVSL. They argued that in order to avoid welfare-reducing outcomes care would be needed to allow for linkages in the production chain, to avoid liberalization of low valued-added products leading to even higher effective rates of protection for the corresponding high value-added upstream industries. They also argued that it would be important to ensure that liberalization involved the removal of subsidies as well as tariff barriers. Yamazawa and Urata (1999) have criticized this view, arguing that the EVSL should not be assessed in isolation but rather as a supplement to liberalization occurring through the IAP process. In his view, any liberalization achieved through EVSL would enhance the IAPs of individual economies and should be welcome.

From a political economy perspective, Yamazawa also argued that as a supplement to the IAP process the EVSL would be most effective if interpreted as an "easy sector liberalization", targetting those sectors where resistance to liberalization is lowest across the APEC economies. This approach in turn was questioned by Dee et al (1998), who argued that it could result in members opting to target small sectors with low protection, thus seriously undermining potential efficiency gains. They argued instead for "twinned" EVSL proposals, where an area of high protection must be nominated for every area of low protection nominated.

APEC and Liberalization: A Lowering of Expectations and a Looming Challenge

The failure of the EVSL had a decisive impact on perceptions of the potential for achieving liberalization through the APEC process. It appeared to demonstrate clearly that moving beyond voluntarism to any form of binding commitment based on negotiated reciprocity is unlikely to be feasible in the APEC context, at least for the time being. At the same time, it may have diminished the incentives for a vigorous pursuit of liberalization through the "concerted unilateral" process, by signalling indirectly to the rest of the APEC membership that two of the three leading economic powers of the region, the United States and Japan, are unlikely to be willing or active participants in APEC's "concerted unilateral" approach to liberalization, and are likely instead to be willing to liberalize only within the context of the negotiated reciprocity of the WTO and perhaps also of traditional preferential regional trading arrangements. Since the U.S. and Japanese markets together account for about three quarters of the APEC membership's gross national product (GNP),[9] this is likely to have led to substantially reduced assessments of the additional benefits attainable from "concerted" unilateral liberalization, and a corresponding reduction in the incentives to participate vigorously in the process.

The resulting disillusion with the process of "concerted unilateralism" occurred also at a time when enthusiasm for further unilateral liberalization in the APEC region had clearly waned in the wake of the East Asian economic crisis of 1997/98. The record on unilateral liberalization in the APEC region in the late 1990s was in fact somewhat mixed. It has been claimed, with some justification, that the lack of any widespread reversion towards protectionism in the aftermath of the East Asian economic crisis of 1997–98 was in part a reflection of APEC's success in solidifying a regional consensus on the benefits of open trade and investment regimes. Some of the "crisis economies", notably Korea and Indonesia, undertook significant liberalization as part of stabilization packages agreed with the IMF. In Thailand, on the other hand, the IMF sanctioned the raising of tariffs on some luxury goods as a revenue-raising measure, and in Malaysia also, some tariffs were raised. Outside East Asia, Chile continued to implement its programme of gradual uniform tariff reductions. Conversely, Australia and New Zealand suspended their tariff reduction programmes, at least temporarily. At the turn of the century, the overall impetus for further unilateral liberalization among APEC members was, on balance, decidedly weak.

No longer able to ride the "wave of liberalization" noted earlier by PECC et al. (1996), APEC's capacity to drive liberalization in the region forward was clearly weakened, at least in the short term. These factors are likely to have contributed significantly to the pressures spurring APEC members to explore alternative modalities for liberalization. It is surely no coincidence that the failure of the EVSL was followed by a dramatic upsurge in interest in new preferential trading arrangements on the part of APEC members.

At the same time, the 2010 target date for the achievement of the Bogor goals by the developed APEC members is beginning to loom uncomfortably closer on the horizon. Major impediments to trade remain in place in these economies, in the form of tariff peaks, tariff escalation, and high levels of protection in sensitive sectors, such as agriculture, and textiles and clothing. It may be reasonable to suspend judgement on the adequacy of progress towards the Bogor goals while a new round of WTO negotiations is under way, during which it can be hoped that breakthroughs can be made in these areas. Following the end of the round, however, the credibility of developed APEC economy commitments to the Bogor goals is likely to come under increasingly intense scrutiny.

Following the failure of the EVSL, a noticeable bifurcation occurred in APEC's approach to its trade and investment liberalization and facilitation (TILF) agenda. Within the APEC process itself, increasing emphasis was placed on trade facilitation, e-commerce, and the theme of "strengthening markets" which was introduced as a central element in APEC's agenda for 1999. The "strengthening markets" theme provided a convenient focus for APEC's efforts in the wake of the East Asian crisis of 1997/98 to build consensus on the importance of improving the efficiency of markets as an essential foundation for economic integration in the region. The APEC Principles on Competition and Regulatory Reform and the Non-Binding Principles on Government Procurement were both agreed in 1999, and considerable effort was subsequently devoted to economic and technical co-operation programmes on corporate and financial sector governance. Trade facilitation had always been a less controversial objective than trade liberalization among APEC members, and is an area of the TILF agenda where APEC can claim some significant achievements. It is noticeable that among the CTI subfora, those dealing with facilitation issues such as standards and conformance and customs procedures receive the strongest support from APEC members and have the most substantive agendas.

In the area of trade liberalization, on the other hand, after the disappointment of 1998 APEC increasingly looked to the successful launch of a new WTO round as the key to maintaining forward momentum. APEC's approach to trade liberalization during 1999 was accordingly heavily focused on developing a common position in support of the launch of a new round at the WTO's Seattle ministerial in December 1999. The relatively bland formula eventually decided by the APEC leaders at their September 1999 meeting firmly supported the launch of the new round but masked ongoing disagreements among members over how far the agenda should extend beyond services, agriculture, and industrial tariffs. It did include a specific call for the abolition of agricultural export subsidies and unjustifiable export restrictions and prohibitions, but consensus could not be reached on other agricultural trade issues or on the approach to be taken on anti-dumping.

The failure of the Seattle ministerial was a major setback not only for the WTO but also for APEC and "open regionalism", since it left the APEC region bereft of any significant initiatives for pressing forward with non-discriminatory liberalization. APEC's credibility also suffered a blow from its inability to act as a cohesive group at Seattle. Some APEC governments were even reported to have taken positions on certain issues at Seattle that contradicted the common APEC position agreed three months earlier by their leaders. On agricultural trade issues, for example, Japan sided with the European Union (EU), its most reliable ally, against the United States and the Cairns Group members, including many APEC members.

In 2000 and 2001, APEC members continued to look for ways of providing impetus for the launch of a new round. The importance attached to the new round no doubt reflects not only its importance for maintaining the momentum of liberalization in the region, but also the recognition that APEC members are likely to be among the biggest beneficiaries of further multilateral liberalization through the WTO, as indicated, for example, in Scollay and Gilbert (2001). The consensus tended to break down, however, whenever the discussion moved beyond statements of general support for a new round to the consideration of the round's possible agenda. The potential agenda issues that were so divisive within the WTO at the Seattle meeting and its aftermath proved equally divisive among the APEC membership. In November 2000 in Brunei, APEC leaders declared their wish to launch the New Millennium round within 2001 but there was little sign of progress towards resolving these familiar conflicts.

Seen against this background, the breakthrough achieved in launching the Doha Development Agenda in November 2001 was an outstanding achievement. Furthermore, in contrast to Seattle, APEC members were able to make major constructive contributions towards achieving the breakthrough. Early agreement by Japan to the draft negotiating text on agriculture, with its reference to the elimination of export subsidies, undermined attempts by the European Union to weaken the text. An apparent softening of the United States' stance on anti-dumping was also an important contribution.

The crucial position of the so-called "Singapore issues" — competition policy, investment, trade facilitation, and government procurement — in the Doha Development Agenda provided an opportunity for APEC to make a distinctive contribution to the negotiations. Proposals to develop WTO disciplines in these areas represent a new departure for the WTO, and have been highly sensitive and controversial. A decision on the commencement of WTO negotiations in these areas is due in 2003. The period leading up to this decision will be taken up with preparatory work, during which many difficult and challenging issues will have to be faced. The ability of developing countries to participate adequately in the process will be crucial to the eventual outcome.

APEC has longstanding work programmes in each of the four "Singapore issues", all of which feature prominently in the Osaka Action Agenda, and has had success in reaching a degree of consensus in each area. This progress is reflected in the APEC Non-Binding Investment Principles, the APEC Principles to Enhance Competition and Regulatory Reform, Non-Binding Principles on Government Procurement, and the APEC Trade Facilitation Principles.

The opportunity therefore exists for APEC to make substantive contributions to the development of the WTO agenda on these issues. This can facilitate progress within the WTO, while at the same time help to ensure that the WTO builds upon, and is complementary to, the approach already taken by APEC, so that the end result is one which meets the needs and aspirations of APEC members.

A second area where APEC has been making a strong contribution to the WTO process is in capacity-building initiatives among developing

APEC members. A matrix prepared by APEC officials indicates an impressive array of capacity-building initiatives by developed APEC members, with Japan and Canada playing leading roles.

The Challenge of Preferential Trading Arrangements

APEC's "open regionalism" was explicitly intended as an alternative to the preferential approach to regional economic integration. Three substantial preferential trade agreements (PTAs) already existed in the APEC region at the time of the Bogor Declaration: the North American Free Trade Agreement (NAFTA), the ASEAN Free Trade Area (AFTA), and the Closer Economic Relations (CER) agreement between Australia and New Zealand. Free trade agreements between Canada and Chile and between Mexico and Chile were agreed upon in the years immediately following the Bogor meeting. Since the failure of the EVSL in 1998, however, the region has seen an explosive proliferation of proposals for preferential trade arrangements, which have been documented in Scollay and Gilbert (2001) and Scollay (2001). The number of such proposals is now more than thirty, of which two have already resulted in agreements while the others are at various stages of negotiation, study, and discussion.

The proposals vary enormously in nature, from bilateral agreements to much larger trading blocs. In some cases, there is an obvious "domino effect" at work, as economies respond to the pursuit of preferential agreement on the part of their neighbours or close competitors by seeking preferential agreements of their own as a defensive measure.

There has been considerable debate over whether and under what conditions PTAs can be viewed as contributing towards APEC's objectives. Proponents of PTAs typically argue that preferential agreements can accelerate progress towards those objectives, and have emphasized the potential role of such agreements as "laboratories" for breaking down domestic resistance to multilateral liberalization. Others have emphasized the discriminatory nature of PTAs, and have expressed concern at the extent to which preferential initiatives may be motivated in some cases by the desire to avoid liberalization of sensitive sectors, and at the potential for increased business costs arising from the development of a "spaghetti bowl" of overlapping agreements with inconsistent provisions. It has been pointed out that the negative effects of the discrimination inherent in PTAs will be minimized if PTA members progressively lower their MFN (Most Favoured Nation) tariffs at the same time as they remove tariffs within the PTA. Another suggestion has been that PTAs could be reconciled with APEC's "open regionalism" if the preferences granted to one another by members of PTAs could be extended to all

APEC members. This suggestion begs the question of what motivates the creation of PTAs in the first place, and is in any case unlikely to be accepted by proponents of new PTAs when there is clearly no intention of applying it within those PTAs already in existence in the region.

These issues received early attention from APEC leaders. The Bogor Declaration called on the APEC Eminent Persons Group (EPG) "to review the inter-relationships between APEC and the existing sub-regional arrangements (NAFTA, ANZCERTA, and AFTA) and to examine possible options to prevent obstacles to each other and to promote consistency in their relations" (APEC/LM, 1994). The EPG's third report emphasizes that any subregional trade agreement (SRTA) must be fully consistent with the WTO (APEC/EPG 1995). It recommends that any new SRTA initiatives within APEC be promptly submitted to the WTO for confirmation that they meet this test and for surveillance of their performance in practice. This recommendation, however, has turned out to contain little substance, given that WTO members have not been able to agree on the interpretation of the WTO rules governing PTAs, and have consequently been unable to reach conclusions as to the WTO-consistency or otherwise of PTAs submitted to the WTO for examination. The requirement for WTO-consistency, thus, in practice imposes only relatively weak constraints on the nature of PTAs that APEC members may pursue.

APEC leaders in 2001 stated that "regional and bilateral trade agreements…should be in line with APEC architecture and supportive of APEC's goals and principles" (APEC/LM 2001). It is, nevertheless, noticeable that the issues raised by the proliferation of PTAs in the Asia-Pacific region currently receive virtually no attention at APEC official and ministerial meetings. This is all the more remarkable in the light of underlying concerns that the proposed Free Trade Area of the Americas, combined with the emergence of an East Asian trade bloc, might divide the Asia-Pacific region into two competing mega-blocs. In its statement to the APEC 2002 Trade Ministers' Meeting, the PECC highlighted the concern that "such a threat to the trans-Pacific dimension of APEC would challenge the very concept of APEC itself. There will be an air of unreality about APEC deliberations if this issue is not squarely addressed." (PECC 2002)

State of Play and Future Prospects

The Shanghai Accord, agreed in 2001 after intensive consultations among APEC members and attached to the APEC Economic Leaders' statement for that year, provides a useful index of APEC members' views at the turn of the century on the feasibility of APEC's TILF agenda, at least in the short term.

There is a strong emphasis in the Shanghai Accord on the consolidation of the APEC process, through "broadening and updating" the Osaka Action Agenda and "strengthening the IAP process". These are useful steps, but they do not of themselves represent fresh progress towards APEC's liberalization objectives.

The inability for the time being of APEC members to reach agreement on further collective steps in the area of trade liberalization is tacitly recognized in the revival of earlier proposals for "pathfinder initiatives" to be undertaken by subsets of APEC members in cases where the full APEC membership is not ready to move forward. The implementation of APEC principles on investment and trade facilitation by "coalitions of the willing" among APEC members could provide logical candidates for consideration as "pathfinder initiatives", especially as these principles have already been endorsed by the full APEC membership.

Any ambitions that APEC should serve as a primary agent of trade liberalization in the Asia-Pacific region are thus clearly "on hold", at least temporarily. The attention of APEC members in regard to trade liberalization matters has shifted decisively to the WTO and the negotiation of subregional PTAs. It remains to be seen whether this shift is temporary or permanent.

In the meantime, the Shanghai Accord lays heavy emphasis on achieving further progress in trade facilitation, with its call for a 5 per cent reduction in transaction costs across the APEC region over the next five years. The focus on trade facilitation is sensible, given that this is the area of the TILF agenda where APEC has demonstrated that it has a comparative advantage, and as such has the potential to make more progress than the WTO. While trade facilitation has been put forward as one of the "Singapore issues" to be potentially placed on the WTO negotiating agenda in 2003, it seems unlikely that the WTO will be able to address issues beyond the customs matters covered by GATT (General Agreement on Tariffs and Trade) Articles V, XIII, and X. Furthermore, it is not clear that trade facilitation issues are in general suitable for inclusion in binding agreements supported by an enforceable dispute mechanism. Greater progress is likely to be achieved through the co-operative, voluntary approach of APEC.

The Shanghai Accord target on trade facilitation, nevertheless, represents a considerable challenge for APEC. On the one hand, the target is modest and ought to be readily achievable, but, on the other hand, measurement of reductions in transaction costs is not an easy matter. If suitable measures cannot be developed, it will not be possible to clearly demonstrate that the target has been achieved, and APEC's credibility is likely to suffer as a result. This difficulty highlights APEC's weakness in not possessing a strong analytical and research division within its Secretariat, which might have influenced APEC leaders to express the target in more readily measurable terms, or alternatively, could be tasked to develop the required measurement methods.

Finally, APEC's role as a forum for discussing and building consensus around contentious issues should not be dismissed. In this role, it may continue to make useful contributions to the WTO process. If preferential trading arrangements become established as the dominant mode of liberalization in the Asia-Pacific region, APEC is also likely to develop added importance as a forum through which potential trade conflicts within the region may be mediated and contained.

Notes

1. The ASEAN group, which has been influential in the development of the underlying philosophy behind APEC, originally defined the "free trade" objective of their own ASEAN Free Trade Area (AFTA) as tariffs in the 0–5 per cent range, but AFTA's free trade goal has more recently been re-stated as zero tariffs.
2. An ambiguity left conveniently unresolved in the concept of "open regionalism" allowed differing interpretations among the APEC membership to be accommodated. The United States has consistently maintained that it can undertake non-discriminatory liberalization only if this liberalization is reciprocated by both members and non-members of APEC. The majority of APEC members, on the other hand, have interpreted "open regionalism" as implying unconditional non-discrimination, without any requirement for reciprocity.
3. The nine principles are: comprehensiveness; WTO consistency; comparability; non-discrimination; transparency; standstill; simultaneous start; continuous progress and differentiated timetable; flexibility; and co-operation.
4. The fifteen areas are: tariffs; non-tariff measures; services; investment; standards and conformance; customs procedures; competition policy; government procurement; deregulation; intellectual property; rules of origin; dispute mediation; mobility of business persons; Uruguay Round implementation; and information gathering and analysis.
5. Despite APEC's claim of a leadership role in launching the ITA, only thirteen APEC members have joined it.
6. "Joint Statement by Ministers", Vancouver, Canada, 22–23 November, 1997.
7. "APEC Economic Leaders' Declaration: Connecting the APEC Community", Vancouver, Canada, 25 November 1997, paragraph 6.

8. *Twelfth APEC Ministerial Meeting: Joint Statement.*
9. This figure is based on gross national product (GNP) as measured in the official national accounts. When GNP is measured on a purchasing power parity basis, the United States and Japan together account for just over half of the combined GNP of all APEC members.

References

APEC/EPG (APEC/Eminent Persons Group). *A Vision for APEC: Towards an Asia Pacific Economic Community.* Singapore, October 1993.

_____ . *Achieving the APEC Vision: Free and Open Trade in the Asia Pacific.* Singapore, August 1994.

_____ . *Implementing the APEC Vision.* Singapore, August 1995.

APEC/LM. *APEC Economic Leaders' Declaration of Common Resolve.* Bogor, Indonesia, 1994.

APEC/MM. *The Osaka Action Agenda : Implementation of the Bogor Declaration.* Part I, Liberalization and Facilitation; Part II, Economic and Technical Cooperation. November 1995.

_____ . *APEC, MAPA 1996, Manila Action Plan for APEC.* Vol. II, Individual Action Plans; Vol. III, Collective Action Plans; Vol. IV, Progress Report on APEC ECOTECH Joint Activities and Framework Declaration on ECOTECH. Manila, 1996.

Dee, Philippa, Alexis Hardin, and Michael Schuele. *APEC Early Sectoral Liberalization.* Australia: Productivity Commission, July 1998.

IAP Study Group. *APEC's Progress toward the Bogor Target: A Quantitative Assessment of Individual Action Plans.* Tokyo: PECC Japan Committee, 1997.

_____ . *APEC's Progress toward the Bogor Target: A Quantitative Assessment of 1997 IAP/CAP.* Tokyo: PECC Japan Committee, 1998.

Pacific Economic Cooperation Council (PECC) et al. *Perspectives on the Manila Action Plan for APEC.* Manila, 1996.

_____ . *Assessing APEC Individual Action Plans and their Contribution to APEC's Goals.* Auckland, 1999.

_____ . *Statement to Meeting of APEC Ministers Responsible for Trade.* Puerto Vallarta, 2002.

Scollay, R. "The Changing Outlook for Asia-Pacific Regionalism". *World Economy* 24, no. 9 (2001): 1135–60.

Scollay, R. and J. Gilbert. "Measuring the Gains from APEC Trade Liberalization: An Overview of CGE Assessments". *World Economy* 23, no. 2 (2000): 175–97.

_____ . *New Regional Trading Arrangements in the Asia Pacific?* Washington DC.: Institute for International Economics, 2001.

Yamazawa, I. *Asia-Pacific Economic Cooperation (APEC): Challenges and Tasks for the Twenty-first Century.* Proceedings of the 25th Pacific Trade and Development Conference in Osaka, June 1999. London: Routledge, 2000.

Yamazawa, I. & S. Urata. "APEC's Progress in Trade and Investment Liberalization and Facilitation". In Yamazawa (2000).

8

INVESTMENT LIBERALIZATION AND FACILITATION IN THE ASIA-PACIFIC
Can APEC Make a Difference?

Myrna S. Austria

Foreign direct investment (FDI) has played a significant role in the growth and dynamism of the member economies of the Asia-Pacific Economic Co-operation (APEC). Most APEC economies are both recipients and sources of FDI. Up to the late 1980s and early 1990s, a number of these economies pursued highly restrictive policies towards FDI for fear that multinational companies would control important activities in their domestic economies (Bora and Graham 1995). However, the development experience of the newly industrializing economies (NIEs) of Asia in the late 1980s has fundamentally changed this view. The capital as well as the technology, management skills, and other expertise brought in by the multinational companies (mostly from Japan and the United States) have played a major role in the unprecedented growth experienced by these economies that has become the envy of other developing economies.

As a consequence, a number of economies began reorienting their FDI regimes towards greater openness and less regulation. This eventually led to the surge of investments into the region during the last decade. At the same time, however, this flow of FDI facilitated industrial adjustment in the source economies as it enabled them to relocate their labour-intensive industries in Asia, where labour is relatively cheap, as part of their global strategy to remain competitive. This was also true of the experience of the NIEs when they themselves later became sources of capital, targetting labour-intensive industries in ASEAN and China (ESCAP 1998). Such a development strategy ultimately increased economic integration among many APEC economies where the production networks of multinational companies located in the region are now interlinked in technologically advanced industries.

The region's dependence on FDI as a source of capital has not diminished and the role of the region in global FDI flows continues to be strong. In light of the general recognition of the importance of FDI in the economic development of the region, an investment environment that facilitates the smooth flow of FDI becomes crucial. To this end, APEC is aiming for free and open investment no later than 2010 for its developed member economies and by 2020 for its developing member economies. As stated in the Osaka Action Agenda (OAA), this vision can be achieved by member economies through the liberalization of their respective investment regimes by progressively providing for most-favoured-nation (MFN) treatment and ensuring transparency; and by facilitating investment activities through technical assistance and co-operation.

To attain the above goal, the OAA has set guidelines for member economies to follow. First, the economies are to progressively reduce or eliminate exceptions and restrictions using, as an initial framework, the WTO (World Trade Organization) Agreement, the APEC Non-binding Investment Principles, any other international agreements relevant to each economy, or any commonly agreed guidelines developed in APEC. Secondly, the economies are to explore the expansion of APEC's network of bilateral investment agreements. The Leaders have also announced, through the annual APEC Economic Leaders' Declaration, a number of broad initiatives that provide the general direction on how member economies should advance the liberalization process of investment in the region.

The objectives of this chapter are: firstly, to assess the role of APEC as an institution in promoting investment liberalization and facilitation in the region, focusing on the process and the mechanisms by which it makes progress towards its goal of free and open investment in the region;

and secondly, to identify areas where APEC can advance further towards the realization of its goal through the APEC process itself and other multilateral efforts on investment, in particular, the new WTO round.

The chapter is organized as follows. The next section discusses the progress of APEC in the area of investment. This is followed by a discussion of the mechanisms and approaches taken to move towards the vision of APEC for investment, highlighting the strengths as well as the weaknesses of such approaches. Next is a brief discussion of the institutional set-up, in particular, the role of the APEC Investment Experts Group, including the factors and pressures influencing the investment agenda and decision-making process. Areas for strengthening APEC's investment policy agenda and process are then identified. The last section provides the summary and conclusion.

APEC's Progress in the Area of Investment

Member economies have undertaken a number of actions to move towards the goal of free and open investment in the region. These include actions taken both at the economy level and at the regional level. Initially, these were simply initiatives that member economies committed to implement individually through the Individual Action Plan (IAP), and collectively through the Collective Action Plan (CAP).

One of the earlier efforts of APEC was the establishment of the Non-binding Investment Principles (NBIP) in 1994. The NBIP are aimed at strengthening the efficiency of investment administration, eliminating investment obstacles, and establishing a free and open investment environment in the region. They are non-binding in nature and absent of the customary provisions that specify procedures with respect to exceptions and reservations. The drafting of the principles exposed the difficulties of arriving at a regional investment agreement. First, the proposal of having an investment code was met with strong resistance from within APEC (Soesastro 1999). A legally binding code would not be acceptable, as this would mean losing some degree of flexibility in domestic policy-making, an issue which developing member economies are concerned about. Secondly, there was also the question of the desirability of having a set of rules on investment, given that the surge of FDI in the region occurred in the absence of a regional or multilateral framework. Finally, identifying the elements or scope of the investment principles was itself difficult because of the considerable diversity in the level of development and investment regimes among the member economies.

Given that a binding code was unacceptable, the NBIP was later established with the principle that it should seek to encourage greater openness, transparency, and consistency in investment policy on a voluntary basis, and not to force any member economy that was not yet ready. Some considered the NBIP to be weak (Soesastro 1999; Petri 1999). One could also argue whether principles that are not binding and, hence, in a legal sense, provide no protection would be of any value.

In retrospect, however, the commitment of APEC to adopt the NBIP showed its commitment to leadership in investment liberalization, especially in the light of the failure of the OECD's effort on the Multilateral Agreement on Investment (MAI). The NBIP marked an important step forward for investment liberalization in the region as they established the norms by which APEC can work towards achieving as a region (Bora and Graham 1995). The output may not be the best but the process and the exercise of formulating the principles are by itself important as confidence-building measures as they familiarize economies with the issues, and as such would help them in strengthening and improving their individual investment regimes (Pangestu 1994; and Soesastro 1999). While it falls short of the ideal, the NBIP can be used, and is now actually being used, as a framework for improving the investment rules and policies in the region.

Nonetheless, there are two implementation issues. First, the implementation of the principles by *all* economies is hindered by the fact that the various economies are at different stages of development and preparedness. Secondly, since the NBIP is a broad statement of principles, the coverage of investment issues is not detailed, making it difficult for economies to decide on how to proceed with implementation. These two implementation issues are, however, addressed by the Menu of Options. As will be discussed later, the Menu is a fitting response to the need to progressively implement the NBIP.

Liberalization of Investment Regimes

APEC member economies have significantly advanced in their commitments to liberalize their investment regimes, as evidenced by the considerable improvements in the area of investment reported in their IAPs since the IAP process was first used in 1996 as a mechanism to monitor and encourage progress towards the Bogor goals.

Indeed, a PECC study (1999, p. 54) shows that "there are now far fewer economies in APEC which can be defined as having relatively closed investment regimes". The study developed an indicator system to measure the degree of openness of investment policy based on the 1996 APEC Investment Guidebook. Changes in investment policy were measured by updating the indicator system using policy changes documented in the IAPs for each economy between 1996 and 1998. The most significant change in policy occurred in the areas of market access, approval procedures, and facilitation. Likewise, the investment liberalization made by member economies has been consistent with the WTO Trade Related Investment Measures (TRIMs) agreement. The same study shows that the gap in the level of openness in FDI regimes among member economies has been narrowed since developing member economies have made considerable commitment in investment liberalization.

Nonetheless, a more recent joint ABAC-PECC survey of business around the region suggests that various impediments to FDI still exist (ABAC Report 2001). The most serious barriers have included performance requirements, restrictions in market access, restrictions related to entry and stay of personnel, and lack of transparency in investment regimes. The same survey shows that performance requirements and restrictions of market access mainly exist in APEC developing economies, while restrictions of entry and stay of personnel are found in both developed and developing economies.

Many of the member economies have complied with most of the NBIP. Bora (2001) has noted that the NBIP might have played a major role in the individual country liberalizations. In addition, for some of the economies where there are restrictions or reservations in their current commitments in the NBIP, actions in the short to medium and long term have been identified (Austria 2001). Likewise, where restrictions/exceptions are temporary, a definite timetable that matches the WTO deadline has been indicated.

While impediments to investment still do exist, what is more important is that significant progress has been made and that the liberalization efforts are in the right direction.

Investment Facilitation and Capacity Building

APEC has been relatively successful in the implementation of the Collective Action Plan (CAP), most of which concerns investment facilitation and economic and technical co-operation. Most noteworthy, however, is the fact that efforts under the CAP have been expanded in the light of the developments in the region by including initiatives that were not originally in the OAA collective action.

Table 1 shows a summary of the initiatives implemented under the CAP since 1996, covering several areas: transparency, policy dialogue, facilitation, study and evaluation, and economic and technical co-operation. One significant achievement in the area of transparency is the publication of the *APEC Investment Guidebook* that is available in both hard and electronic formats on the Internet for easy access by the business

TABLE 1
Accomplishments of the Collective Action Plan on Investment, 1996–2001

Collective Action		Activities Implemented
As stated in the Osaka Action Agenda	Addition since 1996	
TRANSPARENCY		
1. Increase, in the *short term*, the transparency of APEC investment regimes by:		
(i) Updating the *APEC Investment Guidebook* on investment regimes		Published 4th edition of the *APEC Investment Guidebook*
(ii) Establishment of software networks on investment regulation & investment opportunities		Updated electronic version of the *APEC Investment Guidebook*
(iii) Improving the state of statistical reporting & data collection		Conducted seminar on improving member economies' capabilities on statistical reporting and data collection
	(iv) Increasing the understanding among member economies on investment policy-making issues	Conducted policy discussion fora covering the following countries: Chile, PNG, Hong Kong, Australia, Malaysia, Chinese Taipei, Philippines, New Zealand, Peru, China, Thailand, Brunei, Japan, Russia, Vietnam & South Korea.
POLICY DIALOGUE		
2. Promote, in the *short term*, dialogue with the APEC business community on ways to improve the APEC investment environment		Conducted six (6) APEC Investment Symposia and two (2) APEC Investment Mart
3. Continue dialogue with appropriate international organizations dealing with global & regional investment issues		Established policy dialogues to review investment aspects of the following FTAs: Canada–Chile Free Trade Area; ASEAN Investment Area; Mexico–Chile Free Trade Area

TABLE 1 – cont'd

Collective Action		Activities Implemented
As stated in the Osaka Action Agenda	Addition since 1996	
FACILITATION	4. Undertake, in the short term, practical facilitation initiatives by;	
	(i) Progressively working towards reducing impediments to investments including those investments related to e-commerce	
	(ii) Undertake business facilitation measures to strenghten APEC economies	
	(iii) Initiating investment promotion & facilitation activities to enhance investment flow within APEC economies	Conducted six (6) APEC Investment Symposia and two (2) APEC Investment Mart
STUDY AND EVALUATION		
5. Define and implement, in the *short term*, follow-on training to the WTO implementation seminars		Conducted seminar on the WTO–TRIMs agreement
6. Undertake, in the *short term*, an evaluation of the role of investment in economic development in the Asia–Pacific region		Conducted a study on the impact of investment liberalization

TABLE 1 – cont'd

Collective Action		Activities Implemented
As stated in the Osaka Action Agenda	Addition since 1996	
STUDY AND EVALUATION		
7. Study, in the *short term*, possible common elements between existing subregional arrangements relevant to investment.		
8. Refine, in the *medium term*, APEC's understanding of free and open investment		
9. Assess, in the *long term*, the merits of developing an APEC-wide discipline on investment in the light of APEC's own progress through the medium-term, as well as developments in the international fora.	10. Study the advantages and advantages of creating investment rules — bilateral, regional or multilateral — with a view to fostering a more favourable investment environment in the Asia-Pacific region.	

TABLE 1 – cont'd

Collective Action		Activities Implemented
As stated in the Osaka Action Agenda	**Addition since 1996**	
ECONOMIC AND TECHNICAL CO-OPERATION 11. Identify, in the *short term*, ongoing technical co-operation needs in the Asia-Pacific region & organize training programmes which will assist APEC economies in fulfilling APEC investment objectives		Conducted seminars/trainings/workshops on the following: (i) implementation of the WTO-TRIMs agreement; (ii) experiences of economies with one-stop investment agencies; (iii) FDI policy and administration adjustment; (iv) start-up companies and venture capital; and (v) workshops (3) on the Menu of Options
MENU OF OPTIONS	13. Update Menu of Options	Developed menu of options for investment liberalization and business facilitation for incorporation into the IAPs; updated Menu of Options to include other areas.

Source: Convenor's Summary Report on Investment (various years).

community. The *Guidebook* has been updated to reflect changes in the economies' investment regimes. It is now in its fourth edition.

Policy dialogues were undertaken to reinforce business and investment linkages and create new investment opportunities. The dialogues have been implemented through the Annual Investment Symposium since 1996, and Annual Investment Mart since 2000. As an investment promotion exercise, these activities were effective in gathering thousands of potential investors from both member and non-member economies and provided an opportunity for member economies to present investment opportunities in their economies. Hosting of the Symposium and Mart by member economies is on a voluntary basis.

Another notable accomplishment for facilitating investment is the development of the Menu of Options. The Menu is a reference tool that member economies may voluntarily refer to when updating their IAPs and to assist them in identifying policy measures for creating a free and open investment regime. This Menu of Options approach to investment liberalization is a unique feature of APEC as it allows greater flexibility for economies to adopt measures suitable to their individual circumstances. It echoes the NBIP but identifies more concrete steps and actions to implement the NBIP.

On the other hand, economic and technical co-operation activities were basically in the areas of capacity building initiatives through seminars, trainings and workshops covering a range of topics, including those related to the WTO.

As can be seen from Table 1, while there was considerable progress in the implementation of the collective actions, much of the efforts were concentrated on activities that address the short-term objectives of the OAA. Efforts have yet to start along the areas that address the medium to long-term objectives. Until now, most of the initiatives are heavily concentrated on creating awareness and providing information through the Annual Investment Symposium and Investment Mart, but nothing more concrete that would make a maximum impact on investment creation.

Approaches and Mechanisms: The IAPs and CAP

The Individual Action Plans and Collective Action Plan are APEC's primary mechanisms for measuring and encouraging progress towards the Bogor goals. The IAP, in particular, is the primary mechanism for the implementation of the TILF agenda. Many critics of APEC initially casted doubts on the feasibility of APEC's concerted unilateral approach to liberalization, where each member economy announces unilaterally its own liberalization and facilitation programmes and implements them according to its own pace and domestic rules. The approach, however, has certainly helped member economies to start implementing their own liberalization programmes.

Individual Initiatives

The proof of member economies' commitment to investment liberalization will be judged by their IAPs. The IAP approach promotes transparency in the reform process as the IAPs contain information that are of potential value to the region's investment community. To attract investment, business needs a transparent and stable investment environment. If the investment community is able to see clearly the steps an economy will undertake to liberalize, they would consider these in their planning and decision-making process.

The value-added of APEC to the liberalization process of investment can be seen from the member economies' expanded scope of liberalization, compared with other multilateral fora. The NBIP, for example, covers more investment measures compared with the narrow range of operational restrictions brought under the discipline of the multilateral trading system of the WTO's Agreement on Trade-Related Investment Measures (TRIMs). In addition, the Menu of Options covers more areas not included in the WTO's General Agreement on Trade in Services (GATS) and the Agreement on Trade-Related Aspects of Intellectual Property Rights (TRIPs).

However, since most member economies are implementing liberalization measures under more than one initiative (for example, WTO, APEC, AFTA, NAFTA, etc.), it is difficult to tell whether the liberalization measures adopted by member economies are in fact APEC commitments or they were undertaken under other initiatives and only deployed as APEC deliverables (Curtis and Ciuriak 1999). However, since there is a general recognition among member economies of the importance of an open investment regime, it is safe to say that the combined IAP-CAP approach may have helped to speed up the liberalization process.

One weakness of the IAP process, however, is that since the IAP is a listing of efforts to liberalize the investment regime, one cannot conclude that an economy which is not reporting any initiative on a particular area is adopting protectionist policies since it may have started from an already open regime.

Related to this, the listing approach in the IAP could leave everyone unclear about the remaining impediments (Yamazawa 1999). This is best illustrated by the somewhat confusing results of the PECC (1999) study and the ABAC-PECC (2001) survey. As presented earlier, the PECC

(1999) study reported that there are now far fewer economies with relatively closed investment regimes and yet the recent ABAC-PECC (2001) survey shows that impediments still exist. One would expect an improvement in the openness of regimes as APEC moves towards its target dates. Yet, this kind of information is impossible to see from the IAP format. That is, the annual IAP cannot inform the reader the degree of openness of an economy's investment regime nor can it give an indication of how far that economy is from the goal of an open and free investment.

Collective Actions

The IAP-CAP approach to liberalization is again unique to APEC and its significance should be highlighted. The CAP strengthens the IAPs to be implemented in a concerted manner (Yamazawa 1999). The Menu of Options best illustrates this. The Menu was a CAP initiative; yet, it was also instrumental in enabling the economies to identify concrete steps and measures to be included in their IAPs for liberalizing their investment regimes.

The CAP contains what are supposed to be joint actions of member economies. Following the APEC modality, however, participation is voluntary. The voluntary participation defeats what is supposed to be a collective action. Non-participation in an initiative could be due to lack of funding, lack of interest, or the initiative itself is not needed by an economy.

Many of the CAP initiatives are not participated by all member economies. If the objective for collective actions is to generate contributions commensurate with members' capabilities, then surely more is expected from developed member economies. As discussed in the previous section, most CAP initiatives deal with capacity building and investment promotion. While developed economies may no longer see the need for capacity building initiatives, they could take the lead in initiating activities for the shared benefit of the developing member economies, operating under the ECOTECH principle of constructive and genuine partnership.

Certainly, there is much room for improvement in this kind of collaboration and partnership among the developed and developing members in implementing the CAP initiatives.

The Institutional Set-Up: Role of the Investment Experts Group

The Investment Experts Group (IEG) is one of the eleven sub-fora under the Committee on Trade and Investment (CTI). It was established in 1994 in response to the mandate from the APEC Leaders to develop the NBIP. After the NBIP, the group was reconvened in 1995, with no set term, to assist the CTI in the implementation of the collective actions on investment contained in the OAA. The IEG is one of the five CTI sub-fora that are *ad hoc*, and/or informal in nature, with no endorsed terms of reference.[1] The group is composed of government officials, usually from the Ministry of Foreign Affairs or Investment, of member economies. A Chair, selected by the group from among themselves, for a term of two years, heads the group.

Setting Up the Agenda

A review of the various reports of the IEG gives the perception that the agenda is heavily focused on investment promotion activities, instead of improving investment policy. Likewise, there is no cohesive approach on how the collective actions should be implemented. Identification of initiatives and projects is basically *ad hoc* and largely reflects the interests of the economy proposing the initiatives. On some occasions, instruction to look at certain initiatives is received from the APEC Leaders (such as the NBIP, or Menu of Options). There are no set criteria in the selection of projects and, hence, the tendency to accept any initiative or project put forward, without considering whether the result of such an initiative is the most cost-effective way of achieving collective action. Nowhere in the IEG reports is screening or prioritization of projects mentioned.

Likewise, the business sector has not been invited to the IEG meetings. There were efforts to engage the APEC Business Advisory Council (ABAC) at IEG meetings in the past, but these have not borne fruit (ABAC Report 1999). At best, the business sector's involvement was during the Annual Investment Symposium and Investment Mart where they were invited as participants. In recent years, however, the business sector has been invited to provide inputs on the symposium topics or act as resource persons during the symposium. In some instances, the business sector had indirectly influenced the plans and programmes of the IEG, but mainly via economy positions.

Delivery of Work

The IEG meets three times a year, often but not always, in the economy hosting the APEC Leaders' Meeting. The physical meetings are useful in the deliberation of policy-related issues as they facilitate understanding and discussion. However, a review of the minutes of the meetings shows that significant time is spent on reporting the progress in the implementation of initiatives, or reporting of proposed initiatives. It could be more cost-effective if such agenda were done through electronic exchanges, and only the summary or consolidated report be reported during the physical meetings.

Furthermore, a review of the attendance at the meetings suggests that only a few economies send the same representative/s to the meetings. For most economies, different person/s are sent for each meeting. This could affect the productivity of the meetings as the familiarity of the issues and agenda depends on attendance by the same representatives. There have also been instances when representatives could not make decisions and needed to refer the matter to experts when they returned home.

The representative of the economy that proposed the project also does project evaluation upon completion of a project. The evaluation is then reported to the IEG.

Linkages with Other CTI Fora

Linkage is not well defined, basically *ad hoc*, depending on the issue at hand. For example, when the Menu of Options was expanded to include other areas, convenors of the relevant CTI sub-fora were invited during the IEG meetings mainly for information sharing. This is not surprising, however, given the absence of a policy framework that links the works of the IEG with other CTI fora. This is ironic as investment issues are directly related to competition policy and deregulation (Group on Competition Policy and Deregulation), intellectual property rights (Intellectual Property Rights Experts Group), and trade in services (Group on Services).

Effectiveness of the Process

The APEC process has many levels — Leaders' Summit, Ministeral Meetings, Senior Officials' Meetings (SOM), three committees (Committee on Trade and Investment, Economic Committee and Budget Management Committee) and eleven sub-fora for CTI.

The significance of the IEG process cannot be discussed in isolation of the whole APEC process. The consultative process at the various levels can produce initiatives which when implemented can enrich the agenda of APEC. The APEC process institutionalized a reform process. The meetings at the various levels — from working groups, to committees, SOMs, and ministerial meetings — became part of the domestic bureaucratic process of reforms. In other words, the APEC process has mustered domestic political support for the policy reform process. What was politically difficult to implement unilaterally was made politically manageable through APEC (Intal and Austria 2000).

Strengthening the Investment Policy Agenda and the APEC Process

APEC's progress towards its goal of free and open investment in the region has opened an opportunity for APEC to play an international leadership role in investment liberalization. By building on the several steps that member economies have already taken to facilitate investment and liberalize their investment regimes, APEC can send a clear signal that it is prepared to make further progress in this area. This section of the chapter attempts to identify actions, both in terms of the investment policy agenda and the APEC process itself, that need to be made to push further investment liberalization and facilitation in the region.

Investment Policy Agenda

* Expansion of the Menu of Options to include work on investment incentives, and exceptions to MFN and national treatment principles.

    Investment incentives. The NBIP includes investment incentives but one that is limited to those related to health, safety, and environment regulations. When the NBIP was drafted, APEC did not come to an agreement on the use of subsidies and other fiscal incentives to attract foreign investment (Bora and Graham 1999).

    Competition among countries to attract foreign investment through the use of incentives has been pervasive. Studies have shown, however, that investment incentives have the same effect as trade restrictions in reducing allocative and dynamic efficiency (Brewer and Young 1999; and WTO 2000). As competition for investment becomes global, the economic distortions produced by incentives will also increase. The possible impact that this may have on development warrants consideration of the possible need for discipline on investment incentives. APEC can take a lead role in addressing this development issue.

    MFN and National Treatment Principles. While there is general consensus among member economies on the principles of most-favoured-nation (MFN) and national treatment, the IAPs still report exceptions in many sectors or areas. The challenge for APEC is to work towards the reduction of the exceptions to the agreed principles. These exceptions vary across countries and for diverse reasons. Sectors include industries that are important to national security, industries where there are monopolies or significant government ownership, industries that are highly regulated, or industries that are politically sensitive, such as those related to culture or religion. The process will not be an easy task, as it requires economies to resist pressure from the sectors concerned and, in some cases, from policy-makers themselves. This is something that APEC can work at in the medium to long-term. The menu of options could include those that are industry-specific.

• Economies can prepare an inventory of all remaining impediments to investment with a definite timetable for implementation.

To further accelerate investment liberalization in the region, each economy should prepare a complete inventory of its remaining impediments. This will provide useful information to potential investors and will serve as a means of exerting pressure on some economies to accelerate liberalization. For each year, the IAPs can then indicate which impediments these economies are committed to remove in that year and which would still be retained. The IAP can then serve as an annual stock-taking of the remaining impediments. Such an approach will make monitoring of progress easier. It will also give a clear picture each year of how far the economies are from the goal of free and open investment. In case economies make exceptions to removing some impediments, this should be properly indicated and the basis for such exceptions (such as binding multilateral commitments) should be carefully articulated, so that investors can consider ways of accommodating their legitimate concerns.

The problem here, however, is that before one can make a complete inventory of impediments, there must be a clear definition of what open and free investment means. APEC has yet to work this out. The indicators based on that definition will serve as a benchmark or yardstick against which an economy can measure its degree of openness and assess what remaining impediments there are that should be included in the annual IAP.

There has been great improvement in the IAP format on investment since its formulation in 1996. From a mere listing of commitments for the year, the 2001 IAPs indicate for each investment not only the current measures applied but also the position at base year (which is 1996), the cumulative improvements made to date and the planned improvements to be made further. Nonetheless, the improvement still falls short of the ideal. Some IAPs include a blank format. For economies that have complied with the format, it is not clear whether the planned improvements are the only remaining impediments.

• APEC should use its progress on investment to influence the WTO process and agenda and advance the interests of the region in the new WTO round.

   Much of APEC's work on investment is in line with the agenda being undertaken at the WTO. While the time for a negotiation for a multilateral framework on investment may not be ripe yet, APEC can use what it has already achieved to influence the agenda of the new WTO round. The NBIP, for example, has a wider scope than TRIMs, which covers only four trade-related investment measures (local content, foreign exchange, trade balancing and domestic sales requirements), and hence, APEC can push for the expansion of the TRIMs. Also, the Menu of Options includes areas beyond the WTO agenda. The Menu can be used to improve TRIPs and GATS, both of which are highly regarded as reflecting developed country priorities and agenda. APEC could then consider improving or expanding the elements of the WTO work in these areas that could best serve its membership. APEC can also further expand the Menu to include areas that are significant to the WTO agenda.

APEC Process

• Enhance investors' participation in advancing the investment agenda. There should be greater flexibility on APEC's rules regarding participation of the business sector in APEC fora. Currently, the participation of the business sector is limited to attending the Investment Symposium and Investment Mart and in providing inputs to the symposium topics. They should be invited to attend the IEG meetings so that they can provide inputs to the process itself and help shape the policy agenda and initiatives in support of the investment collective plans in partnership with officials from the various member economies. Such involvement is important to ensure that the IEG's work is relevant to real investment problems.

• Strengthen the linkage of the IEG with the Economic Committee and other CTI fora.

   Economic Committee. The IEG's linkage with the Economic Committee, which is in charge of cross-cutting issues in support of the three pillars of APEC, is not clear. However, the work of the Economic Committee in the area of macroeconomic management is increasingly becoming important for those economies seeking to host FDI. That is, investors are not only looking for a liberalized and transparent investment regime but also for a stable economic environment. Hence, the work of the IEG in investment liberalization must be undertaken in concert with the work of the Economic Committee in establishing the other locational determinants for FDI, such as sound monetary and fiscal policies, low interest rates, and inflation, a sensible exchange rate policy and sustainable external balance.

An example of a possible collaborative effort between the IEG and the Economic Committee is in the area of policy dialogues. In the past, policy dialogues had focused only on discussing investment regimes of the various member economies. This could be improved by including a presentation of the macroeconomic environment of the member economies.

Other APEC fora. As discussed earlier, investment is directly related to competition policy and deregulation, trade in services, and intellectual property rights. Hence, collaboration between the IEG and the APEC fora responsible for these areas should be strengthened.

- Use the WTO process to achieve APEC's own objectives and agenda.
  As discussed earlier, there is a need for APEC to work on the exceptions to the MFN and national treatment principles and investment incentives. As these are two difficult issues to deal with, one way of doing it is to build on the existing work of the WTO. As most of the exceptions to the national treatment principles are in services, APEC could push for further work on the GATS. For investment incentives, APEC could channel work through the Agreement on Subsidies and Countervailing Measures (ASCM). APEC could begin work on the expansion of the ASCM, as the agreement applies only to trade in goods and its remedies are effective only when an investment had given rise to trade in goods.
  Considering this, the IEG should take into account developments in the WTO in drawing up its work programme in the above areas.

- Meetings should be focused on substantive issues to save on resources. Considering that participation in meetings involve enormous resources (airfare, hotel accommodation and per diem of participants) for the member economies, especially for the developing members, IEG meetings could be limited to two per year, one at the beginning of the year, focusing on the major projects/activities to be implemented for the year; and another before the Leaders' Meeting, focusing on what should be put forward for the consideration of the Leaders during their annual meetings, through the CTI and SOM, and an assessment of the progress made during the year. Representatives to the meetings must have the authority to make decisions and commitments.

Summary and Conclusions

APEC has made a difference in promoting the liberalization of investment regimes and in facilitating the flow of investment in the Asia–Pacific region. This can be observed from the improved levels of openness and transparency of the investment regimes of member economies. While credit may not go to APEC alone, as member economies are pushing for liberalization under more than one initiative, APEC has helped to speed up the liberalization process. The value-added of APEC is indicated by the member economies' expanded scope of liberalization compared with other multilateral investment fora.

However, more work is at hand as impediments to investment still exist. Investment initiatives should now graduate from promotional activities to something more concrete that could make a maximum impact on investment creation. This includes efforts towards the reduction of the exceptions to the agreed principles on national treatment and MFN; developing disciplines on investment incentives; preparing an inventory of remaining impediments so as to pressure economies on accelerating the liberalization process; involving the business sector in shaping investment policy agenda and initiatives to be implemented so as to ensure that these are relevant to real investment problems; and strengthening the linkage of the IEG with other APEC fora.

The challenge for APEC is to use its progress on investment as the launching pad of initiatives for the much larger WTO round. In particular, APEC can influence the WTO to make use of the NBIP and the Menu of Options to expand or improve work on TRIMs, GATS, TRIPs, and competition policy that would best serve the interests of its own membership. At the same time, APEC can use the WTO process to achieve its own objectives and agenda. Ultimately, a successful WTO round will add credibility to APEC, as this would mean that member economies are binding themselves to implementing their APEC-WTO commitments.

Notes

1. The other informal groups include: (i) Group on Services, (ii) Group on Competition Policy and Deregulation, (iii) Informal Group on Uruguay Round Implementation/Rules of Origin, and the (iv) Informal Experts

Group on Mobility of Business People. The CTI sub-fora that are formal
and have endorsed terms of reference include: (i) Market Access Group,
(ii) Sub-committee on Standards and Conformance, (iii) Sub-committee
on Customs Procedures, (iv) Intellectual Property Rights Experts Group,
(v)Government Procurement Experts Group, and (vi) Dispute Mediation
Experts Group.

References

APEC Business Advisory Council. "APEC Means Business: Restoring Confidence,
Regenerating Growth". Report to the APEC Economic Leaders, Kuala
Lumpur, Malaysia, 1988.
_____ . "Report to the APEC Economic Leaders". Auckland, New Zealand,
1999.
_____ . "Facing Globalization the APEC Way". Report to the APEC Economic
Leaders, Brunei Darussalam, 2000.
_____ . "Common Development Through Market Opening, Capacity Building
and Full Participation". Report to the APEC Economic Leaders, Shanghai,
China, 2001.
Austria, Myrna. "APEC's Commitments on Investments". *Assessing APEC's
Progress: Trade, Ecotech & Institutions,* edited by Richard E. Feinberg and
Ye Zhao. Singapore: Institute of Southeast Asian Studies, 2001.
Bora, Bijit. "Prospects for Harmonizing Investment Policies in the East Asian
Region". Paper presented at the Third Asia Development Forum, organized
by ADB, Bangkok, 11–14 June 2001.
Bora, Bijit, and Edward Graham. "Non-binding Investment Principles in APEC".
CIES Policy Discussion Paper No. 95/01. Australia: University of Adelaide,
1995.
Bora, Bijit, Mari Pangestu, et al. *Implications of the APEC Process for Intraregional
Trade and Investment Flows.* Papers and proceedings presented at the Seminar
on the Implications of the APEC Process for Intraregional Trade and
Investment Flows in Asia and the Pacific, 17–19 September 1997, Bangkok,
Thailand. United Nations Publications, 1998.
Brewer, Thomas, and Stephen Young. "Investment Policies in Multilateral and
Regional Agreements: A Comparative Analysis". *Trade and Investment Policy
Volume II,* edited by Thomas Brewer. United Kingdom: Edward Elgar
Publishing Ltd., 1996.
Curtis, John, and Dan Ciuriak. "APEC After Ten Years: Performance and
Prospects". Paper presented at the APEC Study Centre Consortium
Conference, Auckland, New Zealand, 31 May–2 June 1999.
ESCAP. *Implications of the APEC Process for Intraregional Trade and Investment
Flows.* New York: United Nations, 1998.
Intal, Ponciano, Jr. and Myrna Austria. "APEC: A Review and the Way Forward".
Journal of Philippine Development 27, no. 1 (2000):1–26.
Panagariya, Arvind. "APEC and the United States of America". *International Trade
Policy and the Pacific Rim,* edited by John Piggott and Alan Woodland.
Sydney, Australia: International Economic Association, 1999.

Pangestu, Mari, "APEC Leadership in Liberalization". *CIES Policy Discussion Paper No. 96/07*. Australia: University of Adelaide, 1996.

Pangestu, Mari, and Bijit Bora. "Evolution of Liberalization Policies Affecting Investment Flows in the Asia Pacific". *CIES Policy Discussion Paper No. 96/01*. Australia: University of Adelaide, 1996.

PECC. *Assessing APEC Individual Action Plans and their Contributions to APEC's Goals*. Manila, 1999.

Petri, Peter. "APEC and the Millenium Round". Paper presented at the APEC Study Centre Consortium Conference, Auckland, New Zealand, 31 May–2 June 1999.

Shin-Yuan, Lai. "APEC After Ten Years: Future Directions". Paper presented at the APEC Study Centre Consortium Conference, Auckland, New Zealand, 31 May–2 June 1999.

Soesastro, Hadi. "APEC After Ten Years". Paper presented at the APEC Study Centre Consortium Conference, Auckland, New Zealand, 31 May–2 June 1999.

World Trade Organization. *Report (2000) of the Working Group on the Relationship between Trade and Investment to the General Council*. 27 November 2000. WT/WGTI/4.

Yamazawa, Ippei. "APEC After Ten Years: How Much Has Been Achieved in Liberalization and Facilitation". Paper presented at the APEC Study Centre Consortium Conference, Auckland, New Zealand, 31 May–2 June 1999.

9

THE WHEEL THAT DRIVES APEC
The Critical Role and Mandate of ECOTECH in APEC

MEDHI KRONGKAEW

Introduction

A new metaphor has recently been created for APEC. For a long time, the three functions of APEC have been said to include the support of (a) trade and investment liberalization, (b) trade and investment facilitation, and (c) economic and technical co-operation. These three functions have become the "Three Pillars" of APEC, defining its unique existence and activities. In early April 2001, however, a new analogy was made in Beijing that likened the main functions of APEC to two wheels of a bicycle — the front wheel being trade and investment liberalization and facilitation (TILF), and the rear wheel being economic and technical co-operation (ECOTECH).[1] Since then, this new metaphor has been mentioned in many subsequent APEC-related meetings.[2] It has obviously improved upon the original "Three Pillars" concept of APEC for its dynamic forward movement, and a better sense of balance between trade and investment liberalization and facilitation, and economic and technical co-operation.

However, while this development can be seen as part of the efforts to enhance the status of ECOTECH in APEC, there are many more developments that are required to truly push ECOTECH onto a higher ground of official and popular recognition in APEC. In this short chapter, I would like to discuss some of these developments or changes that are required. However, before discussion of this point, the past achievements of APEC on ECOTECH matters and the reasons behind these achievements will be dealt with. The following section will then discuss forthcoming changes and expectations that may give the APEC forum that handles ECOTECH matters its new enhanced status.[3] Finally, the chapter concludes with some observations on the future success of APEC as a result of these new developments.

Past Achievements in ECOTECH Matters

By now, ECOTECH is a well-known acronym in APEC. What is not well known, however, are ECOTECH's achievements in the APEC process. The ECOTECH agenda is run by the Senior Officials' Meeting (SOM) Subcommittee on ECOTECH, or ESC. According to the terms of reference (TOR) for the ESC, this subcommittee will assist the SOM in co-ordinating and managing APEC's ECOTECH agenda, as well as in identifying value-added initiatives for co-operative action. The main objective of the ESC as stated in its TOR is:

> ...to advance more effective implementation of the APEC's ECOTECH agenda by consulting with and integrating the efforts of various APEC fora through a results-oriented, outcomes-based approach which benefits all member economies; providing a policy management tool for strengthening and streamlining APEC's work; and providing guidance on possible actions which could be undertaken to achieve APEC ECOTECH goals, namely:
>
> • to attain sustainable growth and equitable development in the Asia-Pacific region;
> • to reduce economic disparities among APEC economies;
> • to improve the economic and social well-being of the people; and
> • to deepen the spirit of community in the Asia-Pacific.

The story about the origin and development of the ESC can be found elsewhere.[4] It is sufficient to say here that up to 2001, the achievements of the ESC had been modest. During 1999 and 2000, the ESC succeeded in completing the following tasks:[5]

- examined and reported on the 220 ECOTECH projects that were ongoing or completed in 2000, with assistance from the APEC Secretariat;
- evaluated completed HRD (human resource development) ECOTECH projects;
- reviewed the implementation of Part II of the Osaka Action Agenda (OAA);
- monitored and reported on the implementation of projects/activities that flowed from the Kuala Lumpur Action Programme on Skills Development and the APEC Agenda for Science and Technology Industry Co-operation into the 21st Century, endorsed by APEC Leaders in Kuala Lumpur, Malaysia, in 1999;
- established a system of focal points (co-ordinators) to review progress in the implementation of the six priority ECOTECH themes under the 1996 Manila Declaration. In 2000, the ESC reported on the themes relating to Capital Markets, Economic Infrastructure, and Sustainable Development;
- reported on the implementation by APEC fora of its Guidance on Strengthening Management of APEC ECOTECH activities;
- proposed refinements to the ECOTECH Weighting Matrix, that was designed to provide APEC fora with a better appreciation of the overall ECOTECH priorities, including desired project outcomes; and launched the ECOTECH Clearing House (http://www.apec-ECOTECH.org), a website that indexes all relevant information on APEC ECOTECH activities. The Clearing House also facilitates the exchange of information between potential partners in ECOTECH activity, in particular, the identification of ECOTECH requirements and the capacity to provide appropriate expertise to meet those needs.

The year 2001 can be seen as a watershed year for the resurgent role of ECOTECH in APEC. Many outstanding events happened that year compared to previous years. Apart from the routine activities of surveying and assessing ECOTECH projects undertaken by various Working Groups and other APEC fora, and monitoring activities related to given initiatives, the ESC was involved in three major accomplishments on ECOTECH matters in 2001. These three major accomplishments are discussed below.

1. *The Updating of Part II of the Osaka Action Agenda*[6]
   Building on the success of the review of Part II of the Osaka Action Agenda in 2000, where APEC Working Groups and other

fora were asked to determine what ECOTECH activities had
been accomplished since 1995, and whether there was a need for
its revision, the APEC Ministers in their meeting in Brunei in
November 2000, tasked the ESC to develop further the Joint
Activities/Dialogue sections of the OAA guidelines. This task
became known as the updating of Part II of the OAA where Lead
Shepherds of all existing and new Working Groups were asked to
update their work programmes and activities based on the original
Common Policy Concepts (CPC) contained in the original 1995
OAA Part II.[7] Despite the extensive nature of this task or assignment,
the ESC was able to co-operate with all APEC working groups to
finish the updating on time, and the updated OAA Part II was
submitted to the Ministerial Meeting for endorsement in Shanghai
in October 2001.[8]

2. *The Introduction of ECOTECH Action Plan (EPA)*
    One policy instrument that captures the spirit of the TILF in APEC
    is the annual submission of the Individual Action Plan (IAP) by each
    APEC member. Following the guidelines given in Part I of the
    OAA, the first TILF-IAP was introduced in 1996. In short, a TILF-
    IAP is a policy document specifying how an economy proposes to
    liberalize its trade and investment, and engage in other trade and
    investment facilitation measures. However, while this TILF-IAP can
    be looked upon as an excellent manifestation of APEC voluntarism
    and unilateral liberalization, there is no similar or equivalent
    undertaking on the ECOTECH side. This point was raised during
    the second ESC meeting in Brunei in May 2000, but no serious
    follow up was taken. In November 2000, however, APEC Ministers
    called for a more focused and intensified ECOTECH action agenda,
    and instructed officials to consider the possibility of establishing
    Individual Action Plans on ECOTECH.[9] This was the beginning of
    the major ECOTECH achievement in 2001.
        The debate on the possibility of establishing an ECOTECH-
    IAP started in the first 2001 ESC meeting in Beijing in February
    2001. There were many sceptical members who questioned the idea
    of ECOTECH-IAPs on the grounds of duplication of the
    ECOTECH Clearing House activities just introduced in 2000, on
    the non-quantifiability of the ECOTECH-IAP outcomes, on the
    guise of this ECOTECH-IAP for development assistance, and so
    on.[10] During the second meeting of the ESC in Shenzhen in May
    2001, there were some examples and templates of these ECOTECH-
    IAPs proposed by some economies, but scepticism still remained

very strong. Eventually, however, the co-operative spirit among members prevailed and a compromise was reached for an introduction of this ECOTECH Action Plan (EAP) by members on a voluntary basis for an experimental period of two years. To help members in this new undertaking, this EAP would be limited to the areas of human resources development only. By SOM III in Dalian, China, nine economies had submitted their EAPs, with the possibility of many more offering to show their EAPs later. At the APEC Ministers' Meeting in Shanghai in October 2001, eight more economies had submitted their EAPs. These EAPs represent past, present, and future commitments of some members on the issues of human resources development and human capacity building. Some of these plans could provide best practices for other members to replicate or emulate as a means to improve the human capacity of members in the region.

3. *The Launch of the Human Capacity Building Strategy Report*
The Ministerial Meeting in Brunei in 2000 also instructed that a Human Capacity Building Co-ordination Group (HCBCG) be created to explore the possibility of drafting a strategy report on human capacity building for APEC on an annual basis. This was part of the continuation of the initiatives conceived by the Brunei meeting to increase human capacity and promote human resources development in the APEC region. The ESC was asked to be responsible for this co-ordination exercise. During the first SOM in Beijing, therefore, the ESC prepared to take on the assignment. However, since the subject of human capacity building was very wide and all-encompassing, it requested the SOM to limit the scope of the report to cover only human capacity building in the New Economy, which was also the subject that the Economic Committee was asked to study.[11] The HCBCG worked closely with related APEC fora, such as the Human Resource Development Working Group (HRDWG) and the ISTWG, the Economic Committee, and the High Level Meeting on Human Capacity Building jointly organized by Brunei and China in Beijing in early 2001. The Draft Strategy Report was submitted to APEC members to discuss throughout SOM II, SOM III, and intersessionally before the Informal SOM in October 2001. However, due to the complexities of issues, members could not reach agreement on its Final Report in time for submission to the Ministerial Meeting in Shanghai in October 2001. It was, however, completed before the first meeting of the SOM in Mexico City in February 2002.[12]

In brief, this Report recognizes the importance of education and skills training to attain knowledge on information and communication technology that will change "digital divide" to "digital opportunities" in the New Economy. To do this, five areas of human capacity building were selected as goals or objectives for achievement. They are:

- Build people's capability through education and skills training, particularly through distance and life-long learning based on tripartite engagements among the government, private business, and the academe;
- Increased human capacity through education and skills training will also lead to the achievement of regional development and a reduction in poverty;
- This new development must take place within the environment of equity with regard to gender, ethnic minority, age, health status, and generational differences;
- Private sector and private enterprises, large and small, must be engaged to play an active part in this endeavour; and
- The combined efforts will also lead to well-functioning labour markets, which will contribute to further success of efforts.

Forthcoming Changes and Expectations

It is obvious from the above that, in the past two years, several changes have taken place with respect to ECOTECH agendas and the ways in which these agendas have been pursued in the APEC process. As alluded to in the introduction, ECOTECH has come a long way since its rough beginning in 1997. It is not only that the interest and attention towards ECOTECH issues in APEC are now on par with TILF issues and activities, it is possible that ECOTECH may actually sustain the viability of APEC from now until the end of the second decade of its existence when the first deadline of the Bogor goals is reached. How is this possible? For one thing, the original expectation of a continuous reduction in tariff and non-tariff barriers among APEC members towards the Bogor goals may not be forthcoming owing to difficulties in the domestic economic situations in many member economies. More time and more complex economic and political adjustments may be needed for freer trade and investment in the APEC region in future. However, the Bogor goals are still plausible and feasible if members realize that they need greater and more intensive economic and technical co-operation to push all members to freer trade and investment ten to twenty years from now.

Accepting the fact that progress towards the Bogor goals may not come in a linear fashion, but the possibility that members may succeed in dropping all trade and investment barriers nearer to the deadline if and when their general economic development become more sustained, and members are willing to help share their experiences and best practices with one another, help and share the concerns of development problems with one another, and so on, ECOTECH could effectively push APEC towards its Bogor goals. The following are some of the changes and expectations in ECOTECH matters that could serve to achieve this noble objective.

Many independent observers have commented on the difficulties in the ways ECOTECH agendas or objectives could be set to work. The APEC International Assessment Network (APIAN), for example, has stated that "ECOTECH still suffers from some shortcomings, such as the excessive diffusion of limited ECOTECH resources, a lack of coordination around defined APEC objectives, and inadequate funding".[13] Although there are several improvements in the ways the ESC has helped the SOM to conduct its ECOTECH agendas, more could be achieved by the realization of these measures.

During 2000 and 2001, I myself in my capacity as Chair of the ESC, had suggested formally (that is, in the ESC meetings) as well as informally (that is, through various papers I have written in my personal capacity) about the change and improvement in the role of the ESC in its handling of ECOTECH matters (see, for example, Medhi 2000, 2001a, and 2001b). I have realized, however, that in a consensus-based organization such as APEC (and also its fora, such as the ESC), more concerted efforts among members are needed to bring about those changes and improvements. During the ESC III meeting in Dalian, China, in August 2001, the discussion on the role and mandate of the ESC in its handling of ECOTECH matters had come up again. This time I realized that there must be a group effort in drafting a position or review paper on the role and mandate of the ESC before any concrete change or improvement could take place, so I asked New Zealand to undertake the study of the role and mandate of the ESC in co-operation with interested members.[14]

In the excellent report that New Zealand prepared, six pertinent questions concerning the past and present roles of ECOTECH and the ESC were asked, and some answers to these questions were discussed. These questions and answers came from the review of past records of ECOTECH activities by the New Zealand Study Team, and the opinions and comments from interested ESC members. These six questions that the New Zealand Report posed were:

1. What is the ESC's current role and mandate?
2. Why was the ESC given that role and mandate?
3. What further instructions have there been to the ESC from Leaders, Ministers, and the SOM since its establishment in 1998?
4. What changes in the APEC environment have there been since the ESC's establishment in 1998?
5. What are the achievements of the ESC in relation to the expressed objectives, and what are the problems/obstacles faced?
6. Is there anything in (or not in) the ESC's mandate which restricts its activity in areas where it may be desirable for the ESC to have a role?

The answers given in the New Zealand Report can be summarized as follows:

1. *On the current role and mandate of the ESC*

The Report had made substantial reference to the terms of reference as agreed by the SOM in Penang in February 1998 with regard to the role and mandate of the ESC. In summary, the ESC's overarching role is to assist the SOM in co-ordinating and managing APEC's ECOTECH agenda, by *examining* and *reviewing* ECOTECH activities under way or completed, *identifying* possible ECOTECH initiatives which could be undertaken in the future, *consulting* with various APEC fora and the private sector on how to integrate effort and strengthen and streamline ECOTECH work, *encouraging* participation of the private sector, *evaluating* proposals to include new ECOTECH themes in the 1996 "Framework", *reporting* to SOM on any of the matters above, and *recommending* appropriate action, and *undertaking* ECOTECH-related tasks as directed by the Senior Officials.

From the above account, it may be seen that the ESC's mandate is very wide — there is virtually no limit to the extent to which it can consider, analyse, and report on ECOTECH issues. The ESC can interact with all APEC fora, including committees and working groups. However, while the mandate may be very wide, the power or authority of the ESC may be limited. The ESC's role is to *assist* (italic in the original) the SOM in the management and co-ordination of the ECOTECH agenda; it is not the ESC's role to manage and co-ordinate ECOTECH in its own right. (In a similar way, other fora such as the CTI and Economic Committee revert to the SOM on important issues.) Rather than articulating a narrow list of actions for the ESC, the purpose of the mandate seems to be to ensure that the SOM is provided with appropriate recommendations on a very wide field of ECOTECH issues.[15]

2. On the reasons the ESC was given its role and mandate

The New Zealand Report referred to the decision of the SOM to establish the ESC in 1997. It was not clear from the report how the decision was made to establish this new APEC forum as a subcommittee attached to the SOM rather than as a committee similar to the CTI, although it did report the suggestion by the Canadian SOM Chair in his paper entitled "Implementation of APEC's Economic and Technical Co-operation Agenda", which outlined steps taken to improve the co-ordination of the ECOTECH agenda, tabled at SOM III, which included three options for the management of such an agenda. The three recommendations were that the SOM could continue as the co-ordinating body using a more "hands-on" approach; the SOM Committee of the Whole (COW) could continue to review ECOTECH issues on an annual basis; and an ECOTECH Committee (ETC) could be created.

After reviewing these options, "SOM agreed that while consensus had not yet been reached, there had been a favourable evolution of opinion ... towards a concrete mechanism for coordination, possibly through the establishment of an ETC". Nevertheless, an agreement was reached that, instead of this new APEC forum to help the SOM manage the ECOTECH agenda being set up as an ECOTECH Committee, it would form a subcommittee attached to the SOM, called the SOM Subcommittee for Economic and Technical Co-operation, or ESC.[16] The terms of reference of the ESC which was drawn up later was based on this compromise.

3. On further instructions to the ESC since its establishment in 1998

The New Zealand Report went back to the resolutions from various Ministerial and Leaders' Meetings to see if there were specific instructions to the ESC. For example, it referred to the 1998 Leaders' instruction to Ministers to give further focus to strengthen co-ordination in ECOTECH activities and intensify work in the priority areas. In 1999, it reported the Leaders' decision to direct Ministers to give special attention to improving effective and co-ordinated delivery of APEC's ECOTECH and capacity building programmes. In the 2000 APEC Summit in Brunei, the Report pointed out the Leaders' direction to the Ministers for a more focused and intensified ECOTECH action agenda. Finally, in Shanghai in 2001, the Report mentioned the Leaders' recognition of the importance of substantially enhancing the profile of ECOTECH and improving the co-ordination and management of ECOTECH activities in all fora. The reference to the Management Review of APEC in 2001 pointed out the need to streamline the APEC process and make it more focused and effective, in the light of an increasing number of APEC fora and meetings/ events. In all, the Report suggested that all of the above references were consistent with the ESC's terms of reference as originally drafted. The instructions from the Leaders and Ministers disclosed an ongoing concern with the *coordination and quality* (italic in the original) of APEC's ECOTECH work. The ESC's mandate was specifically designed to address these issues. The comments suggested a need to *implement* (italic in the original) the ESC's mandate, not change it.

4. *On changes in the APEC environment since the ESC's establishment in 1998?*

The New Zealand Report mentioned several changes in the environment surrounding the work of the ESC in the last four years of its existence: the success of the establishment of the Doha round of multilateral trading negotiations; the need for greater relationship between TILF and ECOTECH activities; the trend for greater openness and wider participation in APEC's work from outside organizations; and the importance of other cross-cutting issues, such as human capacity building, the New Economy, and gender integration. However, while the importance of ECOTECH seemed to increase with time, it appears that the direction for the improvement of ECOTECH activities within the APEC process itself was quite vague.[17]

5. *On the achievements of the ESC in relation to the expressed objectives, and the problems or obstacles faced?*

While the New Zealand Report listed several of the achievements of the ESC in a separate annex, some of which were alluded to in the early part of this chapter, it has recognized many difficulties and obstacles that stood in the way of fulfilling its functions, and one of these difficulties was the lack of authority or status on the part of the ESC. However, the Report kept coming back to the strict interpretation of the terms of reference of the ESC that its primary role is to assist the SOM in its management of the ECOTECH agenda, not to manage it on its own account. Accepting the fact that if the ESC has only a recommendatory (rather than decision-making) role, and the effective management of the ECOTECH agenda would be impeded, the Report tried to point out that if the ESC was to be given the status of a committee, its function would be limited to the management of Part II of the OAA only, whereas the ECOTECH activities related to Part I of the OAA would expressly fall under the jurisdiction of the CTI. This, in the opinion of the New Zealand Report, seems to be inferior to the current status and position of the ESC as a subcommittee attached to the SOM because the SOM would have the power and authority to enable the ESC to maintain a very broad oversight of all ECOTECH activities, including the ECOTECH aspects of projects being carried out by CTI sub-fora under Part 1 of the OAA. In short, the ESC does not have to change its mandate to consider issues such as the most effective institutional structure for advancing ECOTECH.

On the restrictions of the current mandate for the role of the ESC, the Report discussed several issues that might restrict the current role and functions of the ESC. For example, on the organization of the ECOTECH agenda, the Report recognized the multiplicity of fora, initiatives and priorities which make it difficult to have a measurable impact on public well-being. It even quoted a passage in the Second APIAN Policy Report that the vast lists of ideas, goals, and projects loosely grouped under the ECOTECH umbrella need to be reviewed and reduced to a more manageable set of coherent programmes. The Report suggested that it might be possible to establish a shorter list of priorities for APEC funding, and to direct scarce resources to those issues.

6. *On strengthening outreach and engagement with other organizations*

The Report referred to the endorsement of Ministers and Senior Officials to the APEC Secretariat's communications strategy to guide future communication and outreach efforts. It also referred to the Ministerial Statement made in Shanghai in 2001 where it recognized the need for APEC to interact with bilateral, regional, and international organizations and financial institutions with a view to fostering co-operation, broadening support, and leveraging financial resources to boost ECOTECH activities. There is no conflict in this line of activities with the original terms of reference, as Paragraph 5 states that the ESC will "encourage active participation of the private sector in the activities of economic and technical co-operation".

The New Zealand Report made a brief reference to the APEC project cycle, that is, how APEC projects are being submitted, approved, managed, and evaluated. On this point, the ESC has no direct involvement with the project cycle, from early inception to final evaluation. Although it was the ESC which designed and suggested the use of the ECOTECH Weighting Matrix, a kind of tool that ranks the worthiness of a project on economic and technical co-operation aspects, the ESC has no part in the implementation and enforcement of this tool. Because of this lack of direct involvement in the cycle of ECOTECH projects, it was argued that it would be difficult for the ESC to provide leadership on ECOTECH. What makes this more complicated is that the Japanese had already provided a large sum of research funds to APEC for use in the TILF areas which were overseen by the CTI. ECOTECH projects are not eligible to use this fund.[18]

The intra-APEC relationship between the ESC and other APEC fora was also discussed in this section. It has been observed that, since the inception of APEC, APEC Working Groups have operated relatively independently from policy oversight of the SOM, the Ministerial Meeting and the Leaders' Meeting. The only time that Lead Shepherds of Working Groups meet face to face with SOM Leaders is during the Joint Fora Meeting which usually takes place after SOM I. Even on this occasion, some Lead Shepherds may decide not to join. The sensitivity of the independence of the Working Groups is so pervasive that it is difficult even to raise the issue whether the ESC Chair should have the right to attend a Working Group meeting without asking for prior permission, let alone any indication of oversight or control by the ESC.

Apart from the Budget and Management Committee (BMC), which is very much an accounting unit for project approval in APEC, the three APEC fora, namely, the CTI, the ESC, and the Economic Committee, are more or less of equal rank and stature, but the intra-APEC relationship between the three is almost non-existent. In fact, meetings of all three fora during the three SOMs take place on the same days and at the same times. Thus, it is not possible for the chair of each forum to attend the meetings of other fora (unless, of course, he or she asks someone else to chair the meeting). Although the Leaders had said in Shanghai that TILF and ECOTECH should be mutually reinforcing, there is yet no plan for this intra-APEC relationship among APEC fora to take place any time soon.

Finally, on the issue of the profile of the ESC as a subcommittee or a committee, there is a subtle difference between Version 1 and Version 2 of the New Zealand Report. It seems that Version 1 of the Report shows an inclination to support the status quo, that is, keeping the current status of the ESC as a subcommittee, whereas in Version 2, this support for the status quo is not as clear. Perhaps the Report has received strong comments from some members who are really in favour of changing the ESC to the ETC, or ECOTECH Committee. The resolution of the ESC meeting in Mexico City in February 2002 on this issue was that the ESC would continue to debate in its subsequent meetings until a consensus or a compromise is reached.

Comments on the Recommendations of the Report

After taking into account all the written comments from members, the New Zealand Report makes the following recommendations, with which I largely concur albeit with some qualifications.

On Defining ECOTECH

The New Zealand Report had several recommendations on defining ECOTECH. First, "ECOTECH" for the purposes of the ESC's work should be taken to mean all economic and technical co-operation work undertaken under the APEC umbrella, rather than only the work that flows from Part II of the Osaka Action Agenda, which is generally funded by the Operational Account. I agree that ECOTECH should include all activities that flow from both Part I and II of the OAA, and not just from Part II, as the dividing part may seem to suggest. However, to interpret ECOTECH in this way does not assume that the ESC must remain a special subcommittee attached to the SOM to be able to undertake this role to assist the SOM in carrying out its duties.

Secondly, consideration should be given to including emerging cross-cutting themes (such as human capacity building, the New Economy, and gender integration) as priority areas within the "Framework for Strengthening Economic Co-operation and Development". I agree that constant awareness and consideration on cross-cutting issues are desirable but must be weighed against the net benefits and costs of such efforts. For example, while the awareness and concern for gender integration in APEC should be supported in general, the practice of splitting everything along the gender line may be counter-productive as not every issue has critical gender implications. Emphases on too many cross-cutting issues could also be similarly costly. On this score, the ESC has made a smart move to choose only human capacity building as its only subject of focus for its first foray into the ECOTECH Individual Action Plans, as pointed out earlier.

Additionally, in order to seek a more focused and results-oriented ECOTECH programme, APEC should earmark resources for a shorter list of strategic priorities, drawing from the categories of ECOTECH activities set by the Leaders and Ministers (the four goals, the six themes, the four principles, the thirteen areas from the OAA Part II; the fifteen areas from OAA Part I; and the five key initiatives.) In my view, the shorter list of strategic priorities could be supported by the argument above. There are no iron-clad reasons that ECOTECH must always contain the six themes in the Manila Framework. Efficiency and practicality should be a better guide for setting the priority for policy action.

On Integrating ECOTECH

To integrate ECOTECH more fully, the report suggests that the ESC should examine options for furthering the mutual reinforcement of ECOTECH and TILF, for example, by removing the formal separation of activities by funding source (operational account, or TILF account), or by formal consultations between the ESC and CTI with a view to distilling a common set of capacity building/technical co-operation objectives. I concur that the idea of formal consultation between the ESC and the CTI, with a view to distilling a common set of capacity building/technical co-operation objectives, should include the same between the ESC and the EC as well.[19]

On Co-ordinating ECOTECH

The New Zealand Report also recommended that consideration should be given to whether the ESC should have direct oversight responsibilities in the process through which projects are conceived, developed and approved — for example, by endorsing or ranking Working Group project proposals (under OAA Part II) before submission to the Budget and Management Committee (BMC) (such endorsement could be by assessing it against the "Guidance on Strengthening the Management of APEC ECOTECH Activities" and/or the ECOTECH Weightings Matrix), or by having the ESC Chair attending the BMC. I strongly support the suggestion of the ESC to have direct oversight responsibilities in the process through which projects are conceived, developed, and approved. This should also extend beyond the realm of the APEC project cycle into the operations of the Working Groups as well. In addition, the ESC Chair should be invited to sit with the BMC as a full deliberating and decision-making member, and the same invitation should be extended to the CTI and Economic Committee Chairs as well.

The report also advised that consideration should be given to whether the ESC should work more closely with other APEC fora on ECOTECH issues — for example, by having Working Groups report directly to the ESC, having ESC members "adopt" a Working Group to follow, either by attending meetings and/or receiving the communications of that group, formal consultations between the ESC and CTI, or reviewing the reporting requirements of the fora, including ways to increase the level of feedback to the fora on how reporting is used, and reduce the compliance burden (for example, by rationalizing the reporting requirements and making better use of the information collected.) A response has been made to the point above regarding the new relationship between the ESC and the Working Groups. Care must be taken not to institute additional layers of administrative duties but to create more co-ordinated working relations.

Lastly, the Report recommends that the ECOTECH Sub-Committee should be renamed the ECOTECH Committee (ETC) with a mandate substantially the same as the current mandate of the ESC. I suggest that the SOM should continue to have its special relationship with regards to the ESC role and mandate, but the rationale behind the agreement to establish the ESC as a subcommittee is no longer valid in today's environment. The conversion of the ESC to the ETC is a major institutional change that will enhance the position and importance of ECOTECH in particular, and of APEC in general.

Summary, Conclusions, and Future Prospects for ECOTECH

In this chapter I have tried to recount the recent developments and successes of ECOTECH in carrying out its co-ordination, dissemination, and participation functions. It was pointed out that, in addition to the general survey of completed ECOTECH projects, the ESC (mainly through designated officers of the APEC Secretariat) also conducted the follow-up of such ECOTECH initiatives as the Agenda for Science and Technology Industry Co-operation, the Kuala Lumpur Action Programme on Skills Development, and the progress on the implementation of the APEC Food System. However, none of these activities can match the three most outstanding ECOTECH accomplishments: the updating of Part II of the OAA; the introduction of ECOTECH Action Plans (EAPs) on human resources development; and the launch of the first Human Capacity Building Strategy Report. This has enhanced the posture of ECOTECH in the APEC process so much that the new analogy for ECOTECH is the second wheel of the APEC bicycle, not the third pillar of the APEC structure.

In this chapter, I have also discussed the paper prepared by New Zealand on the role and mandate of the ESC in its present and future handling of ECOTECH in APEC. This is a well-prepared paper and I agree with some of the ideas and suggestions. After taking into account all the points debated concerning the present and future role and mandate of the ESC, I have developed the following suggestions or recommendations in the institutional aspects of ECOTECH and its operational agent.

- The ESC should be upgraded from a subcommittee to a committee, to be called the Economic and Technical Co-operation Committee, or ETC, with an organizational structure similar to the CTI, and report to both the SOM and the Ministerial Meeting.

- This ETC should be supported by a much stronger APEC Secretariat having the traditional "house-keeping" duties of meeting organization needs and record keeping, and new "analytical" duties of assessment and evaluation of ECOTECH projects and activities, either alone or in conjunction with outside experts or organizations.

- The new ETC should oversee the functioning of existing and new Working Groups. The purpose is not so much control, but better co-ordination of the outcomes of the activities of the Working Groups and the objectives of ECOTECH, and indeed APEC, as a whole.

- The engagement with organizations outside the formal APEC process should continue to be promoted and strengthened through this new ETC. This includes regular utilization, consultation, and liaison with such organizations as the Pacific Economic Co-operation Council (PECC), ABAC, APIAN, ASC, and other NGOs (non-governmental organizations) and international financial organizations such as the World Bank and the Asian Development Bank.

- The CTI and ETC should work more closely together, for example, on the approval of projects by the Budget and Management Committee. At this juncture, there is no need to be fastidious about the clear demarcation between what is ECOTECH in TILF under the jurisdiction of the CTI, or what is ECOTECH under the ETC. It is more important to share activities or interest in similar activities than to insist on exclusive territories or functions. For example, the CTI can continue to carry out its programmes on human capacity building under the WTO rules of trade liberalization, but the ETC should be informed of the initiatives, and invited to share the experience.

- The EAP, which is the creation of the ESC, should continue to be supported by the ETC. Pending the assessment and evaluation of the EAP on human capacity building in 2001 and 2002, improvements and adjustments should be made on the subjects and execution of the EAP — that is, they can continue to be in the areas of human capacity building or in other ECOTECH areas.

- Whereas the collective action element in the EAP that offers opportunities for members to work together on common goals (such as complete Internet access among members within 2010) remains an important undertaking under the present EPA, the ETC should encourage all members to engage in individual, unilateral undertakings to improve the ECOTECH elements within their own economies. This could set examples for others to emulate.

After intense activities on ECOTECH by the ESC in 2001, which brought about much success in its outcomes, as discussed above, the mood of the ESC has become a little sombre in 2002. The debate on the role and mandate of the ESC during SOM I and SOM II perhaps acted as a brake to the rapid movement or motion of the ESC in the previous two years. The cautious approach on the future of ECOTECH and the ESC may be necessary if APEC members are satisfied with the function of this regional grouping. However, too much caution could rekindle historical fear that the developed members of APEC are not really interested in ECOTECH because their main concerns are more on trade liberalization, and the debate and exchange of views within the ESC and SOM meetings simply serve to underscore the wish to play down the present and future role of ECOTECH and the ESC. It is regrettable if this is true.

Other observers have been more forthright on the future role and mandate of the ESC. Andrew Elek (2002), for example, went straight to the point and said that the ESC of the SOM needs to be given the unambiguous responsibility, combined with the necessary authority, to respond to objectives set by the APEC leaders. To achieve this, Elek suggests that the ESC needs to be redefined as a full committee of APEC, to be called an ECOTECH Committee or ETCC, with broad authority to shape the work of APEC on matters other than TILF. To him, the ETCC would facilitate the work of the Task Force set up to implement new APEC objectives, such as region-wide access to information and communications technology (ICT) in addition to co-ordinating the general ECOTECH activities of the Working Groups, such as HRD. Elek realizes the sensitivity and complexity of the relationship between the new ETCC and the existing structures of APEC fora, and has discussed several options on how to cope with these issues. However, Elek's vision has gone beyond this organizational issue into the more substantive ECOTECH activities in future (of which achieving complete Internet access among APEC members by the year 2010 is one). Once this new form of ECOTECH operational committee is accepted, APEC members can move forward to discuss the type of activities that this new APEC Committee could be engaged in in the future.[20]

As the deadline of the Bogor goals is nearing, concerns have been expressed in the APEC fora that if the momentum of trade and investment liberalization slackens the future promise of APEC could be jeopardized. It is not uncommon, therefore, to see some APEC members pressing for greater and faster commitments towards free trade and investment among APEC members. While all APEC members are proponents of freer trade and investment, the levels of economic development of all members are not the same. Therefore, it is difficult for them to observe exactly the same rules and same timetables for free trade and investment. This is why ECOTECH is of critical importance because it can help to accelerate the development of members; it can share development practices with other members; more developed members can help less developed members through technical or financial assistance; and so forth. APEC is a unique international organization or association based on voluntarism and unilateral liberalization. The success of APEC cannot be measured by how many trade agreements have been concluded and enforced, but on how committed members are in working together towards the Bogor goals, on the willingness to help one another, and on sincere wishes for greater participation from people or organizations outside the APEC official circle. These are within the realm of interest of ECOTECH in APEC, and as such, ECOTECH is truly the wheel that drives APEC now and will drive it in the future.

APPENDIX

TERMS OF REFERENCE OF THE SOM SUB-COMMITTEE FOR ECONOMIC AND TECHNICAL CO-OPERATION

A. Background
1. SOM has been mandated by the Leaders to co-ordinate the APEC Economic and Technical Co-operation (ECOTECH) agenda. In Vancouver, Ministers have committed to further strengthen economic and technical co-operation in APEC by fully implementing the *Framework for Strengthening Economic Co-operation and Development*, which was agreed in Manila. In this connection, Ministers endorsed the proposal by Senior Officials to establish a SOM Sub-Committee for Economic and Technical Co-operation.
2. The SOM Sub-Committee will assist the SOM in co-ordinating and managing APEC's ECOTECH agenda, as well as identifying value-added initiatives for co-operative action.

B. Objectives
1. The main objective of the SOM Sub-Committee is to advance more effective implementation of APEC's ECOTECH agenda by consulting with and integrating the efforts of various APEC fora through a results-oriented, outcomes-based approach which benefits

all member economies; providing a policy management tool for strengthening and streamlining APEC's work; and providing guidance on possible actions which could be undertaken to achieve APEC ECOTECH goals, namely:

- To attain sustainable growth and equitable development in the Asia-Pacific region;
- To reduce economic disparities among APEC economies;
- To improve the economic and social well-being of the people; and
- To deepen the spirit of community in the Asia-Pacific.

2. The pursuit of the ECOTECH goals through concrete projects will take into consideration members' diverse and complementary capabilities and guided by the principles of:

- Mutual respect and equality;
- Mutual benefit and assistance;
- Constructive and genuine partnership; and
- Consensus building.

3. The SOM Sub-Committee will serve as a forum to discuss, formulate as well as co-ordinate action-oriented integrated strategies in consultation with existing APEC groups and the business community, as necessary to implement the *APEC Framework for Strengthening Economic Co-operation and Development*, which has identified the following six priority themes:

- Develop human capital
- Develop stable, safe and efficient capital markets
- Strengthen economic infrastructure
- Harness technologies for the future
- Safeguard the quality of life through environmentally sound growth
- Develop and strengthen the dynamism of SMEs

C. Activities
1. The SOM Sub-Committee will:

- Report to the SOM on its proposed work programme and assist the SOM to effectively implement the *1996 Framework for Strengthening Economic Co-operation and Development*. In so doing, the SOM Sub-Committee shall ensure that all the elements of the Framework are developed.

- Review progress of APEC activities towards achieving APEC ECOTECH goals.
- Identify and recommend for Senior Officials' consideration specific issues and value-added initiatives to assist the achievement of ECOTECH goals, taking into account the economic situation, requirements, and capacities of all member economies.
- Examine and evaluate ECOTECH programmes and activities and recommend to Senior Officials means to achieve visible, targeted, and result-oriented deliverables to address member economies priorities.
- Assist the SOM to improve the management and co-ordination of ECOTECH activities among APEC fora, including APEC working groups and policy level committees, with a view to improving the identification and co-ordination of new cross-cutting issues.
- Evaluate proposals to include new priority areas within the *Framework for Strengthening Economic Co-operation and Development.*
- Encourage active participation of the private sector in the activities of economic and technical co-operation. Consider the recommendations of ABAC regarding the process of economic and technical co-operation in APEC.
- Undertake ECOTECH-related tasks as directed by the Senior Officials.

D. Organization and Operation
1. A Chairperson will be appointed who will be devoted to meeting the objectives of the SOM Sub-Committee.
2. A Vice-Chairperson(s) will be appointed to assist the Chair in managing the tasks and work programme of the SOM Sub-Committee.
3. The Chairperson and Vice-Chairperson(s) will serve for a term of two years.
4. Membership of the SOM Sub-Committee will be open to all economies.
5. The SOM Sub-Committee shall meet regularly.
6. The SOM Sub-Committee will report regularly to the SOM.
7. The operation and effectiveness of the SOM Sub-Committee will be reviewed at the end of a two-year term.

Notes

1. Such an analogy was made by Mr Wang Guangya, the 2001 Chair of the Senior Officials' Meeting (SOM) in his opening remarks at the Policy Dialogue Meeting on ECOTECH, organized jointly by the Foundation for Development Co-operation (FDC) and the Chinese National Committee for PECC, in Beijing, on 19 April 2001.
2. For example, it was discussed in both the second and third meetings of the Economic and Technical Co-operation Subcommittee (ESC) in 2001. See ECOTECH Report, 2001.
3. At present, the main body that handles or manages ECOTECH matters within APEC is the SOM Subcommittee on Economic and Technical Co-operation (ESC). The structure of this subcommittee may change with the new enhanced status.
4. See, for example, Medhi (2000, 2001a, and 2001b).
5. This information is obtained from the Website of the APEC Secretariat based in Singapore. See, http://www.apecsec.org.sg.
6. The Osaka Action Agenda is a policy document agreed upon by APEC Ministers at the Ministerial Meeting in Osaka in 1995. Part I of the OAA is about measures to promote trade and investment liberalization and facilitation; Part II is about economic and technical co-operation activities divided along the line of the existing APEC Working Groups (for example, on human resources development, tourism, telecommunications, energy, and so on).
7. In 2001, one Working Group, the Trade and Investment Database Working Group was disbanded. Two new Working Groups, the Agricultural Technology Co-operation Working Group (ATCWG) and the Small and Medium Enterprises Working Group (SMEWG) were set up from the Agricultural Technical Co-operation Experts' Group and the Policy Level Group on Small and Medium Enterprises, respectively. A new Group on Economic Infrastructure (GEI) was established in 2000 as a sub-forum under the ESC to take care of infrastructure issues.
8. One of the reasons for the successful co-operation of the ESC-Working Groups was the establishment of a new procedure whereby member economies were asked to volunteer to liaise closely with selected Working Groups to ensure that the updating was finished on time. There is always great sensitivity among Working Groups in the way each carries out its work. This procedure of ESC members "latching on" to the work of Working Groups could be construed as an interference, unless all Working Groups can be assured that the ESC does not wish to establish another layer of control over the work of the Working Groups. Trust must be established that the ESC is simply doing the assigned job of co-ordinating ECOTECH work within APEC, or among all APEC fora.
9. However, the main credit should be given to Mr. Kono Yohei, then Foreign Minister of Japan, who suggested the idea at the Ministerial Meeting, which was later agreed upon by all ministers.

10. For discussion on these debating points, see Medhi (2000).
11. Ambassador Elard Escala, Vice-Chair of the ESC, was asked to chair this Co-ordination Group.
12. However, by SOM I in Mexico City in February 2002, the HCBCG had completed its task. In the discussion at the ESC I, members decided that it was appropriate to submit the Strategy Report to the SOM for endorsement, but without the attachment on possible implementation activities as that was considered to go beyond the mandate of the Ministers. The attachment, however, would remain as an informal document for consideration by the relevant committee during the implementation phase of the strategy.
13. APIAN, "Learning from Experience", the First APIAN Policy Report, November 2000.
14. The main reason I asked New Zealand to volunteer to do this was that New Zealand had just undertaken the ECOTECH Clearing House project where all information relating to ECOTECH projects in APEC were electronically archived for easy use and reference. Among APEC members, it probably had the greatest and most recent experience in ECOTECH matters. I also appreciated the position of New Zealand that, despite its early reservation (one could even say objection) to the ECOTECH Action Plan (EAP) idea, it became one of the first members to submit their EAPs.
15. It seems that New Zealand interpreted a somewhat restrained role for the ESC in the context of the overall function of APEC organizations. If this interpretation is correct, it could explain why New Zealand had a somewhat reserved position regarding ESC support for the launch of the EAPs in 2001.
16. I have mentioned in my other paper (Medhi 2000) that some developed member-economies objected to the creation of this special APEC forum to co-ordinate the ECOTECH work, the reason being that such creation might dilute the importance of the TILF, which was the primary objective of APEC, and might turn APEC into a mutual aid-giving and aid-receiving organization, while some developing member-economies had insisted that this special forum was needed to co-ordinate ECOTECH activities, as an important objective of APEC was economic and technical co-operation, not aid-related developmental activities. Therefore, a committee equivalent in structure to the CTI was necessary. In the end, a compromise was reached whereby this forum was set up, not as a committee like the CTI or the Economic Committee (EC), but as a sub-committee attached to the SOM.
17. On the future direction of ECOTECH activities, I have argued that those involved in the APEC process at all levels were not sure of what that direction should be. A more urgent issue was not the way to move forward but the way to move out of the problems facing ECOTECH work. See Medhi (2000).
18. In 2000, the Japanese Government was considering changing this rule so that the so-called TILF Fund could also be used for ECOTECH projects. However, the lack of final agreement between the two administrative

organizations representing Japan (the Ministry of Foreign Affairs and the Ministry of International Trade and Industries [MITI]) prevented such change of rule to take place.

19. Although I have heard some suggestions concerning the merging of the EC with the ESC once the ESC has taken the form of the ETC.

20. This was exactly what the 2002 APEC Summit host, Mexico, and the 2003 APEC Summit host, Thailand, planned to do in their ECOTECH Workshop in Acapulco in August 2002.

References

APEC International Assessment Network (APIAN). "Learning from Experience". First Policy Report of APIAN, November 2000.

_____ . "APIAN Update: Shanghai, Los Cabos and Beyond". Second Policy Report of APIAN, October 2001.

Elek, Andrew. "Achieving APEC's ECOTECH Targets: A Progress Report and Proposals". Foundation for Development Co-operation (FDC), 2002.

Medhi Krongkaew. "Problems and Prospects of ECOTECH in APEC: A Way Out or A Way Forward?". Paper presented at the Annual Japan APEC Study Centre Consortium, organized by the Institute of Developing Economies, Chiba, 17 December 2000.

_____ . "ECOTECH IAP: A New Challenge for APEC?". Paper presented at the International Workshop on Promoting ECOTECH in APEC: Bridging the Digital Divide and Other Issues, organized by the Foundation for Development Co-operation (FDC) and the China National Committee for Pacific Economic Co-operation, in Beijing, 20 April 2001a.

_____ . "The Current State of Economic and Technical Co-operation in APEC: A New Beginning or an Old Revised Agenda?". Paper presented at the APEC Roundtable and APIAN Workshop on APEC at the Dawn of the 21st Century, organized by the Institute of Southeast Asian Studies, Singapore, 8–9 June 2001b.

New Zealand Study Team. "Position Paper on the Role and Mandate of the ESC, Version 2". New Zealand, 2002.

10

POTENTIAL IN SEARCH OF ACHIEVEMENT
APEC and Human Resource Development

Nigel Haworth

APEC's human resource development (HRD) activities are second only in importance to the trade and investment liberalization and facilitation (TILF) agenda. No other issue, apart from TILF, has drawn such universal and consistent commitment from member economies involved in the APEC process. The significance attached to HRD in APEC derives from two factors. First, few now challenge the view that in a progressively more integrated global economy, in which new technologies are increasingly the key to international competitiveness, the quality of human resources present in an economy or enterprise is the key to economic and commercial success. Improving HRD is now a *sine qua non* in national and enterprise planning. It follows that any efforts on this front in a regional body such as APEC will be supported, particularly where there is also advantage created for the TILF agenda. HRD for

TILF is now an important sub-set of the wider HRD agenda in the region.

Secondly, the consensus around HRD makes it an ideal rallying point for institutional identity within APEC. APEC needs more than the TILF agenda to provide long-term substance. This need has three dimensions. There is a natural desire to use the framework provided by APEC for activities beyond the TILF focus. Equally, however, for economies to be involved in APEC, but not wholly convinced by the TILF model, HRD provides an area for involvement which is universally recognized and legitimized. Finally, for some economies and notably Japan, HRD is a strategic issue, central to the needs of overseas subsidiaries operating in APEC member economies.

The Institutional Framework: A Preliminary Note[1]

To set the scene, some discussion of the APEC HRD Working Group (WG) is needed. APEC's early agenda for HRD, laid down in Beijing in 1995, was formulated for eight priority areas of work. These were:

- The provision of quality education for all;
- The development of regional labour market analyses;
- An increase in the supply and quality of managers, entrepreneurs, and training in the areas central to economic growth;
- A reduction in skill deficiencies and unemployment by designing appropriate training priority areas and outcomes;
- An improvement in the quality of curricula, teaching methods, and materials;
- An improvement in access to skill acquisition;
- The preparation of individuals and organizations for economic and technical change; and
- Support for the TILF agenda.

These priorities were much the same in 2002, with one exception. The seventh priority was, as a result of the active intervention of the Clinton-led U.S. government, subsequently amended to read as follows:

- (To enhance) the quality, productivity, efficiency, and equitable development of labour forces and work-places in member economies.

To respond to these priorities, the HRDWG originally created five subgroups (known as networks). These were:

- Business Management Network (BMN)
- Industry Technology Network (HURDIT)

- Economic Development Management Network (NEDM)
- Education Forum (EDFOR)
- Labour Market Information Network (LMI)

In 2000, after considerable discussion, the network structure was rationalized into three: EDNET (primarily education issues); the Labour and Social Protection Network (LSPN, primarily concerned with labour markets, labour management issues and social safety nets); and the Capacity Building Network (CBN, with a focus on management capacity building in public, private and business sectors). The new structure reflected post-1997 emphases in member economies and in Leaders' and Ministers' statements. As a result of restructuring, the WG reduced the frequency of annual meetings from two to one, resulting in savings for the economies, but also a significant reduction in the level of interaction in the WG.

The networks have developed an array of projects designed to respond to the established priorities. At the May 2002 meeting of the WG, some 42 projects were included in the annual work plan, with 18 new projects proposed. In 2000, it was calculated that the WG undertook about 50 per cent of all APEC HRD work. In other words, other APEC bodies, principally other WGs, carried out about 50 per cent of HRD activity in APEC. This opens up still unresolved issues about the HRD's co-ordinating role that the WG might (or should) have across APEC. Usually 120–150 people attend the annual WG meeting, the substantial majority of whom are officials from Education, Labour, and HRD ministries and departments.

Decision-making in the WG follows APEC practice. APEC functions on the basis of consensus decision-making. The model was adopted from ASEAN and was the only basis upon which the ASEAN economies would commit to APEC. The impact of a consensus-based model is that from the top down, decisions tend to be defined by the least common denominator. In APEC decision-making, decisions made at the Leaders' Meeting filter down to the Working Groups (where the majority of the APEC activities take place) through ministerial meetings and meetings of senior government officials. This process tends to be anodyne. Controversial issues are generally deflected or accommodated such that their controversial aspects are sidelined. Only in the case of the largest and most powerful economies is it possible to sustain controversial issues over time. Even then, as in the case of the United States and labour standards, consensus requires considerable diplomatic dexterity to preserve anything approaching a challenge to that consensus.

Often then, the effect of the decision-making process is to allow the uncontroversial to proceed, and challenges to fall away. An essential conservatism marks the creation of WG agendas, except in times of significant stress. The 1997 crisis generated that level of stress.

When the conservatism of the decision-making process is combined with the technical orientation of many economies in the HRDWG, it is not surprising that the work of the HRDWG usually takes on technicist and unitarist characteristics. It is technicist in that it is predominantly about upgrading HRD practices in technical terms. It generally eschews involvement in the politics of production and policy-making, focusing instead on the functional improvement of education, training, and production systems. Put another way, APEC is broadly comfortable with contemporary relations of production in market systems. Its aim is to improve the efficiency of those relations, not to challenge them in any substantive way. This is not surprising. The ethos of APEC is to avoid political controversy whenever possible, a quality with which government officials are most comfortable. APEC is also, through both TILF and ECOTECH, embedded in a worldview predicated on the superiority of market relations. Such consensus as APEC creates holds that view as a central tenet.

This also explains the unitarism of APEC's HRD approach.[2] The APEC worldview generally assumes one maximizing mode of economic advancement — regional and global integration. Participants in that process — institutions, social groups, and individuals — will rationally share that view. In the APEC process, HRD is configured in tune with that worldview. The key actors in that view are business and government — wealth creators, on one side, and wealth creation facilitators, on the other. Other sectors of society are assumed to depend materially upon the arrangements struck between the two key actors. It is logical for those other sectors to conform to the dominant worldview. Hence, APEC has established a vehicle for business-government discussion — the APEC Business Advisory Council (ABAC) which, apart from channelling the views of business into the APEC process (particularly at the annual Leaders' Meeting) also undertakes an analysis of the extent to which APEC is achieving its goals (that is, supporting or achieving that worldview). In this framework, it is unnecessary for other sectors of society to be represented, for two reasons. First, governments represent their sovereign peoples and do so in APEC. Secondly, the other sectors have nothing useful to add to a process that already protects their best interests.

This means that for much of its life, business participation has been promoted in WG activities. Indeed, a pressing concern of WG members has been the need to increase business participation. Equally, there has been little interest on the part of most economies in bringing other sectors of society into WG activities. This has been especially true for the international labour movement, which has developed a detailed strategy for involvement in APEC. There have been two regular exceptions to this — the United States and Canada.

Three Key Dynamics[3]

Three dynamics have supported the development of a powerful HRD agenda in APEC. The first is the tension between the TILF and ECOTECH agendas. This is a tension inherent in the development of the organization, but it also reflects the *realpolitik* of APEC membership. APEC initially found its purpose in what became known as its TILF agenda. The TILF agenda captured an Asia-Pacific commitment to a global move towards trade liberalization located in the Uruguay Round. Some economies were essentially single-issue members of APEC, believing that the only value-added, by participation in the APEC process, was in the trade area. The role played by government officials in trade-related departments and ministries in member economies was particularly important in establishing TILF's priority. Even today, the Committee on Trade and Investment (CTI) is *primus inter pares* in the APEC institutional structure, a status challenged only by the APEC Finance Ministers and their semi-autonomous activities.

For member economies emphasizing the TILF agenda, any subsequent APEC agendas were to be dependent upon and supportive of TILF. Inevitably, there would be other issues that would arise in the APEC process. For the TILF-orientated economies, the preference was, first, to minimize the frequency of such irruptions and, secondly, to subordinate them to TILF. This position on other issues was usually couched in terms of two arguments. First, the priority of TILF was simply asserted, particularly in relation to the Uruguay Round and its creation, the World Trade Organization (WTO). Secondly, the diversity of circumstances faced by APEC member economies was argued to be such that most other agendas would be unable to find sufficient common ground for effective action.

However, economies such as Japan and Canada were running a more traditional regional development agenda before APEC was created, and they sought to include their perspectives in the APEC process. A home for this agenda was found in the 1995 Osaka Action Agenda (OAA). Part II of the OAA commenced with the following statement:

> APEC economies will pursue economic and technical co-operation in order to attain sustainable growth and equitable development in the Asia-Pacific region, while reducing economic disparities among

APEC economies and improving economic and social well-being.
Such efforts will also facilitate the growth of trade and investment in
the region.

Note the relationship between the two sentences in the quotation. The
raison d'etre for ECOTECH was separate from the TILF agenda, although
supportive. Thus, Part II of the OAA defined APEC's economic and
technical co-operation activities and became a convenient framework in
which two competing views of co-operation were to be found. The one
saw any ECOTECH activity undertaken by APEC to be subordinate to
the TILF agenda. The other gave ECOTECH a high degree of autonomy
from TILF. APEC was able to resolve this difference by means of two
processes. The first is the capacity to work with ambiguities; the second
is the opportunity in a consensus-based organization to choose which
activities are supported, which are tolerated, and which are to be opposed.
Thus, economies wedded to the TILF agenda picked and chose which
ECOTECH activities they would participate in. Thus, for example,
previous New Zealand governments did not share the U.S. view on
labour issues, actively promoted within the WG. However, New Zealand
did not oppose the U.S. agenda but simply ignored it. Thus, New
Zealand did not send a representative to the Labour and Social Protection
Network of the HRD Working Group, chaired by the United States, and
did not become involved in the projects emerging from that network.

The second dynamic intersects with the first. The 1997 Asian
economic crisis was a shock to the APEC process. APEC's relevance to
the region was widely questioned and for good reason. In the immediate
circumstances of the crisis, the TILF agenda appeared to offer little
succour to the most affected economies. On the other hand, to the
extent that APEC could offer short-term support, the ECOTECH
dimension was the most relevant. Hence, APEC undertook significant
support work in areas such as defining HRD responses to the crisis. The
most prominent intervention was undertaken by the WG Task Force on
the HRD dimensions of the crisis. The Task Force produced case studies
of the most affected economies and an overview analysis, the latter
subsequently submitted to APEC Leaders in their 1998 meeting.[4] One
aspect of the work of the Task Force was the symposium on the crisis
held in Taipei in June 1998. Two aspects of that symposium were to
reverberate. The first was the breadth of discussions that developed. It
transcended the "safe" ground usually traversed in APEC meetings, in
particular raising fundamental questions about the applicability of the
trade liberalization process in a period of crisis. Secondly, the symposium
deliberately drew on the expertise of "non-APEC" groups and individuals,

anticipating the subsequent calls within APEC for such engagement. For many, the modest success of these interventions reinforced the view that a greater autonomy for ECOTECH within the APEC process was both possible and desirable. For others, the "stretching" of the APEC process explicit in the work of the Task Force raised concerns about the downgrading of the TILF agenda.

The third dynamic relates to the state of the international trade liberalization debate and the particular effects of regional trade agreements (RTAs) and the WTO Ministerial Meetings in Seattle and Doha. APEC has played an important role as a regional cheerleader for the WTO process. Much of the APEC trade effort has been devoted to supporting and extending the WTO agenda. This role has been complicated by the emergence of RTAs and the shifting fortunes of the WTO. RTAs are in vogue, generating a complex debate about their impacts and their relationship to the WTO agenda. Some suggest that RTAs are pragmatic steps in support of the WTO trade liberalization agenda. Others, noting the crisis in the WTO after the Seattle meeting and the modest progress made at Doha, imply that RTAs may become practical alternatives to a failing WTO approach.[5] ECOTECH plays an important role in regional integration in both perspectives. Those who see a future in the WTO agenda, and a role for APEC in supporting the WTO, see ECOTECH in two ways — as a back-up area of activity when the trade debate is in a lull, and in terms of capacity building for the trade effort. Those who believe that the WTO trade agenda will lose impetus see ECOTECH as a free-standing alternative framework in which an alternative mode of regional co-operation might be fashioned.

The impact of these three factors has been to create space in which the ECOTECH agenda can flourish, and HRD is the most powerful theme in that agenda. This can be seen in the outcomes of Brunei's and China's years of leadership in APEC.

Progress from Brunei and China: The Inexorable Rise of HRD and Human Capacity Building

Brunei's year of leadership generated new levels of debate about HRD in APEC and also heralded the emergence of human capacity building (HCB) as a concern. As is often the case in APEC, several processes came together. Brunei needed an issue or issues upon which it could build its years of leadership. Each lead economy wishes to make its mark on the APEC process and Brunei chose HRD as a major emphasis. This included a shift in terminology to HCB.[6] Simultaneously, APEC began an appraisal of its ECOTECH agenda, a process lodged in the ECOTECH Sub-

Committee of the Senior Officials' Meeting. This process took particular notice of the HRD dimensions of APEC's work. Meanwhile, the HRD Working Group restructured itself, in particular, creating a Capacity Building Network. The ECOTECH Sub-Committee established the Escala group to study HCB in APEC, with a focus on issues related to the New Economy (thus also making a link with the Economic Committee's interest in these issues). Finally, emerging from the Leaders' Meeting and the work of the Economic Committee, a focus on the "New Economy" was linked to HCB.

The "Brunei Vision" for HCB and the New Economy had three key dimensions: a measurable outcome, that is, universal access to the Internet across member economies by 2010; the centrality of HCB in reaching that goal; and the importance of wide stakeholder participation in the process. Thus, Brunei offered a vision with clear targets, an emphasis on the regional impacts of the New Economy and a capacity to provide focus for APEC's ECOTECH agenda.

China took this vision forward smartly in two directions. The first was in the priorities established for its year of leadership and agreed to by the Leaders in the Shanghai Leaders' Declaration and Accord. It is interesting to observe the ordering of issues presented in the Declaration. The first key issue is the promotion of sustainable growth, couched very much in terms of the impact of the 1997 crisis. Then comes sharing the benefits of globalization and the New Economy, in which HCB and ECOTECH are prominent. Only then does trade achieve centre stage, in the section on supporting the multilateral trading system. Finally, the Leaders talk of broadening APEC's goals, a process which also emphasizes ECOTECH and HCB as well as the trade agenda. Building on Brunei's vision, China firmly placed HRD/HCB in the vanguard of the APEC process.

The second was less visible, but important. This was the major effort invested in the WG by China in the lead-up to 2001. Not only did China put into the WG a highly-skilled team of officials, but also took over the role of Lead Shepherd of the WG, nominating a senior, experienced and competent official to that task. China provided widely praised leadership for the WG, and in the process ensured that it contributed fully to the achievement of China's vision for HRD and HCB in APEC. That vision emphasized the ECOTECH aspects of capacity building in line with the traditional development agenda noted above, rather than with the TILF-dominant view. This is not to say that trade was not important to China. Accession to the WTO ensured a central role for trade in 2001. However, China's interest in HRD is particular to the pressing problems it faces in restructuring a planned economy. Capacity building, particularly for management, is a paramount concern of the Chinese Government. Not unreasonably, China sought to take advantage of its leadership position in APEC to gain ground on its capacity building challenge.

The Beijing Initiative

China demonstrated its commitment to HRD/HCB by convening the Beijing High Level Meeting (HLM) on Human Capacity Building in May 2001. The HLM was notable for its size (over 500 participants), the level of private and business sector participation, and its emphasis on New Economy issues. Its purpose was to give focus to APEC's (and China's) approach to HCB. This focus was captured in the preparation of the Beijing Initiative during the HLM, and its subsequent generation of "concrete deliverables" launched at the Shanghai Leaders' Meeting. These include the related APEC HCB Promotion Programme and the APEC HCB Implementation Programme. These programmes envelop the "tripartite" relationship between government, business, and training in a very large project designed to deliver online training for IT professionals, virtual classrooms for Internet literacy, and a cyber forum for APEC HCB. Cisco Systems, Sun Microsystems, Oracle, McGraw-Hill, Tsinghua Tongfang Co. Ltd., and the China Petroleum and Chemical Corporation were the key private and business sector participants, alongside twelve of the APEC economies and a substantial network of training and education institutions. In May 2002, some 650 people were selected from 1,500 applicants to take part in the first training programme associated with this project.

The APEC HCB Promotion Programme is the largest HRD project ever attempted in APEC. In many ways, it constitutes a flagship project able to provide a focus for HRD activities in APEC.[7] Its involvement of big players in the private and business sectors is notable. This has been a desire of the APEC HRD process for many years and has required the commitment and energy of an economy like China to achieve. There is no doubt that many of the companies involved in the project are there because of the China factor and the doors that will, potentially, be opened (in terms of markets, access to top policy-makers and, often, for the recruitment of top officials into the private sector). Yet programme delivery extends well beyond China into other APEC economies, and the project's outcome will in all likelihood be a positive-sum outcome for companies and APEC.

A Pause for Review

Before attempting an assessment of the future options for HRD in APEC, we should review what we know so far. HRD concerns unite

APEC economies, possibly even to a greater extent than the TILF agenda. There is an institutional framework in place to deliver HRD (the WG) and in recent years impetus has been given to HRD activities in APEC by, first, the impact of the 1997 crisis; second, the emergence of an ECOTECH agenda with (more or less) autonomy from the TILF agenda; third, the efforts of Brunei and China in their years of leadership. These circumstances provide a platform upon which further HRD developments are possible. Thinking about that platform brings us to the present day and the threats and opportunities facing APEC's HRD agenda.

HCB/HRD in APEC: The Institutional Challenge

There are many challenges to the HCB/HRD agenda. The most significant challenges are:

- The problem of rhetoric versus action;
- The commitment of member economies' institutions;
- Institutional Shifts in the Working Group system;
- Output Integration;
- Buy-in by wider constituencies; and
- Issue definition.

The Problem of Rhetoric

There is an old adage in human resource management that the most important resources held by a company are its human resources. In periods of growth, this adage tends to reflect management practice. During a downturn, the adage loses traction and it is often human resources that are the first to be shed. This is true both for employees in general and for HR staff in particular. There is often a discontinuity between the rhetoric and the practice.

In many ways, the same discontinuity exists in APEC's HBC/HRD work. From the leaders down, the rhetoric of HCB/HRD is legion. Yet the ability of the area to generate practical commitment, measured especially in terms of resources, is often at odds with the rhetoric. Indeed, close observation of the key APEC institution in this area, the HRD Working Group, suggests that many economies are in a holding pattern when it comes to resource commitment to regional initiatives. Some key economies have expressly stated that they are now holding a watching brief on the area, rather than supporting actively new initiatives. A reasonable conclusion is that the vision of a regional HCB/HRD strategy does not command *effective* universal support. This can be explained in a number of ways. Most importantly, the translation of the Leaders' vision into action at the level of competent government agencies is inconsistent. The usual (and often credible) reason given for this is resources, but it is also often an issue of political will in member governments. It is one thing for Leaders to have a view; it is another for cash-strapped agencies to carve out funds for projects and their related expenses, especially when political masters and mistresses are unconvinced about the returns to expenditure. The effect is to produce "minimalist" responses from the agencies, even in the face of initiatives such as those emerging from the Beijing Initiative.

The Commitment of Member Economies' Institutions

A related issue is the institutional fit of HCB and HRD with the institutions of member economies. Unlike areas such as transport or fishing, where most economies have discrete institutional responsibilities lodged in a single agency, HCB/HRD tends to be a divided responsibility. In the case of New Zealand, for example, HRD falls under at least three government departments (Education, Labour, and Economic Development) and a host of subordinate agencies. Effective co-ordination and commitment are often difficult to sustain in this fractured environment. To this must be added the possibility that many agencies, which are charged by member governments with participation in the HRD process, are either unable or unwilling to undertake the preparatory work that lays the foundation for effective participation in the WG or its projects. Government departments have many calls on their resources and time, and APEC may not be assured high priority.

Changing Nature of the Working Groups

APEC's Working Groups were originally established to provide a source of technical and specialist inputs into the APEC process. Their advice and recommendations were to provide government officials with high quality advice, to be accepted or rejected as the official process chose. To some extent, this is still the case. However, there is an observable decrease in the proportion of specialists attending Working Groups. Officials increasingly dominate Working Group activities, with two effects. The first is a decrease in the quality and amount of non-government, technical, and specialist debate in APEC. The second is a diminution of the intellectual life of APEC. There are many reasons for this change — budget constraints, especially during and after the 1997 crisis, choices made by governments and non-governmental organizations (NGOs) about funding priorities, and a loss of sense of purpose in the APEC process, for example. The net effect of this shift is to limit APEC's effectiveness.

Limited Integration

Much of APEC's work is piecemeal and fragmented. This is not to say that much of APEC's work is not good. Many projects maintain the highest standards. However, there are consistent problems associated with identifying and integrating different compatible APEC outputs. This also carries with it the potential for wasteful duplication of effort.

Limited Stakeholder "Buy-in"

The wider community, including business, does not "buy-in" to APEC. Again, there are many reasons for this, mostly reflecting APEC's inability to sustain stakeholder participation. Some Working Groups with particular technical interests — telecom, energy, for example — are more successful in terms of business buy-in than others. The reason for this is clear. The issues being addressed have direct significance to the business sector and its companies. In other areas — HRD, for example — relevance has been much harder to establish. It is interesting to note that, despite its work in various areas, ABAC appears to be unable to generate wide levels of active business interest in APEC.

In relation to the wider community, APEC has not generally solicited active participation. There have been exceptions, such as sustained work on gender. The example of organized labour makes the point. Some economies have included organized labour in their APEC activities on essentially two grounds — they offer an important, non-governmental perspective on issues and, quite independently, they are significant members of civil society and should be included in APEC deliberations as of right. Many economies have not accepted these arguments and have actively opposed labour representation in APEC councils.

Issue Definition

Institutional concerns are compounded by conceptual difficulties. HCB/HRD covers the gamut of issues from basic education to the outer margins of the New Economy discussion. The creation of a coherent strategic vision uniting twenty-one economies across that range of issues is an intimidating prospect. The tendency has been, therefore, to respond in a piecemeal way, depending on the interests of particular economies. It is this piecemeal approach to complexity that gave rise to the ESC debate on HCB/HRD and the Estrada initiative. There is also implicit in the Leaders' commentary from Brunei a view that coherence should be sought round the theme of new technology, the New Economy, and the digital divide. Of course, that simply raises another set of complexities as observed in the contending definitions of the New Economy that are currently circulating in APEC.

The New Economy focus at the heart of the HLM is contested terrain. It is common to observe that new technologies, especially in the field of communications, are inducing rapid shifts in the world economy. The precise nature and impact of these changes is far harder to determine. For APEC in particular, contending analyses suggest quite contradictory policy outcomes. The sceptical approach emphasizes the gradual impact of technological change and, therefore, an adaptive approach to economic change. More dramatic analyses imply that regions of the globe (not just economies, sectors, or companies) may be excluded from the wealth creation impacts of technological changes, perhaps on a permanent basis. In this view, the aim of the policy must be to promote a "leapfrogging" of development stages by disadvantaged economies in order that "catch up" is achieved before permanent disadvantage sets in.

These brief points indicate the complexity of issue definition in this area, and, for APEC, the consequent difficulty in defining a common approach across member economies.

Thinking about the Future

When thinking about the future of HRD in APEC, a distinction emerges between the HRD focus provided by the Leaders, Ministers, and the wider APEC process and the operation of the WG.

The Wider Process

In the wider process, HRD will continue to be an important issue, second only to trade. However, future HRD directions are difficult to predict in this wider process. Leaders' Meetings generally stick to generalities when addressing HRD. The Brunei and Chinese initiatives on the New Economy and capacity building were notable for their specificity. It is possible, even likely, that other lead economies will be equally focused in their view of HRD, but this is up to the serendipity of the APEC process. Ministers' meetings are more likely to influence the priorities of the WG and the other HRD work undertaken elsewhere in APEC. For example, the Washington Ministerial in 1999 placed labour market and social safety net issues firmly at the centre of WG responsibilities, and was a key factor in the creation of the LSPN and its work programme within the WG. The WG studies Leaders' and Ministers' directives in its annual work plan assessment and takes care to reflect in that plan any shifts in direction indicated by the two groups.

A number of APEC-wide issues are currently on the table and may have long-term significance for APEC's HRD work. These include:

- *The future development of the ECOTECH agenda and the related issue of ECOTECH Action Plans (EAPs).* This is a thorny issue at present. EAPs were proposed as the ECOTECH equivalent of the TILF Individual Action Plans (IAPs). Proposed by the ECOTECH Sub-Committee (ESC), they were endorsed in the Shanghai Leaders' Meeting and by May 2002 seventeen APEC economies had submitted them. They were intended to be a voluntary method for benchmarking best practice in the ECOTECH area across member economies, whilst giving greater institutional status to ECOTECH within APEC. HRD is, naturally, a central theme of the EAP process. In recent discussions in the WG on the issue of EAPs (24th APEC HRD Working Group Meeting, Hanoi, May 2002) it became clear that there is widespread disillusionment with the notion of EAPs. The most positive comment was that they were a new phenomenon and should be given time to mature; the most negative comments were that they were useless and should be abandoned forthwith. It may be possible to improve EAPs in order to overcome this generally negative view. To do so, EAPs must become relevant to the work of the WG. If, for example, EAPs were couched in such a way as to address the priorities and workplan issues that drive the work of the WG, perhaps by focusing on best practice examples and similar experiences, they might take on a more immediate meaning for WG members.

  The adverse commentary on EAPs reflects a broader concern about ECOTECH, at least in the WG. The WG has its own logic and institutions that respond more readily to Leaders and Ministers than to the notion of ECOTECH. The idea that the WG interacts or reflects a wider ECOTECH agenda is not widely understood or shared in the WG. In fact, broad knowledge of APEC is less widespread in the WG than one might expect. Most officials in the WG attend in terms of their (narrow) technical concerns, rather than in terms of the broader APEC process. The "higher mathematics" of APEC escapes most WG participants, generally much to their relief. In other words, effective, useful outcomes from the WG are far more significant for many participants than the regional integration agenda. As a result, impositions on the WG from the APEC process that obstruct or weaken those outcomes will deter officials from participating in the WG.

- *Human capacity building and the new economy.* Under Brunei's and China's tutelage, HRD has been transmogrified into HCB with a strong emphasis on the New Economy (in turn, reflecting Leaders' commitments and the work of the Economic Committee). Thus, for example, we see the Escala project on HCB and the New Economy (under the auspices of the ESC), completed in 2002, the emergence of the HCBPP under Chinese leadership, and the inclusion of a strong HRD component in the recently produced e-APEC strategy. HRD now has three locations in the APEC process — in the WG, in other WGs and, now, in projects and activities managed at the APEC-wide level. Two striking issues emerge from this. The first is co-ordination. How will the APEC HRD process be managed to reduce duplication and effort, improve co-operation and sustain quality across these three locations? Secondly, there is the problem of implementation associated with high-level statements such as the Escala document and the e-APEC strategy. A substantial gap exists between the applied focus of projects in the WG and the high-level goals and outcomes defined in these statements. Attaching substance to these high-level statements will require work to be carried out to integrate the statements with the work plans of the WGs. One way to ensure that this integration takes place would be to involve key members of the WG in the development of similar high-level statements. Whilst attempted in the past, this has not been successful for two reasons: first, WG specialists have not been involved from the inception of projects and find difficulty in establishing a clear role for themselves; secondly, there is a resourcing issue — participation often requires substantial expenditures. APEC economies must accept that the implementation of high-level statements sooner or later translates into expenditure at the level of the WGs.

- *Relations with Non-APEC Institutions.* This has two dimensions: co-operation between institutions, and the involvement of non-APEC institutions in the APEC process in general, and the WG in particular. A variety of international and regional agencies work in HRD in the APEC region. There is much potential for both unnecessary duplication and effective co-operation across these institutions. Despite much rhetoric to the contrary (particularly after 1997), many collaborative opportunities remain unexplored. Action is needed to break through the institutional and attitudinal barriers that prevent such co-operation.

    One possible approach would be, with the support of Leaders and/or Ministers, to conduct an exchange on HRD and capacity building priorities between APEC, ASEAN, the Asian Development Bank (ADB), the PECC, the International Labour Organization (ILO), the International Monetary Fund (IMF) and the World Trade

Organization (WTO), from which collaborative work could be developed and in which duplication might be identified. If found to be useful, the exchange could be made a regular feature of regional dialogue. Probably the easiest approach to this would be a small informal workshop, involving the leadership of the WG, the APEC Secretariat, and perhaps two representatives of key sister multilateral organizations. The intention would be to explore overlaps, duplication, and possible areas of collaboration. Information exchanges might be established, perhaps on a clearing-house basis, using electronic means. Subsequently, a pilot collaboration might be launched. Such an event, which only requires some leadership and energy to organize, might well repay its cost multifold.

The Working Group

The WG is among the most active of APEC institutions. It generates many useful projects, most of which are completed on time with reasonable-to-good quality outputs. It is, on the whole, well managed and led and has usually enjoyed strong leadership. Officials meet regularly. It has a strong collective memory. It has also developed a strong tradition of auto-criticism, in part derived from the active participation of non-officials.

The future effectiveness of the WG depends on a number of factors, including:

•   *Leadership.* The Lead Shepherd must continue to provide strong leadership. In an area such as HRD, leadership that provides clear focus and direction is essential. In recent years, the leadership of the WG has been transformed into a team-based management operation in which the Lead Shepherd manages the WG in conjunction with the three network co-ordinators. This has been a positive innovation, although it has had significant implications in terms of time and resources. The compliance costs of managing WGs are growing as, for example, demand from the Senior Officials' Meeting for returns grows. Team-based management shares these costs with the WG management team, increasing the workload of all concerned. Team-based management has also coincided with an era of network co-ordinator activism, stimulated by the restructuring of the WG networks in 2000. Network co-ordinators have pushed hard to reduce the operational side of WG activities, and increase the discussion of substance (see below).

- *Resources.* Economies must consider the resources that they are willing to make available to the WG. In particular, attendance in the WG is not a sufficient condition for effective WG outputs. The substantial work of the WG is done in projects and it is here that economies must place their efforts. The key to this is the identification of issues and projects that will add value to an economy's HRD activities.

- *Building on success.* The WG has a sound platform of success in terms of quality project development and completion and a respected contribution to the wider APEC process. Quality project development has been driven by effective leadership at WG and network levels, and the presence in the WG of great expertise in project assessment and monitoring. The WG has increasingly emphasized the importance of quality project design, an issue taken very seriously during the network assessment of projects. The prioritization of projects for funding by the WG also markedly reflects project quality and relevance.

- *Flexibility in the workplan.* The WG's workplan is currently less a strategic plan for the WG and more a simple reporting mechanism. Greater involvement by more economies in the preparation of the workplan, and a deeper sense of ownership of the workplan by economies might generate a more dynamic, strategic approach to the WG's work. Increased involvement and ownership would, arguably, contribute to improved prioritization of issues and project development, improved project design, and an improved quality of participation in projects.

- *The victory of substance over procedure.* This is perhaps the most pressing issue facing the WG at present. The WG embodies vast experience in the development, application, and evaluation of HRD policies in the region. It is also able to call on an impressive depth of expertise from non-officials in the WG process. Currently, however, much of the annual WG meeting is given over to operational issues, rather than discussions of substance. The network co-ordinators are currently canvassing a re-ordering of the WG process, whereby less time is spent on administrative matters and more on substantive discussions in the networks and in the WG as a whole. This proposal has been well received and is likely to be set in place in the 2003 meeting of the WG. One result of more substance is likely to be increased involvement by the private and business sectors and HRD experts currently not associated with the WG.

One feature of the substance versus procedure question is the debate about the future role of the APEC Secretariat. An option for consideration is the extension of the role of the Secretariat to take on much wider administrative responsibilities in relation to the WG structure. If the Secretariat were to take on a larger role, the work of the HRD WG, particularly in its annual meeting, could be more focused on issues of substance. A new administrative configuration would require additional resources in the Secretariat and the development of a new relationship between the Secretariat and the WG leadership.

- *Involvement of civil society, including business and private sectors.* The WG has a long tradition of such involvement but it has been reduced in recent years. The reasons for this reduction are complex, but primarily relate to the shift in the content of WG meetings from substance to procedure and the replacement of non-official participants by officials. There is a consensus in the WG that this tendency must be reversed and that greater levels of civil society participation are needed. The network co-ordinators plans for increased substance in the annual meetings of the WG are predicated on the active participation of more representatives of civil society.

- *Effective articulation with the wider APEC process.* This issue has been mentioned above. The development of HRD activities beyond the WG requires the WG and the wider APEC process jointly to consider carefully the issues of duplication and co-ordination. Quality concerns may also be important.

- *Articulation with non-APEC institutions.* Again, this has been covered in some detail above. The WG membership offers access to many HRD networks that extend far beyond the WG and APEC. It is ideally placed to take part in the types of inter-organizational dialogue that is suggested above.

Conclusion: A Vision

The trans-Pacific nature of APEC offers significant opportunities for regional leadership. This is already the case in many areas of APEC's work. This advantage could be taken further. By developing its technical foundation in analysis and policy formation, APEC could become the dominant regional institution for the intergovernmental (and wider) exchange of best practice and experience in both TILF and ECOTECH areas. This is particularly true for HRD. If the three proposed developments — an emphasis on substance, increased participation of civil society, and articulation with non-APEC institutions — are successful, there is an opportunity for the WG to make itself the paramount forum for HRD in the Asia-Pacific region. It could become an event to which government officials, international institutions, companies, and scholars feel obliged to come, because of the substance and networks involved in its activities. No such forum currently exists, yet the importance of HRD in regional development calls for such an initiative. This is at the heart of the network co-ordinators' current thrust for substance and participation in the work of the WG. This is the supreme challenge facing the WG in the coming years.

Notes

1. This section is taken in part from N. Haworth, "Human Resource Development and Regional Integration in the Post 1997 Asia-Pacific Region: Social Protection, Production Volatility and the Voice of International Labour" (Paper presented to the CAPSTRANS Conference and Symposium on "Social Transformations in the Asia Pacific", Universities of Wollongong and Newcastle, 1–6 December 2000.

2. "Unitarism" is a term introduced by Alan Fox in his classic delineation of approaches to industrial relations.

3. What follows is drawn in part from an unpublished paper, "Human Capacity Building in APEC: Preliminary Comments on the Beijing High Level Meeting", presented to the ASC Conference, Tianjin, May 2001.

4. "The HRD Dimension of the Asian Financial Crisis: Towards the Definition of an APEC Response", Keynote speech at the APEC HRD Working Group Symposium on the HRD Impacts of the Asian Financial Crisis, Taipei, June 1998, and presented to APEC Leaders, Kuala Lumpur, November 1998 as the APEC position paper. Singapore: APEC Secretariat, 1998.

5. Recent (mid-2002) U.S. decisions on steel and agriculture subsidies will do little to allay that suspicion.

6. HRD is, for some, identified with traditional "development aid" agendas; HCB captures two things: the approach to economic and technical co-operation adopted in APEC and an approach to capacity building more in tune with the idea of the "New Economy".

7. The idea of a flagship HRD project was originally launched during the Beijing meeting.

SECTION V

NON-GOVERNMENTAL PARTICIPATION IN APEC

11

BUSINESS INVOLVEMENT IN APEC

Michael C. Mullen

APEC and the Business Community: Involvement and Expectations

One characteristic makes APEC unique in the long history of government-to-government international organizations: it has allowed the private sector to play a more direct and influential role in its deliberations than any similar organization. The business community's involvement in APEC has been the impetus for some of the organization's most significant accomplishments. The private sector's high expectations are a healthy impetus to APEC action: when business invests time and resources in an issue, it expects concrete results in the relatively near term. These expectations can be disappointed when the APEC process, based on forming a consensus that even one member can disrupt, produces inadequate or no results, and takes too long to do so.

The opportunities and modalities of business involvement in APEC are as broad and varied as the APEC structure itself. One of APEC's genuine strengths has been the window it provides for private sector initiative and entrepreneurship, and the commitment of resources, interest,

and energy from the business community has helped APEC achieve very
practical goals, such as the online training being provided by the private
sector through the APEC human capacity building promotion plan.
Through APEC, business has been able to co-operate with governments
to effect change in policies in the direction of more liberalized trade and
greater business facilitation — in other words, change that has a positive
impact on economic growth and raising living standards in the region. It
is against this benchmark of concrete changes in government regulatory
and other policies that business judges the results of its involvement in
APEC.

The breadth and scope of formal and informal vehicles for business
involvement in APEC is striking. The APEC Business Advisory Council
(ABAC) was created by the Leaders as the official voice of the private
sector and meets directly with the Leaders, providing an annual report
with specific recommendations. Numerous other levels of the APEC
hierarchy include interactions with the private sector that range from
ongoing, substantial participation in the group's activities to one-day
conferences associated with major meetings. Virtually every Working
Group and other APEC subgroups officially welcome the participation
of business, and private sector representatives are often included in
official delegations to a range of APEC meetings. This chapter will
examine the processes and results that have evolved from this varied
landscape of activities.

The APEC Business Advisory Council

The major vehicle for private sector input to APEC is the APEC
Business Advisory Council. The ABAC includes three senior business
representatives from each economy appointed by their respective Leaders.
In addition to the meeting the Leaders have with each other, the ABAC
is the only group they meet with each year. Owing to the ABAC's role
as the official voice of the business community within APEC, a detailed
analysis of how this organization has developed and the challenges it is
facing is warranted.

ABAC's Mandate

Leaders declared in Osaka in 1995 that:

> Recognizing that business is the source of vitality for the Asia-Pacific
> and the driving force for regional economic development, we will
> appoint the members of the APEC Business Advisory Council to
> provide insights and counsel for our APEC activities.

ABAC's mandate is

*   To provide APEC Leaders with advice on the implementation of APEC's agenda and other specific business sector priorities.
*   To respond when various APEC fora request information about business-related issues, or the business perspective on specific areas of co-operation.

Since its creation in 1995, ABAC has forwarded six Reports to the Leaders, with recommendations on a full range of issues relevant to the achievement of APEC's goals of free trade and investment liberalization by 2010/2020. The ABAC has often supplemented these Reports with specific letters on individual issues to Ministers, particularly in advance of Ministerial Meetings. ABAC usually meets four times a year, in January/February, May, August, and coincident with the annual APEC Leaders' Meeting.

APEC's Response to ABAC

Over time, a certain frustration has been expressed over the slow pace of progress in implementing ABAC's recommendations. Implementation never happens or, at best, lags significantly. Feedback to ABAC on recommendations from the official side of APEC is minimal, and the business community and ABAC have concluded that Leaders and their representatives in official APEC circles do not always consider their input seriously.

The reality may not be as grim as this suggests. In some cases, ABAC and official APEC have complemented each other's efforts. For example, ABAC and APEC united to push strongly for the launch of a new WTO (World Trade Organization) Round. ABAC's support for efforts to develop an air services agreement reinforced governments' negotiation efforts, resulting in the signing of the first multilateral agreement in 2001. Efforts to encourage the public and private sectors to collaborate behind borders on the E-Commerce Readiness Initiative were advanced within ABAC, through relevant APEC Working Groups, and at senior government levels, resulting in almost all APEC economies completing assessments. The APEC Business Travel Card and the e-IAP initiative to put APEC's Individual Action Plans on the Internet are two more examples of APEC implementing ABAC recommendations.

Other initiatives and recommendations advanced by ABAC have not fared so well. Implementation of the APEC Food System, an attempt to resolve fundamentally important food security and economic development issues, has made little progress since its endorsement in

Auckland by the Leaders in 1999, a fact reflected both in APEC's self-assessment in 2001 and the resultant call in the 2001 Leaders' statement for accelerated implementation. Repeated ABAC recommendations on the adoption of international financial and insurance standards have received little attention in most APEC economies.

ABAC's Attempts to Improve its Approach

To its credit, in 2001 ABAC began to confront its own frustration and look at how it could improve its interaction with the official APEC process. While not wanting to lose its direct link to the Leaders, as called for in its mandate, ABAC realized that Ministers, Senior Officials, and APEC Working Groups play key roles in implementing APEC's agenda and Leaders' instructions over the course of the year.

With strong support from the 2002 Mexican Chair, ABAC looked first at structural problems. Traditionally, the ABAC Report to Leaders would be published about a month before the annual Leaders' Meeting. By this point in the APEC work cycle, priorities and consensus on most policy issues would already be close to final, with only a few outstanding points directed to Trade and Foreign Ministers and, subsequently, the Leaders for final resolution. However, ABAC recommendations arrived too late to have an input for 2002. The following year, under a new APEC chairmanship, priorities and emphases often shifted and thus, the ABAC recommendations made the previous year did not command the attention merited in planning the new APEC work programme.

Realizing that its work schedule was not well synchronized with official APEC, ABAC held its first organizational meeting for 2002 in Shanghai in October 2001 so that it could begin substantive discussions at its February 2002 meeting. Its goal was to provide the major part of its recommendations to APEC Trade Ministers before their May meeting in Puerto Valarta, thereby giving Ministers a greater opportunity to take these recommendations into account in implementing policy initiatives.

Furthermore, ABAC's intention was to devote more attention to the implementation of earlier ABAC recommendations. Using past ABAC reports and the matrices of APEC actions on past ABAC recommendations created by the APEC Secretariat, the ABAC Action Plan Monitoring Committee (APMC) would prepare an evaluation of APEC implementation. The evaluation would be vetted by the APEC Secretariat to ensure that all APEC implementation actions were included. APEC fora responsible for the implementation of ABAC recommendations would also be asked to provide their implementation plans.

However, ABAC needs to go beyond establishing this kind of feedback process. The Council should focus on providing more advice on how to implement its recommendations and the concrete steps that are required by governments to turn their policy ideas into reality. Beyond being advised on what to do, the Leaders need the business community's expertise on how to build a blueprint to achieve desired goals. The ABAC represents a wealth of expertise on practical approaches to achieving economic objectives and could greatly enhance its contribution to the APEC process by focusing this talent on specific plans to implement its recommendations.

By making the above structural changes, ABAC hoped to obtain some feedback on its recommendations from the Leaders at Los Cabos, and thereby begin a discussion on the next steps for the Dialogue. Putting a focus on implementation should also help the ABAC to prioritize the relatively long lists of recommendations being provided each year.

How APEC Can Improve Its Response

Traditionally, the ABAC Chair has briefed the Senior Officials Meeting (SOM) on ABAC's work programme at the end of each meeting. The matrix of APEC actions based on ABAC recommendations has been circulated to Senior Officials for their information, but the follow-up process seems to end with the distribution of this list. If APEC is serious about considering ABAC recommendations and making APEC responsive to the business community and its concerns, then Senior Officials and others on the official APEC side have a responsibility to examine their procedures and practices as they relate to ABAC and improve them.

Senior Officials could begin by taking the matrix developed by the APEC Secretariat and instructing the relevant fora to report back on actions taken where none seems to be under way. If no action has occurred, APEC groups should submit an implementation plan or explain why no action has occurred. The APEC Secretariat could co-ordinate this function. In accordance with a recommendation made by ABAC in its May 2002 "Pre-Report" to the APEC Trade Ministers, the Executive Director of the APEC Secretariat could make a report each May to the ABAC on what has been done to date, and what has been planned, based on the recommendations made in the previous year's report.

The full text of what ABAC would like to see APEC do in the form of a formalized feedback system was contained in ABAC's "Pre-Report" to Trade Ministers of May 2002.

> *APEC Formal Feedback to ABAC on its Recommendations*
> **Background:** ABAC has noted that little action has been taken on many of its past recommendations. ABAC often lacks feedback that its recommendations were ever evaluated by APEC.

Action required:
ABAC recommends that APEC create a formalized feedback system for informing ABAC what action or evaluation APEC undertakes on future ABAC recommendations. Specifically, ABAC recommends that the APEC Secretariat be tasked to collect this feedback from all APEC fora and formally present it to ABAC prior to the second (April/May) meeting of ABAC each year (covering recommendations ABAC made the previous year). The APEC Secretariat Executive Director should attend the second ABAC meeting of each year to discuss the results of the Secretariat's report directly with the ABAC.

Additionally, to begin this feedback process, ABAC would like to know, at its meeting in Hong Kong in August 2002, what action has been taken on the six ABAC recommendations from the past that are listed below. ABAC believes these recommendations were especially relevant and achievable, but feels it has not received sufficient feedback on what happened to them. ABAC invites the Executive Secretary of the APEC Secretariat to attend the Hong Kong meeting to discuss these past recommendations:

- **International Standards:** Status of participation of member economies in international standards and mutual recognition agreements. This has been a repeated ABAC recommendation.
- **APEC Food System:** Response to and implementation of the ABAC's 2000 and 2001 recommendations on the APEC Food System.
- **Government Online:** ABAC's 2000 recommendation of a clear timetable for putting government services online.
- **Participation in ROSCs and FSAPs:** ABAC's 2000 recommendation that APEC economies participate in and undertake completion of the IMF's and the World Bank's Report on Observance of Standards and Codes (ROSCs) and Financial Sector Assessment Programmes (FSAPs) process.
- **Development of Bond Market Coordinating Bodies:** ABAC's 2000 recommendation that APEC economies commit to establishing high-level domestic coordinating bodies to oversee the development of bond markets.
- **Strengthen IPR Enforcement:** ABAC has repeatedly made recommendations on this subject, the first time in its 1996 report. It supports the establishment of IPR Service Centres to accumulate information on IPR infringement measures taken by rights holders, share information between governments and business communities, promote public awareness, and strengthen enforcement through capacity building.

At the direction of Ministers, the Senior Officials should task the APEC Secretariat with this standing formal feedback function and the one-time review of the selected past recommendations above.

APEC responded well to this call from ABAC and agreed to send the Executive Director of the APEC Secretariat to the August 2002 ABAC meeting to report on the items listed above.

Better APEC-ABAC Interaction

While the ABAC Chair has been briefing the SOM, he has not really been integrated fully into the Senior Officials' Meetings. At the least, the ABAC Chair should brief on ABAC's work at the beginning of the SOM so that this is factored into later discussions during that meeting. The ABAC Chair should be welcome to participate in the full SOM and be included in discussions of those issues of interest to ABAC.

Senior Officials should also ensure that Ministers provide feedback to ABAC on recommendations. A good first step would be to provide a substantive response to any specific letters sent by ABAC to APEC Ministers.

The ABAC Dialogue with Leaders

The Leaders' annual Dialogue with ABAC remains the strongest illustration that, at the highest level in APEC, the views of the business community are welcome, relevant, and useful. Unfortunately, the Dialogue itself has become too staid, stilted, and scripted, with little or no give and take or spontaneity. The Leaders and the Chief Executive Officers (CEOs) who serve on the ABAC have tremendous demands on their time; thus, Senior Officials have a responsibility to make sure that the Dialogue provides them value added, not a staged performance. The consequence of not reforming the Dialogue will be greater difficulty both in securing the participation of the Leaders and convincing the CEOs of leading companies to serve on the ABAC.

The Dialogue must be revamped if it is to serve more than a symbolic purpose. One idea is to break the Leaders and ABAC members into 3–4 smaller discussion groups, with each group focusing on a different set of issues/recommendations. This permits more informal give-and-take, allowing a richer exchange of views with possible next steps identified.

One of APEC's unique features is the institutionalized role the business community provides through ABAC. Few other international bodies have such a relationship, and APEC should be rightly proud of this partnership. ABAC has shown its willingness to do its part to make the partnership more dynamic and the interactions more worthwhile. APEC officials have an equal responsibility to improve the relationship with ABAC, and restructuring the Leaders' Meeting with ABAC is the critical first step in this process.

ABAC's Domestic Relationships with Government and Business

ABAC's Independence from/Dependence on Government

The ABAC deals with a number of other challenges that impact on its ability to represent the business community effectively and interact with the official side of APEC. When the ABAC was established, the policy was that it would be self-funding. A system of dues for each delegation was developed based on the "APEC formula" used to determine APEC dues for governments. In fact, the ABAC dues for many delegations are paid by the governments, but a few members pay the dues themselves from their corporate funds, or large national business organizations pay the dues. This arrangement, together with the fact that the Leaders personally appoint the ABAC members and in some economies are personal friends of the ABAC members, raises a question about how independent the ABAC is from the government. This tension can actually be observed in ABAC deliberations — some members are clearly reluctant to endorse positions they know their governments do not support, even when an objective analysis might indicate that the issue makes good business sense.

How ABAC Represents the Larger Business Community

Questions have also been raised about how three executives can effectively represent the entire business community of a large and complex economy with a wide variety of geographic and sectoral interests. Several Asian economies have powerful national level business organizations which are involved in selecting their ABAC members, and these organizations are also effective at amalgamating business opinion on issues so that their ABAC members can be confident they are representing majority opinions. Other economies, such as the United States, must rely on more informal approaches to providing access to their ABAC members for the business community at large. The U.S. National Center for APEC, Secretariat to the U.S. ABAC members, facilitates this process by organizing events open to all where the ABAC members meet with other business executives to share views. However, in every economy, effective outreach to the larger business community is a challenge for the ABAC members, and an additional time demand on their already overburdened schedules. Each APEC economy has been careful to include a representative of small/ medium enterprises (SMEs) in its three-person delegation. These representatives have formed a committee which puts forth cogent recommendations regarding SME interests, but the demands of time/

resources in serving on the ABAC fall particularly hard on the small business representatives.

Business Participation in Ministerial Meetings and Working Groups

Apart from the ABAC, numerous formal and less formal avenues exist for business to participate in the APEC policy process.

The Finance Ministers

Below the level of the APEC Leaders and the ABAC, the business community is active at many levels in APEC and in many of the APEC Ministerial and working-level groups. At the level of the Ministers, the APEC Finance Ministers established in 1995 the APEC Financiers Group, which consists of representatives of financial institutions from each APEC economy. While this group has had some interesting dialogues with the Finance Ministers, it does not have a permanent secretariat, the attendees change from year to year, and some business members have complained that the group's recommendations do not seem to have been incorporated in a structured way in the Finance Ministers' discussions. As an *ad hoc* arrangement, the Financiers Group is not working well. The Finance Ministers need to give the Financiers Group a more institutionalized presence in their deliberations, with a permanent ability to maintain continuity from one year to the next, or they could turn to an established group of financial industry representatives to provide this function. The ABAC has a Financial Task Force made up of industry leaders and this group could fulfill this function.

The Energy Ministers

In 2000, the APEC Energy Ministers held a full-day public and private sector dialogue and a separate dialogue with the Energy Business Network (EBN), a grouping of energy-related private sector companies that was formed in 1999. The EBN has a permanent secretariat which consists of one staff member from the U.S. PECC office, and the group has continued to meet actively and offer recommendations to the Energy Ministers. APEC agreed with an EBN recommendation to send advisory teams organized by the Energy Business Network and the APEC Energy Working Group to visit an APEC economy at the request of the host government to review natural gas policy from the perspective of agreed APEC principles. To date, Thailand has hosted two such expert groups and Peru one, and in 2002 a very successful advisory team visit to the Philippines focused on that economy's new energy law. Composed of both public and private sector representatives, the energy advisory team visits have been viewed as very beneficial by both the team members and the host economies.

The SME Ministers

The APEC SME Ministers hold joint meetings with the SME Business Forum. They have also met with the Women Leaders' Network and an E-Commerce Workshop. While the rhetoric of APEC meetings includes countless references to the importance of small businesses in the region, it is hard to identify many discrete actions that have been implemented that specifically address small business issues. On the other hand, much of APEC's work to reduce trade barriers, lower tariffs, simplify customs procedures, facilitate business travel, and agree on equipment standards benefits large and small business alike.

APEC Working Groups

APEC's eleven working groups have been the venue for some of the business community's most productive engagement in the organization's work.

The Telecommunications Working Group has seen the most intensive engagement by the private sector, and was a major reason for the successful APEC Mutual Recognition Arrangement (MRA) on telecommunications equipment in 1998. This landmark agreement opened a market of several billion dollars annually by providing procedures and policies for conformity assessment of telecommunications and related equipment. The TEL Working Group has also produced much of APEC's best work on e-commerce, with the private sector being the driving force behind this effort.

The Transportation Working Group also has a very active business component and often includes private sector representatives in official delegations. It was successful in navigating the Air Services Initiative, which is the first plurilateral open skies agreement in the world, signed by a subset of APEC economies in 2001. The Air Services Agreement is a "pathfinder" initiative, with additional APEC economies joining as and when they are ready, and includes eight specific steps to take the region closer to an open market in air services.

Dialogues, Subgroups, and Expert Fora

APEC has shown some flexibility in adopting a structure to accommodate the specific interests of major industries. The one positive result of the Early Voluntary Sectoral Liberalization process was the creation of the

Automotive and Chemical Dialogues. These groups bring together public and private sector representatives for detailed discussions of issues germane to their industries, and the ability to focus on specifics is showing promising results. The Automotive Dialogue has promoted greater co-operation between small business suppliers and major car producers in the region. The Chemical Dialogue has just started in 2002, and is focusing initially on the harmonization of safety standards and labelling.

At the working level of APEC, there are many different ways in which business representatives can advise APEC officials. For example, business representatives have participated in meetings of the Intellectual Property Rights Experts Group since 1996, and the Fisheries Task Force of the Pacific Economic Co-operation Council (PECC) has worked with the Fisheries Working Group since 1991. Other working level APEC groups hold annual dialogues with the private sector — for example, the Infrastructure Workshop, the Sub-Committee on Customs Procedures, and the Trade Promotion Working Group. Many other groups have *ad hoc* contacts with business and others, such as the Informal Experts Group on the Mobility of Business People, include business representatives as members of their delegations.

APEC also receives recommendations and policy advice from a range of international business organizations, including the Pacific Basin Economic Council (PBEC), the Pacific Economic Co-ordination Council, the South Pacific Forum, and other bodies. The PECC and the South Pacific Forum have official observer status in APEC.

The Shanghai Model Port Project — How a Public/Private Collaboration in APEC Produced Real Change

China Customs, together with U.S. Customs and a coalition of private sector companies with significant business interests in the APEC economies, formed a public–private partnership whose goal was to make Shanghai a model of a modern customs entry point by the time of the 2001 APEC Leaders' Meeting in Shanghai. Planning began in 1998, and the Shanghai Model Port Project (SMPP) started officially in early 1999 when U.S. Customs, China Customs, and the National Center for APEC signed a Letter of Intent to conduct the project. American President Lines, Applied Materials, Compaq, DHL, FedEx, Ford, General Electric, General Motors, Hewlett-Packard, JBC International, Mattel, Microsoft, Oracle, Procter and Gamble, TNT, and UPS participated in this Project and provided invaluable support to achieve the Project's goals.

Customs modernization offered a unique opportunity as an area in which China could exercise leadership during its year in the APEC chair. China Customs declared that the overall objective of the Project was to shift the entire mode of operations from the current system of enforcement based on supervision, control, and inspection to a new approach based on forming relationships of trust with the companies who are their main clients. The project fulfilled a longstanding desire on the part of U.S. Customs and private sector companies to convincingly demonstrate the value of improved customs practices in the APEC region. The Project was designed to implement the twelve action items in the APEC Customs Collective Action Plan.

The programme had four main components:

*   Training on advanced customs procedures, provided by U.S. Customs and private corporations, both in China and the United States. The training component created a core cadre of officers with advanced training within Shanghai Customs who will provide models and share the benefits of their training throughout China Customs. The training was funded by the private sector members of the Project and through a grant from the U.S. Trade and Development Agency.
*   A major upgrade of Shanghai Customs information technology, funded entirely by China Customs. This effort required the majority of the resources to be devoted to the Project. In addition to upgrading the current system, the hardware/software provided as part of the SMPP allowed China Customs to implement seven new applications designed to automate various Customs processes and comply with China's WTO obligations.
*   An Intellectual Property Rights (IPR) Information Center, initially an online resource designed to enhance real time communications between China Customs and IPR holders and improve IPR enforcement capabilities.
*   A new express package facility at the Pudong Airport which became operational in July 2001. China Customs significantly overhauled their express package clearance procedures incident to building the new facility, and as a result shippers enjoy one of the world's most advanced operating environments in this facility.

Shanghai Customs showcased the achievements of the SMPP during the October 2001 APEC meetings. U.S. Ambassador to China Sandy Randt and China Customs Deputy Commissioner Zhao presided over a ceremony at the express package centre to highlight the potential of the China market for global commerce and the contribution that modernized, efficient customs operations can make to business. President George

Bush sent a congratulatory letter on this occasion, acknowledging the successful conclusion of the Shanghai Model Port Project.

Through similar projects, the private sector has contributed significantly to APEC's understanding of key issues. Nine companies formed the Asia Pacific e-Learning Alliance and in 2001 issued a detailed report with recommendations on how governments can foster an environment where the Internet is used more effectively to achieve educational goals. Public–private partnerships are currently being formed on projects to promote standards for healthcare institutions in APEC and to devise the right policy on biotechnology.

Business Conferences

As an added opportunity for top business leaders to participate in the APEC Leaders' Meeting, a CEO Summit is organized each year. Normally, several of the Leaders, together with other leading political, academic and business representatives, speak to this gathering, which has included between 300 and 1,000 top business executives. The CEO Summit is a highlight of the annual APEC calendar, but the meeting does not have an institutional presence in APEC, does not produce recommendations from the private sector for APEC governments, and does not maintain any kind of continuity from one year to the next.

On a smaller scale, one to two-day business conferences are often organized around APEC Ministerial and Working Group meetings, or separately, on topics of major interest, such as intellectual property, or trade promotion. Like the CEO Summit, these events are characterized by a series of speeches by public and private sector leaders, with limited time allocated for any discussion. They usually, therefore, do not provide a forum for genuine give and take between the business communities and the governments. Like the CEO Summit also, these are often interesting and informative events for the attendees, but they generally do not produce specific recommendations that are submitted to APEC governments, and little follow-up occurs on any concrete results that are generated.

Both the PECC and PBEC also organize specific events that are sometimes keyed to APEC proceedings or issues. The most recent example was the February 2002 PBEC-sponsored event on agricultural biotechnology that was immediately preceded by the first APEC High-Level Policy Dialogue on Agricultural Biotechnology in Mexico City; the PBEC invited the government representatives to hear the private sector views in its meeting and also gave a summary of the results of its meeting directly to the Policy Dialogue.

Some Key Questions

What Motivates Business to Engage in APEC?

While the WTO and other regional and bilateral free trade agreements tend to focus on trade and investment liberalization and lowering tariffs, in addition to these attractive features, APEC also offers the private sector business facilitation. APEC's business facilitation activities consist of a long list of interesting initiatives in which the business community sees real value: customs harmonization and simplification, agreements on standards and conformance, mobility of business persons, and many others. Businesses are strongly motivated to engage on these issues which are important to their operations. The Information Technology Agreement (ITA) is an example of a trade liberalization initiative that has provided strong motivation for business engagement. The Air Services Agreement is an example of a business facilitation activity where the private sector has played a critical role.

APEC's third major area, economic and technical co-operation, is also a motivation for business to engage in the process. The APEC Food System was conceived by the private sector and think-tanks, which concluded that only a broad-based and balanced approach to food, including sound rural development, could overcome the deep-seated obstacles to liberalization in the agricultural sector by the 2010/2020 Bogor target dates. As was demonstrated in the Shanghai Model Port Project, companies will contribute resources to training and other ECOTECH activities designed to build capacity in the governments of APEC developing members. The motivation for these contributions is usually two-fold: the increased capacity will help the company's business in the host country, and participation in the training activities will help build relationships that the company may find useful. For example, in 2001 New York Life hosted a training session for insurance regulators in the region, and Citigroup provided a seminar on advanced risk management issues.

How Important is Business Involvement in APEC?

The business community plays an important, but not necessarily crucial role in the APEC process. APEC is, in the final analysis, a government-to-government organization, and governments have demonstrated that they are not compelled to accept or act on the views of the private sector. There is no question that business involvement has been critical to some of APEC's biggest successes, such as the ITA and the Air Services Agreement. Furthermore, most observers recognize that business input on issues helps to produce the right policies. However, governments must answer to a larger constituency than the business community, and business views therefore do not always receive the support required to actually implement a programme or change government policy. The relatively small number of ABAC recommendations that have actually been implemented from six annual reports of more than thirty pages each is a good barometer of the private sector's success is getting its voice heard.

However, if the Bogor goals are to have any meaning, APEC will be facing a time compression in the next eight years. As time compresses, business inputs, resources, and creativity will be more necessary than in the 1995–2002 period, when APEC's deadlines seemed distant and governments could put off concrete action.

How Effective are APEC's Formal Structures for Accommodating Business Input?

Theoretically, APEC has a very clear structure for accommodating business input. The APEC Business Advisory Council was created by the Leaders at the Osaka meeting in 1995 as the official voice of the business community, with the dual missions of providing advice and recommendations directly to the Leaders and reviewing APEC's progress toward the Bogor goals, as reflected in the Individual Action Plans. However, as noted above, APEC's official response to the ABAC recommendations has been less than satisfactory. It has actually been APEC's informality that has provided the best opportunities for the private sector to move issues onto the agenda and achieve concrete results. The ability to include business in Working Group and other sub-fora meetings and interactions between the business community and their Senior Officials have been the source of several initiatives of real interest to the private sector.

Recommendations

The following recommendations arise from the analysis presented above:

* APEC needs to develop a structured and responsive process for evaluating recommendations from the business community, particularly the APEC Business Advisory Council, taking implementation actions on recommendations where warranted, and explaining the rationale for not taking action where justified. The responsibility for implementing this process resides with the Senior Officials, with support from the APEC Secretariat. The decision by the Senior Officials to send the Executive Director of the APEC

Secretariat to the August 2002 ABAC meeting to discuss the implementation of ABAC recommendations is a step in the right direction.

• The changes the ABAC made to its reporting schedule in 2002 are a positive step. APEC needs to respond by developing a process to include the ABAC in Ministerial and Senior Officials' Meetings in a meaningful way that goes beyond receiving a briefing from the ABAC Chair.

• The ABAC needs to refine and prioritize its recommendations and provide guides to APEC governments on how recommended actions can be implemented. The wealth of business expertise on the ABAC can contribute enormously to developing concrete plans and programmes to achieve APEC goals.

• As both the public and private sector participants have noted repeatedly, the ABAC meeting with the Leaders needs to be restructured to provide a more interactive give-and-take participation, and clear commitments to pursue follow-up actions.

• The Finance Ministers should incorporate engagement with the business community more directly into their policy-making process on an ongoing basis through a permanent relationship with an established, as opposed to *ad hoc*, private sector body. Other Ministerial Meetings would also benefit from a more structured interaction with the private sector with more continuity from meeting to meeting.

• APEC should focus on generating more public–private partnerships, such as the Shanghai Model Port Project, to achieve concrete results that can benefit both the business community and the government. The ABAC should be a wellspring of such projects.

• The annual CEO Summit could be improved by narrowing its focus to one or two main issues of key importance to both the host economy and the broader APEC community. Various public–private sector discussions could be held on these issues, and the result would be a more coherent set of policy views than is currently generated from an agenda that attempts to cover a large spectrum of interests.

12

CIVIL SOCIETY PARTICIPATION IN APEC

STEWART GOODINGS

Introduction

This chapter is designed to examine APEC's experience and current practices with civil society participation in various fora, to assess the situation in APEC compared with some other multilateral organizations and to offer some suggestions for strengthening such participation in the work of APEC.[1]

Background

The term "civil society" is not well known or accepted in APEC circles. Other terminologies are more commonly used, such as "non-member participation", "involvement of outside groups", "interaction with the community", and "the private sector". For the purposes of this chapter, civil society includes those organizations and individuals not employed directly by governments and who do not work in the business/commercial private sector. *Inter alia*, this would include academic and research organizations, advocacy groups such as women's and environmental associations, labour unions and other workers' bodies, religious and community groups, and international agencies not directly connected to any government, and so forth.

Two sectors — the academic and business sectors — are already well represented within APEC, through two main bodies, namely, the APEC Study Centres Consortium and the APEC Business Advisory Council (ABAC). ABAC, in particular, has a privileged place in APEC's structure as an Official Observer, by being able to meet annually with Leaders and to make reports and interact frequently with other senior levels of the organization, such as Ministerial Meetings and Senior Officials' Meetings (SOM). While the Study Centres do not enjoy a similar level of access, this collective of academics in each member economy holds an annual meeting within the framework of APEC's schedule of meetings and has credibility among member economies.

However, the set of organizations generally referred to as "civil society" has not enjoyed either the formal access to ABAC, nor anything like the overall credibility of the APEC Study Centres (ASC). Their participation in APEC activities has been governed by a document called the "Consolidated Guidelines on Non-Member Participation in APEC Working Group Activities." These guidelines are restrictive, time-consuming, and cumbersome to administer, and the overall message they convey has been that APEC is reluctant to allow outside organizations to get involved.

In the last two or three years, however, this has gradually started to change. In 2000, in Brunei, paragraph 29 of the Leaders' Declaration stated the following:

> The people of the region are APEC's most valuable asset. We continue to believe that APEC must be a process which is open and transparent and which draws on the talent and creativity of our people. We strongly encourage the continued engagement and outreach APEC has developed with our community and seek to develop partnerships with groups which share and add impetus to our goals.

During Brunei's year as host, an Ad Hoc Study Group of APEC officials was created, which reported in 2001, and whose main conclusions were the following:

> It is beneficial for APEC to benefit from the expertise and insights of non-governmental groups that have a contribution to make...

> SOM should send a message to Working Groups encouraging them to make efforts to identify and draw such groups into their work.

The Ministers at the meeting in Shanghai subsequently accepted this report, and in paragraph 72 of their Joint Statement gave the following direction:

> ... instructed relevant APEC fora to identify and invite the participation of outside groups that can make a contribution to their work.

In addition to these Leader and Ministerial statements, several other practical initiatives have shown the willingness of APEC to broaden its outreach interests. In May 2001, China and Brunei co-hosted in Beijing a High-Level Meeting on Human Capacity Building, which included as participants a number of senior representatives of the educational and private sectors. For several years, the Women Leaders' Network has held meetings of women leaders from the private and non-governmental sectors in conjunction with APEC Ministerial Meetings, while the last two HRD (Human Resource Development) Ministerial Meetings have incorporated special working sessions with labour leaders and representatives of international organizations. In May 2001, Mexico hosted a Dialogue on Globalization and Shared Prosperity in Merida, which brought together representatives from most member economies, including the academic, business, and other interested sectors to meet with government officials with the aim, as Leaders put it, of making sure that all sectors of society "participate in and benefit from the APEC process and globalization at large."

Current Situation

Despite this strong encouragement from the Leaders and Ministers, however, there is not much evidence that APEC fora have made efforts to reach out to organizations not already involved with APEC. Only three fora — the HRD Working Group, the Agricultural Technical Co-operation Working Group, and the *ad hoc* Advisory Group on Gender Integration (AGGI) — replied to the email canvass carried out in March and April 2002. In the case of the HRDWG, two non-governmental organizations were listed as having taken part in the 23rd meeting of the Working Group in 2001, while nine specific projects were listed in which non-governmental representatives were included. As for the Agricultural Technical Co-operation Working Group, no outside groups apparently attended the actual Working Group meetings, though some experts and individuals from such organizations did take part in one-off symposia or conferences sponsored by the Working Group. The AGGI group noted that it had met with the Women Leaders' Network in 2001 and there were non-governmental organizations (NGOs) in attendance.

In addition, two member economies included NGO representatives in their delegations to the AGGI.

What should we conclude from this? It is possible that there is more widespread non-governmental participation in APEC fora activities than was reported in this survey. Perhaps the Lead Shepherds and Chairs of the various groups were simply too busy to gather accurate information or to respond. As a former Lead Shepherd, I know how onerous the reporting expectations are for Working Groups. With little staff support and a small APEC Secretariat in Singapore with limited capacity to assist the Working Groups, it is possible that Lead Shepherd/Chairs have not been able to take action on this particular direction from the Leaders and Ministers. In fact, it may simply reflect a more fundamental issue for APEC — how to sustain, with the current level of resources, an increasing level of responsibility by the various fora?

The guidelines for non-member participation remain another obstacle to obtaining greater civil society input. Their complexity, multi-level approval process, and restrictive language have all combined to deter potential interested organizations from applying, and to frustrate Lead Shepherds who are genuinely open to greater civil society representation in their fora. However, at the most recent SOM (SOM II, at Merida), the Senior Officials did make two important amendments to the current application of these guidelines: first, SOM agreed to delegate to Working Groups its authority to approve non-member participation for a trial period of two years, and secondly, SOM affirmed that the Guidelines should be equally applicable to Working Groups, the Committee on Trade and Investment, and the Economic Committee. These decisions were made following the presentation by Canada of proposals to simplify the Guidelines. These two changes do, in fact, make it easier for APEC fora to apply the Guidelines, and make them applicable across the board to all APEC committees. Yet it remains the case that within individual fora, a single member economy can veto the participation of an organization which nearly all other economies wish to be involved. It will be interesting to see whether the gradually more positive approach in APEC to outside involvement will translate itself into meaningful interaction with other organizations or whether one or two member economies will continue to frustrate the widespread wish to broaden APEC's engagement with the wider community.

Leaving aside the formality of Leaders' declarations, official Guidelines and instructions to fora, the reality is that the culture of APEC is only gradually opening up to interaction with NGOs, which takes place more frequently and normally in other multilateral organizations. Perhaps because of its history, perhaps because of the suspicion among some member economies about the advocacy activities of some NGOs, perhaps because of different traditions of relations between government and citizens in some APEC members, there has been a reluctance in APEC to go beyond business and academia in the outreach activities.

Yet, APEC is not the only multilateral organization which must deal with this issue. How have some other international economic organizations managed their relations with civil society? The next section will focus on the experience of five such organizations — the World Bank, the World Trade Organization (WTO), the International Monetary Fund (IMF), the Organization for Economic Co-operation and Development (OECD), and the Organization of American States (OAS).

Multilateral Comparisons

These five organizations share some important characteristics — they are all intergovernmental bodies under member governments, as with APEC — but unlike APEC, they all possess large professional secretariats. In terms of their approaches to relations with civil society, while each has particular methods that are unique to that organization, a number of common elements stand out:

1. Gaining access to knowledge, expertise, and capacity relevant to their work is the key objective. These organizations recognize that NGOs have information and perspectives that will enable the multilateral organization to accomplish their objectives more effectively. The exchange between multilateral organizations and non-governmental expertise is constant, intense, mutually beneficial, and often unstructured. It takes the form of informal discussions with academics and advocacy experts on draft staff papers, colloquia or seminars on sectoral issues, advisory mechanisms and peer review committees, etc. Levering alternative sources of funding for projects, gaining access to grass-roots organizations to help with pilot programmes, and linking civic groups interested in combating poverty and related social ills are also organizational objectives.

2. Transparency and openness and enhanced mutual understanding are sought through well-developed and interactive Websites and a series of formal consultation instruments at many different levels, including the highest governance level. These organizations do not rely on a single method of communication with NGOs; rather they encourage and enable interaction in many different parts of their structures.

3. The multilateral organizations have substantial secretariats to undertake analysis, write reports, and develop policy proposals.

While policy remains the exclusive role of member governments through the usual governing structures, the underlying research and development of ideas and analysis is done largely by professional secretariats.

4. All the multilateral organizations have set up both organizational units within their secretariats and formal consultation mechanisms to facilitate non-governmental interaction. This enables day-to-day communication, plus a more formal opportunity for outside groups to put forward their views on the priorities, programmes or research work of the institutions.

It would be wrong to conclude that the processes for interaction between these five organizations and their respective NGO interlocutors is always smooth. Sometimes the dialogue is fractious. Sometimes, both sides end up being frustrated with the result. The WTO has suffered unpleasant demonstrations at its meetings, and it must be admitted that some NGOs are simply not interested in talking, they just want to protest. Despite the setbacks, and the small group of anarchists who would not be satisfied with any kind of civilized dialogue with those who believe in globalization, the fact remains that these five multilateral economic organizations have committed themselves to a long-term policy of constructive interaction with those NGOs who have both an interest in and a capacity to contribute to their agendas. If anything, the extent of the interaction has intensified in recent years, in recognition of the fact that to accomplish their organization's goals, they need to be understood by their respective communities, and they need the input of those who have valid experience and opinions to offer.

Implications for APEC

There are both systemic and cultural difficulties in APEC when it comes to encouraging greater involvement of non-governmental organizations within both APEC fora and activities. The Secretariat does not at present have the capacity to provide a point of expertise and co-ordination for this topic, while among the Lead Shepherds and Chairs, some have the staff support to work on this issue, and others do not. In addition, the current guidelines for participation of non-members do not offer a positive welcome to NGOs. It must also be recognized that for some member economies there are reservations about allowing access to APEC for organizations which may have negative views on trade liberalization and globalization generally.

Before recommending a set of proposals for strengthening the input of outside organizations in APEC, I will examine each of the ten most frequent practices of other multilateral organizations and consider their potential applicability to APEC:

1. *Websites.* As with the other multilaterals, APEC has a Website, a very good one which is accessed by a large number of people on a regular and increasing basis. Yet it does not have a "chat" capability to enable interested organizations and individuals to interact with Secretariat staff or Lead Shepherds, whereas three of the multilateral organizations studied have such a capacity. Cost considerations would need to be explored.

2. *Guidelines and accreditation procedures.* Other multilateral organizations have a process whereby organizations can be accredited, following an application process, which then enables them to receive certain documents and to attend certain meetings as observers and/or participants. Inviting NGOs to apply for accreditation would also be a way of identifying the degree of interest that exists in the member economies in an association with APEC. Such organizations would over a period of time become familiar with APEC and would be able to make an increasingly useful contribution to the mandate of the organization. While the existing Guidelines are a form of accreditation, they are exclusionary in orientation, and only pertain to the particular forum in which the outside organization seeks participation.

3. *Staff.* All other multilateral organizations have designated staff or units to engage in communication with civil society. This is not the case with APEC. Whether a full-time position could be designated to deal with this issue or allocating a portion of an existing staff's time to the issue would depend on resources, and may be considered in the broader question of strengthening the Secretariat's ability to support the growing APEC agenda.

4. *Advisory committees.* At the level of formal structures, APEC has one — ABAC — composed solely of business executives. The three Observer organizations — ASEAN, the Pacific Economic Co-operation Council (PECC) and the South Pacific Forum (SPF) — have business and academic participants but do not go beyond these two categories. There are also the APEC Study Centres with membership from the academic sector. If APEC wishes to create an NGO advisory structure, it could follow the model of ABAC, and invite Leaders to nominate three members of the civil society community from their own countries. A variety of options for establishing some sort of NGO advisory group could be explored, starting "small" with groups associated with particular Working

Groups, for example, a labour/management group connected to the Human Resource Development Working Group (HRDWG).

5. *Special committee to manage and monitor relations with civil society.* Nothing like this exists in APEC although similar bodies do function in most of the multilateral organizations studied. The *ad hoc* Task Force created in 2000 by the SOM to examine interaction with the broader community could be revived as a two or three-year pilot project to monitor developments (somewhat like the AGGI, which was maintained to monitor the implementation of the Framework for the Integration of Women in APEC). Such a committee could develop a certain expertise on non-governmental organizations and serve as a useful point of contact for NGOs that have a legitimate interest in the work of APEC.

6. *Seminars and symposia.* Holding occasional meetings dealing with issues of substance and inviting NGOs with an interest and expertise in these topics is a logical continuation of current practices in APEC. This is presumably one of the rationales for the Leaders' directive to the Working Groups to identify and invite outside groups to take part in their work. Preliminary research indicates this is not working.

7. *Annual meetings of NGOs in conjunction with Ministers/Leaders' meetings.* To some extent, this has already occurred in the APEC context, at several Ministerials, though the non-state participants have tended to come from only two sectors — business and education. Prior to the New Zealand AELM (APEC Economic Leaders' Meeting), there had been a number of "people's summits", organized by NGOs around the time of the AELMs, but these were anti-APEC events and did not involve any constructive interaction with APEC's Leaders or officials. The experience of other situations, such as in the OECD or Free Trade Agreement of the Americas, suggests that useful interaction can take place when there is goodwill on both sides. At present, there is nothing to prevent a host economy from organizing an NGO seminar in conjunction with a Ministerial or Leaders' Meeting and, in fact, Mexico has organized a Dialogue on Globalization and Shared Prosperity in 2002, with participants coming from a variety of non-governmental spheres.

8. *Briefings with NGOs.* The Secretariat responds in a professional manner to information requests from outsiders, whether individuals or organizations but no attempt is currently made to "reach out" to the NGOs to keep them informed of APEC activities, or to seek their views. Current staff limitations may preclude this approach on a widespread basis, although briefings to a carefully chosen group of

NGOs could be carried out easily by the Executive Director or the Deputy Executive Director whenever they visit member economies on business.

9. *Consultation on work plans.* The multilateral organizations with programme delivery functions, such as the World Bank, engage in extensive consultations with civil society before implementing their strategies in a given country. While this is less relevant for APEC, it would be quite feasible for several Working Groups and other fora to seek the views of relevant NGOs as they develop their workplans for the coming year, either by face-to-face meetings or via the Internet.

10. *Joint research and programme activities.* At the level of individual fora, there have been instances of co-operation between civil society and particular Working Groups. For example, some representatives of Asian labour groups contributed to the work of the HRDWG Task Force on the human resource and social impacts of the Asian financial crisis several years ago. Another example is the women's organizations which helped to develop the Framework for the Integration of Women in APEC. Recognizing that APEC has limited resources to do its own research, it makes sense to try to benefit from the knowledge that many effective think-tanks, research organizations, trade associations, and community groups bring to different topics.

Recommendations for APEC

Based on these emerging trends in other multilateral organizations, and with a view to moving forward in a constructive manner on this policy issue while respecting the traditions of APEC, the following specific suggestions are proposed:

1. *Follow up with Lead Shepherds and Chairs.* It appears that little has happened as a result of the directive from the Ministers and Leaders to APEC fora to identify and invite outside organizations to participate and contribute to the work of the different fora. It is suggested that the Executive Director and the respective programme staff pursue this matter with the various fora. This could also be done at the next joint fora meeting.

2. *Create a focal point in the Secretariat.* At present, it is unrealistic to expect that this issue will move forward unless there is some additional staff capacity in the Singapore Secretariat to act as a point of expertise and co-ordination. As a start, it is suggested that an existing staff person be designated to devote 50 per cent of her/his

time to this responsibility of encouraging and monitoring civil society involvement in APEC, and of being the point of contact for any outside enquiries on this issue.

3.   *Revise and monitor the Non-member Guidelines.* Now that the process has been simplified on a trial basis, the language of the Guidelines needs to be clarified and made more welcoming. The trial period should be monitored by APIAN to assess whether delegating authority to the various fora has actually made any difference to the number of NGOs involved in APEC activities.

4.   *Hold a seminar on best practices.* This is a tried and true APEC approach, to examine how member economies deal with a particular issue, and to draw on the expertise of other organizations which have experience on the same subject. It is suggested that either the APEC Study Centres Consortium or the ESC sub-committee of SOM be mandated to organize such a seminar, preferably to be timed in such a way that the Senior Officials could participate.

5.   *Revise the APEC Website.* APEC's Website is a popular way to access information about the organization and its activities; however, it is not very user friendly to those who are not familiar with its processes and mechanisms. A particular section could be added to the Website focusing on civil society to enable interested outside organizations to make a greater impact on APEC.

6.   *Invite the APEC Study Centres to make an annual presentation to the SOM and Ministers.* Mexico took the lead on this by inviting some ASC representatives, including people from APIAN, to make a presentation to the SOM II in May 2001. Extending this opportunity to the Study Centres would be both a practical and symbolic sign that APEC wants to hear from the non-governmental sector of society. Over time, it is possible that NGOs, in addition to the academic community, may come to play a larger part in the work of the ASCs. Without viewing this initiative as an "ABAC equivalent", it would send a signal to the outside world that APEC is continuing on the path of gradually opening itself to the experience and opinions of non-governmental actors.

Conclusion

Encouraging greater participation of civil society organizations in APEC would accomplish two things: first, it would enhance the credibility of the organization because it would be seen to be more open, more transparent, more accountable, more willing to listen to the world outside its doors. Secondly, the quality of APEC's output would be improved as a result of input from knowledgeable NGOs.

APEC has already moved a certain distance in involving non-state actors in its work. So far, these have mainly been business and education representatives. Now it is time to advance further into the broader world of civil society, provided it is done in a carefully planned way and is mindful of both APEC traditions and its financial and human resource limitations.

As far as the Leaders and Ministers are concerned, their directions are very clear. What remains is for the staff and fora chairs of APEC to take meaningful action to implement the clearly expressed views of their leaders.

Notes

1. This chapter is based on two previous papers prepared for the APEC Study Centre Consortium meetings in Auckland (1999) and Bandar Seri Begawan (2000), on my personal experience as Lead Shepherd of the HRDWG from 1996–98, my attendance at ESC meetings in 1999 and 2000, and the results of an email canvass of Lead Shepherds/Chairs of APEC fora carried out in March and April 2002.

SECTION VI

APEC AND THE SECURITY AGENDA: FIRST THOUGHTS

13

APEC'S ROLE IN POLITICAL AND SECURITY ISSUES

JOHN MCKAY

Introduction

APEC is usually regarded as an exclusively economic and trade organization, with its primary targets focused on trade and investment liberalization and facilitation, and it appears certain that at least in the near future this agenda will remain as the primary goal. However, at various times in APEC's history, questions have been raised about the potential for the organization to play a constructive role within the region in a range of political and security issues. Generally, these calls have been met with scepticism if not downright hostility. Noordin Sopiee (1997), for example, stated his strong opposition to APEC's entry into any kind of security role:

> It would seem that there are few things more likely to damage and even destroy APEC than to put security on its agenda. The poison would run through APEC's entire frame. It would be time to write the epitaph on an endeavor that can be powerfully used to bring all APEC countries closer together, that can forcefully bring prosperity

to the entire superregion and that can, with persistence and patience, help build the Asia Pacific community that all APEC countries need.

In an similar vein, Bergsten (1997) has noted a number of arguments against including security issues in APEC's brief, even going so far as to warn the APEC community to be on its guard against those who might seek to encourage such a security role!

> At this point, there is no discernible push to include security topics in APEC. The issue could thus be left quiescent. We should be alert, however, to oppose its revival, as it will almost certainly be proposed if APEC continues to prosper and those in charge of security policy look for effective avenues to pursue it in the Asia Pacific context.

However, not all commentators have been so final in their judgements. In a recent book on APEC, John Ravenhill (2001) has speculated on whether the future of APEC might not in fact depend on its willingness to confront the really big issues in the region.

> The Auckland APEC Leaders' Meeting perhaps points the way for the future: the focus was less on APEC's economic agenda than on political and security issues in the region, and the meeting arguably made an important contribution to resolving the East Timor crisis. Whether an institution whose principal focus is the minutiae of trade facilitation and whose achievements remain modest will continue to attract participation at the highest political level remains to be seen. Therein lies APEC's most pressing dilemma.

Another recent study of APEC has reached a similar conclusion:

> Community building in a broad sense may constitute APEC's most important function. In the longer term, the peace, stability and prosperity of East Asia can only be assured if inter-state relations change their quality in ways which make major wars unthinkable. This means establishing a security community. To fulfil this function better, the Leaders' Meeting ought to be less shy about formally integrating security issues into their discussions, even if this seems to duplicate the work of the ASEAN Regional Forum (Maull 2002, p. 35).

At the risk of being charged by some with committing a serious APEC heresy, I want to revisit this old argument about the role of APEC in political and security affairs in the region. My rationale for doing this is based on six critical questions:

1.   What real merit do the arguments put forward by Bergsten, Sopiee, and others have, both at the time they were first posed, and more

particularly now? Their dismissal of APEC's role in this area was, in fact, based on very little analysis, relying instead on firm but unsubstantiated assertion. I want to look at the issues in more detail than, as far as I know, has ever been attempted previously.

2.　In the period since the end of the Cold War, the whole concept of "security" has been drastically rethought in many quarters. The old emphasis on "traditional" or "hard security", involving war, threats of attack, alliances and so on, has been extended to include much broader questions of *human security*. Even the concept of what constitutes a security threat is being re-thought, and the events of 11 September 2001 have given much impetus to this approach. What merit do these new concepts of security have, and if we accept their relevance, does this have implications for the role of APEC in the new "security" agenda?

3.　Has APEC been less than honest about its role in security matters over the years, and in reality, has the organization always had a central concern over these issues? If this is true, and I want to argue that it is, what is to be gained or lost by acknowledging this reality?

4.　In terms of the real politics of the region now, what are the chances of some of the real opponents of any involvement of APEC in security issues changing their opinions?

5.　Given the seriousness of a number of security issues in the region, and given the manifest failure of any other regional organization to deal with these questions, especially the ASEAN Regional Forum, is there a possibility that APEC will of necessity have to assume this role as well, however reluctantly?

6.　In terms of APEC's longer-term future, is Ravenhill right in suggesting that trade and economic issues alone will not be capable of maintaining a high-level interest in the organization?

The chapter is divided into four major sections. The first section looks at the whole concept of security, the ways in which new definitions have been proposed, especially in the post-Cold War context, and the relevance of these new ideas for the Asia-Pacific. In the light of the discussion on what exactly constitutes the security agenda in the current climate, the second section considers the most important elements of the security problems in the region. This is a vast task, and one which will be presented as succinctly as possible, with the discussion structuring around the question of the need for a new security architecture. What should or might such a new system look like, and in particular what are the tasks that any effective regional organization concerned with enhancing security would have to accomplish. The third section looks at the recent record of trying to build effective mechanisms for the promotion of security in the region. A number of authors have raised serious questions about the effectiveness of those organizations that already play some kind of security role in the Asia-Pacific, and their analyses are evaluated here. In particular, the role of the ASEAN Regional Forum is discussed and whether it can be revitalised to play the central security role that some have always envisaged. The fourth section looks at APEC itself, considering the arguments for and against a broadening of its agenda into political and security matters, what roles it has played or might play, and the likely attitudes of various key APEC members on this question.

Revisiting the Concept of Security

The current debate about the re-definition of the whole concept of security is based on three separate but related threads. The first concerns the place of economic relations within the security domain. It has often been contended that trade and other economic linkages play a positive role in the development of stable and productive links between nations, but this has been challenged in a number of recent studies. Secondly, the scope of what constitutes the security domain is under question, with a number of writers arguing that we must look at definitions that are much broader than have been conventionally used. Thirdly, even those writers who still concern themselves with the traditional questions of security studies now argue that new kinds of threats to stability must be included in this analyses.

Economic Growth, Trade, and Security

In the literature on international relations and security, there has been a long-running debate about the relationships between economic change and the degree of resultant stability or instability in the security environment. On the one hand, some analysts have argued that economic growth will inevitably lead to greater interdependence between nations and a general desire to avoid any conflict that might interrupt economic progress. Hence, economic growth and change would lead to regional stability. Furthermore, as growth proceeds, there has been a tendency in many countries for more democratic forms of government to emerge, and some commentators have gone on to argue that two democracies will never go to war — the so-called democratic peace theory (Richardson 1997). This view has been put very strongly by Kishore Mahbubani, who has argued that one of the major reasons for Asia's recent economic dynamism is that a tidal wave has hit the region:

> .... the tidal wave of common sense and confidence. Over the past decade or two an immense psychological revolution has occurred

and is continuing in most East Asian minds: increasing numbers realise that they have wasted centuries trying to make it into the modern world. They can no longer afford to do so. After centuries their moment has come. Why waste it over relatively petty disputes or historical squabbles? (Mahbubani 1998, p. 118).

In a controversial theoretical analysis by Etel Solingen (1998), the themes of democracy and peace have also been linked to the possible relationship between economic liberalization and regional stability. She argues that the architecture of regional order depends upon the construction of various kinds of coalitions. Basically, two forms of coalition are possible. *Internationalist coalitions*, made up of supporters of economic liberalization, usually create co-operative regional orders that encourage peace and stability. On the other hand, opponents of economic liberalization give rise to *statist/nationalist coalitions* that are prone to create and reproduce zones of war and militarized disputes. Thus, the fostering of economic reform can be regarded as a major contribution to regional security. I will return to this argument later.

In marked contrast, some analysts have argued that the process of growth itself can lead to instability, especially in the current phase of capitalist development in which there have been marked shifts in power distribution between nations as well as a seemingly inevitable widening of the gap between rich and poor, both between and within nations. The intense competition that now characterizes the world economy can lead to serious rivalries and disputes that can escalate into armed conflicts. At the same time, the increased national wealth that has resulted from rapid growth can be used to purchase ever more sophisticated and destructive weapons, intensifying the damage resulting from any conflict. Few, if any, nations in the region can be regarded as supporters of the *status quo*, especially in the economic realm, and intense competition has been an inevitable consequence of the greater integration into global markets. Zysman and Borrus (1996), for example, have argued that there are several important lines of fracture that result from economic competition. Efforts by middle-power and mid-technology countries, such as Korea, to break loose from the existing hierarchy of economic power by moving towards higher value and higher technology products could create serious rivalries of development strategies. China and India may in turn provide alternative and competing lines of development, making economic competition within Asia into a form of security competition. Moreover, there is always a danger that Asia may be transformed into a more self-contained economic bloc competing with the United States and Europe (see also Friedberg 1993; and Betts 1993).

These old debates have taken on new forms and increased relevance in the period following the Asian financial crisis of 1997/98. After some four decades of rapid economic expansion, the crisis called into question for the first time the inevitability of Asian expansion and led to a re-evaluation of earlier assumptions that the new century would indeed be the Asian Century. The crisis, and the role of the West and the International Monetary Fund (IMF) in its management and seeming resolution, has created in some Asian minds a new sense of vulnerability and, for some, a blaming of the United States in particular, and U.S.-dominated institutions such as the IMF, for these problems. The "politics of resentment" (Higgott 2000) have, in my view, created a new and more unstable environment in the region, and this compounds the already serious security issues facing Asia.

These theoretical controversies, to which I will return in more detail later, are crucial to APEC as an organization devoted to the promotion of economic progress. If economic prosperity leads automatically to a more peaceful region, APEC needs only to continue its present path to make a significant contribution to peace and security. If, on the other hand, economic growth is more problematic in its security implications, then a more complex set of policy and institutional solutions needs to be designed.

Broadening the Security Agenda

Another basic conceptual problem concerns the changing nature of international relations and the focus of concern for states. During the Cold War, there was a simple and overriding imperative for survival and defence, and this is still true for relations between the two Koreas, for example. In many other domains, however, the very concept of security has been extended to include ideas of *economic security, environmental security*, and *food security* as well as concerns with international crime, illegal migration, and various pandemics. Some would argue that the most useful new overarching concept is that of *human security*, which reflects some of the concerns of traditional security, but with a wider concern for the individual as the object of security, and for the ways in which increasingly global systems impact on the family and other small local groups. It also looks at "structural violence" emanating from non-territorial threats (Tow, Thakur and Hyun 2000; and McRae and Hubert 2001). The emphasis on human security received much initial impetus from a UNDP report (United Nations 1994) which proposed that two forms of security are vital for the individual: *freedom from want* and *freedom from fear*. This formulation is still very influential in most accounts of the concept.

In a recent study, Alan Dupont (2001) has argued that in East Asia a new class of non-military threats has the potential to destabilize East Asia and reverse decades of economic and social progress. Here he includes issues such as overpopulation, pollution, deforestation, unregulated population movements, transnational crime, and AIDS. This broadening of the scope of security issues to include, at the very least, questions of national trade and economic priorities has a number of important consequences. At the level of analysis, the traditional separation of international relations from defence studies is no longer valid; indeed, any meaningful study must also include a range of other viewpoints and disciplines. Similarly, at the level of government, ministries of foreign affairs, trade and defence, at the very least, all need to make policy inputs to security questions, which simply does not happen in most countries.

The gathering pace of globalization is also adding a number of complications. Growing international linkages and interdependencies are, at least in the view of some, weakening the power of the nation-state. Actors on a range of scales, from local communities through cities to regions of various kinds, are now part of global networks in their own right. In many countries, the nation-state is no longer the sole arbiter of policy, even of policies that have implications for security, especially if one accepts the new, broader concept of security discussed above. The entire post-war security system has been built around relations and treaties between sovereign states, but this concept looks shaky in some parts of Asia where economic and political weakness and fragmentation through religious or ethnic conflict are causing serious problems of instability. Indonesia is a prime example here.

Some of the best of this new literature are not arguing that traditional security concerns have become obsolete; this is clearly not the case. Rather, there is a search for conceptual linkages between the old issues and the new ones. Tow & Trood (2000) have suggested four potential linkages between the two schools of thought, and these are analysed later.

1. *Conflict prevention.* Traditional security studies have spent much time dealing with the ways in which conflict can be prevented, and this is very much at the centre of the debate about human security. Co-operative security arrangements, and a broader sensitivity to the interests and priorities of other nations or peoples, can be much more cost-effective than waging war, and prevent large-scale human suffering.
2. *Reducing vulnerability.* Traditional studies have dealt with the nation-state as the subject of security, and have employed concepts of state sovereignty and social contract to deal with overriding issues of *order*.

Human security stresses human welfare goals and sees the state only as a means to achieve these goals, and only one means among many. A meeting point between these concepts can be the use of various instruments, such as collective security, to overcome behaviour that could threaten states, communities, or groups.

3. *Who is to be governed and secured?* A number of recent studies have argued that security is a civilizational problem. This acknowledges that fault-lines do exist between peoples, which is an area of concern in traditional security as well as human security analysis.

4. *Collective Security.* Both traditional and new concepts of security concede that there is a crisis of collective security at regional international levels, and the development of new institutions and mechanisms is regarded by both as a high priority.

Attempts to push the new agenda of human security have been met with strident criticisms, including some objections from various parts of Asia. Some critics have seen the human security agenda as yet another example of a Western model of economic and political development being foisted on Asia. The emphasis in much of this agenda on the individual is seen as potentially undermining the jurisdiction and power of the nation-state. In some versions of the human security blueprint — for example, that put forward by the Canadian Government — options for humanitarian intervention in crisis-ridden countries are left open, something which is vehemently opposed by many Asian countries. Most governments, notably that of Japan, favour an emphasis on "freedom from want" rather than "freedom from fear", but as a number of commentators have pointed out, this limitation makes the concept essentially indistinguishable from a conventional notion of development, and hence the real point is lost. Still other commentators have questioned just how much the idea of human security adds to the much older formulations of *comprehensive security*. For example, Japan as long ago as 1980 put forward a policy of comprehensive security to safeguard the economic livelihood of the Japanese people, protect vital markets and sources of raw materials, and guarantee Japanese investments. The idea was taken up in a number of Southeast Asian countries, including Singapore, which proposed a concept of *total security*. Acharya (2002) has attempted to answer these criticisms, arguing that many of the basic ideas of human security were in fact first articulated by Asian scholars. He also stresses some important differences between the formulations of human security and comprehensive security. However, he concedes that the basic unit of analysis in human security has shifted to the individual and the community, away from the emphasis on state security and regime stability which is central to comprehensive security. This is its strength, he argues, but this is bound to cause suspicion in many regional governments. Again, I will return to this issue later in this chapter.

The Security Agenda in the Asia-Pacific Region and the Search for a New Regional Architecture

The recent terrorist attacks in New York and Washington have added still more weight to calls for a new security architecture in the Asian region. Yet one more concern has been added to an already complex and potentially dangerous situation. Few would disagree that the region already contains the most difficult and intractable security problems facing the world community. Some of these issues are residues from the Cold War, and indeed, it might be argued that in East Asia the Cold War has not yet ended. Others are of a long-standing nature, but are not related to the Cold War itself, while still others have resulted from the end of the Cold War in the wider world, and the consequent re-evaluation and repositioning that has taken place, including some movements in Asia itself. A further layer has been added by the traumatic financial crisis that afflicted Asia in 1997/98, and which in some ways is still with us. Finally, we are now seeing the reverberations in Asia of the terrorist attacks in the United States in 2001. Given these multi-layered problems, it is clear that the existing security arrangements are quite inadequate and need to be completely reformed — yet, this is a frighteningly complex task. Asia is unique in that five major powers have a vital interest in the region — China, India, Japan, Russia, and the United States — and balancing their concerns is extremely difficult. China and the United States, in particular, have not generally favoured multilateral solutions to such problems, preferring bilateral negotiations. At a more general level, serious questions are being asked about the security implications of the rapid economic growth and consequent pressure for social and political change that have characterized the region in the last forty years. As was noted earlier, some see increased prosperity and greater economic integration as a positive influence, but other commentators have warned of the dangers of increased nationalism and competition in the region, coupled with the increased capacity for building larger and more destructive forces that growth has brought.

The aim here is not to review all these complex issues in detail: that in itself could fill several volumes. Rather, as a necessary prelude to a consideration of the adequacy or otherwise of existing regional security organizations, a very brief analysis of the basic nature or essence of the various security challenges facing the region is presented here. It is argued here that it is only after we have evaluated precisely *what we need regional organizations to do* that we can make sensible suggestions about the design of new or revamped institutions. This is a complicated task, because the multiple layers of security concerns, some old and some new, create different demands and priorities that are to some extent contradictory. No attempt will be made to examine the complex issues of West and Central Asia. Clearly, current events in that area will have a significant impact on the entire world, including East Asia, but the details of that situation and the possible regional approaches to peacemaking there are not considered here. However, since India is such an important player in the eastern part of the continent, not least in its relations with China, its regional role is included here.

Asian Security Issues Old and New

The Legacy of the Cold War

Asia is the one remaining major region of the world in which a number of very significant security issues have been left over from the Cold War. Principal among these are the questions over the Korean Peninsula and the Straits of Taiwan, and these are certainly the most serious security concerns in the region. Both are characterized by the central role being played by the United States, and many of its attitudes and policies are essentially the same as they were during the Cold War. In essence, for the United States, the major concern is still the need to take a stance against communism, although the rhetoric has shifted to express primary concern for upholding democracy and human rights.

Following the apparent success of the summit in Pyongyang between Kim Dae Jung and Kim Il Sung in June 2000, there were grounds for cautious optimism. However, the whole process has now stalled and some very difficult issues remain. Given the intensity and duration of the disputes between the Democratic People's Republic of Korea (DPRK) and the Republic of Korea (ROK), any kind of resolution will demand a great deal of time and patience, and a willingness to compromise. However, there seem to be some problems with the very process in both the ROK and the United States. Many commentators in Seoul have argued that the North is receiving too many concessions without having to make any real commitment in return on key issues of disarmament and the dismantling of the DPRK's nuclear and missile capabilities. Others argue that far too much aid is being given to a nation with a very poor human rights record. These criticisms seem to be supported by a significant majority of voters in the ROK. Indeed, it has been suggested that because of this lack of popular support, Kim Dae Jung is now a lame-duck President. These arguments are echoed in the United States, where many Republicans have criticized the former Clinton Administration for also giving many concessions and promises of financial assistance without adequate safeguards or returns. As a result, funds have still not been released by Congress in line with the agreements made in Geneva in 1994, much to the anger of the DPRK. The whole process of reconciliation received a major jolt with the comments about the DPRK in President Bush's "axis of evil" speech. This has caused great consternation in both Seoul and Pyongyang. Some progress has been made on much less contentious issues, such as the facilitation of contact between divided families, and on building transport and communications links across the 38ᵗʰ parallel. These are useful confidence-building exercises but the problems go beyond the ROK and the United States. Some commentators remain sceptical about the level of support for the whole process in the DPRK, especially among the military. Many have also perceived a profound ambivalence in both China and Japan. China does not welcome a continued unstable situation on its borders, nor the influx of large numbers of refugees from the famine in the DPRK. On the other hand, some have argued that China sees some value in having an unpredictable and threatening regime in Pyongyang to use as a weapon against U.S. influence in the region, and to avoid having a possibly pro-United States united Korea on its borders. Similarly, Japan worries about instability so close, but is also uncertain about the nature of a unified Korea.

The situation across the Straits of Taiwan also continues to cause serious concern. In Chinese eyes, the result of the 1999 presidential election in Taiwan has increased the chance of some kind of Taiwanese independence which, China has always stressed, would lead to war. On the Taiwanese side, the strident threats made by China have seemed only to harden public opposition to reunification with China, especially on the terms offered by China. Taiwanese perceptions of what has happened in Hong Kong after the handover have also served to justify Taiwanese fears. On the other hand, the continued growth of investment and trade links between China and Taiwan means that both sides have a strong interest in containing the situation. This economic impetus can only have been strengthened by the recent agreement to allow both to become members of the World Trade Organization (WTO). However, the strong stand taken by a number of American members of Congress on the need to stand against communism in support of Taiwan illustrates that the old attitudes of the Cold War are still alive in this region.

This latter point leads to the crucial questions being asked about future China–U.S. relations, and more generally about the stability of the China–U.S.–Japan strategic triangle. In particular, China fears that any deployment of a national missile defence (NMD) system by the United States would work against its interests and disturb the current balance in the region. Many Chinese analysts believe that in spite of the rhetoric about defence against "rogue states", such as the DPRK, it is China that is the real target of the proposed system. This view is supported by U.S. statements that its foreign policy focus has now shifted from the Atlantic towards Asia, with China as the central concern of military planning.

What challenges, then, do these relics of the Cold War pose to the regional security organizations in East Asia, and what could we expect of any revamped groupings? These issues encourage the retention of the defensive attitudes that characterized the Cold War, a very polarized worldview that has no problems in identifying "the enemy". It also encourages a firm discipline by nations sharing similar values behind the clear leader, the United States. While not underestimating the real dangers inherent in the Korean and Taiwan Straits issues, nor downplaying the need to maintain the security of both South Korea and Taiwan, it is argued later in this chapter that this Cold War mentality creates problems for other aspects of the regional security agenda. The secret for any new arrangements in the region will be to update our strategic thinking without creating the risks of unacceptable development in these two key areas. I will return to this tricky problem later.

Other Longstanding Security Issues

Asia also has a number of other old security issues that are not really relics of the Cold War, but still pose risks at the same level of magnitude. Of particular concern here are tensions in the relationships between India and Pakistan, and between China and India. The demonstrations of nuclear capability by both India and Pakistan in 1998 have, of course, added to the weight of these problems. The China–India–Pakistan triangle is difficult enough in itself, but it is further complicated by some echoes of Cold War attitudes and relationships, and by very recent developments involving U.S. strikes against Afghanistan.

Pakistan justified its development of nuclear weapons by pointing to the need to counteract the overwhelming superiority of India in conventional armaments, and the development of its missile delivery systems has been dominated by the need to deter strikes from India. However, Indian defence analysts have consistently argued that India is quite confident of its ability to deal with any threat from Pakistan with its existing arsenal, and that it is really fear of China that has prompted the Indian nuclear developments (see, for example, Jasjit Singh 1998). Long-term rivalry in the region between India and China now seems to be a reality, and this is complicated by some Cold War legacies, particularly involving U.S. positions. India has suffered from its identification with the Soviet Union during recent decades, while Pakistan was seen as a Western ally, a perception which was enhanced during the Soviet intervention in Afghanistan. Considerable U.S. aid was given to Pakistan, but this support waned during the 1990s as Pakistan developed closer ties with China. Suggestions that China gave some practical help to Pakistan in its nuclear development programme, while North Korea shared some of its missile technology, added to these suspicions. At the same time, the United States attempted to rebuild its relations with India, culminating in an official visit by President Bill Clinton. Now, with the new imperative of gaining access to bases for its strikes into Afghanistan, the United States is moving back to a close relationship with Pakistan, promising much needed aid and technical assistance.

The central problem between India and Pakistan remains that of Kashmir, but neither side is showing any signs of compromise. Nor is either side willing to accept any kind of outside mediation, arguing that this is a matter only for the two protagonists. In that sense, there are some similarities with the China–Taiwan issue, which China insists is a purely internal matter.

The more general problem for security raised by the Indian and Pakistan nuclear tests, as well as the nuclear programme of North Korea, is the old issue of nuclear non-proliferation. This was dealt with during the Cold War under the 1968 Nuclear Non-Proliferation Treaty (NPT), but serious questions have to be asked about the continued viability of this mechanism (Ungerer and Hanson 2001). India and Pakistan have both made it clear that they regard adherence to the NPT as unacceptable unless the "old" nuclear powers, and in particular the United States, adhere to the original bargain enshrined in the NPT. Non-nuclear nations originally agreed not develop such weapons in return for a pledge that the established nuclear powers would progressively dismantle their arsenals, something which has never happened. Given the interest of five major powers in the Asian region, a major goal in seeking to develop a pentagonal balance of power system in the region would be to encourage nuclear disarmament as well as non-proliferation. This is essential to prevent Japan from ever building its own nuclear capability, as well as reassuring nations such as South Korea that certainly have the capacity to acquire such capabilities. A stable balance of power will be difficult to achieve, which will be discussed in the following sections.

Post-Cold War Uncertainties

It is clear that the hopes for an uninterrupted period of peace and goodwill following the end of the Cold War were sadly misplaced. The "end of history" debate now looks extremely hollow, even naïve. Some analysts now suggest that we are already into the second phase of the post-Cold War era, in which optimism has given way to fears about how to manage a fluid, multipolar world. Paul Dibb (2000) has labelled this current phase the "Age of Discontinuity", and more recently the "Age of Strategic Surprise", arguing that these are indeed difficult and uncharted waters.

These uncertainties have resulted from a whole series of factors, the most basic of which is uncertainty about the precise locus of power in the new strategic context. While some commentators expected that the United States, as the victor in the Cold War and clearly the dominant military and economic power in the world, would enjoy unchallenged power, this "unipolar moment" has not really eventuated. Rather, we have a complex multipolar world in which there is intense jockeying for power and influence. Perhaps we should have expected such a situation. Torbjorn Knutsen (1999), for example, has argued that if one examines the history of the world order, it is typical for the victors in any major war to enjoy a brief period of hegemony and pre-eminence, but this will soon give way to the *phase of challenge*, which in turn will become the *phase of disruptive competition*. However, our security organizations, including those in East Asia are plainly unprepared for the new realities. Part of the problem is that the United States itself has yet to come to terms with the new context of strategic relations. Much thinking in the United States, especially in Congress, is still firmly anchored in the old Cold War mentality. There is an understandable reluctance on the part of the United States to take all the responsibility for global security, yet there is also unwillingness to share power and decision-making. This results in a curious mixture of protest about being expected to be the "world's policeman", coupled with a tendency to indulge in what is becoming known as "unilateral militarism". In Asia, this confusion (or perhaps schizophrenia) is especially acute. At certain times, Asian nations have worried about the United States disengaging from Asia and leaving a dangerous power vacuum, while at other times there have been complaints of undue U.S. involvement, even meddling, in the region. In part, this reflects the uncertainties of the Asian nations themselves — many are yet to work out whether they fear most undue U.S. interest in the region, or the lack of it. Perhaps what is needed in the region is the acceptance of the legitimate interests of five major powers — China, India, Japan, Russia, and the United States — which need to be included in a new balance of power arrangement. As Dibb (1995) has pointed out, the creation of a stable, pentagonal balance of power regime in Asia is a daunting task, and there is little experience of such relations in the region. Henry Kissinger (1994) has also reminded us that the United States has always refused to take part in balance-of-power systems, arguing that such a concept is incompatible with America's idealistic tradition. Similarly, many commentators have argued that China has problems in accepting the compromises that are essential to make such systems work.

The broadening of the definition of security explored in the previous section poses particular challenges for regional organizations. There is now a good argument to be made about the centrality of economic and trade issues in the current security debate. However, a number of nations, including China and Australia, seem to be persisting in their insistence that some organizations (such as APEC) should only deal with trade and investment issues, while other, quite separate, bodies are devoted to "security". Thus, we need to think carefully about this separation, which is becoming increasingly difficult to sustain.

Consequences of the Asian Economic Crisis

As if the issues outlined above were not enough, a series of new security tensions face the region in 2002. In part, these are the outcomes of the Asian crisis itself, but others are related to those more general processes labelled "globalization", which some would argue were partly responsible for the convulsions which gripped the region in 1997/98.

Richard Higgott and others have argued that an immediate result of the crisis and its management has been the creation of what is becoming known as the "politics of resentment".

> The ambivalent relationship that has always existed between the states of East Asia and the United States, and the U.S.-led international institutions, has been brought into sharp relief by the collapse of the East Asian currencies and the subsequent process of international financial institutional intervention. As time progresses, the nature of the bailout seems increasingly ambivalent and problematic for many Asian policy-makers. They do not like it, but it is difficult to know what they would have done without it. The authority of the IMF would have been accepted more readily by the State policy elites of East Asia if the interventions had indeed rapidly restored market confidence and stability. But they have not. Rather, for many in the region, the crisis appears to have presented the IMF with the opportunity to force open East Asian economies (Higgott 2000, p. 279).

The consequences of this seething resentment are still working themselves out in various ways, but Higgott and others have argued that one result has been a widespread disillusionment with multilateral institutions such as APEC, which are often regarded as Western-dominated.

An immediate outcome has been the revival of the old East Asia Economic Caucus idea under the ASEAN Plus Three (China, Japan, and South Korea) formula, and the re-emergence of proposals for an Asian monetary fund, which was originally proposed at the height of the crisis but vetoed by the United States (Kwon 2002). There have also been calls to build a strong free-trade zone in Northeast Asia, which can later be extended to the rest of Asia (Cai 2001). This would build on the strong production network that seems to be emerging in the region (Peng 2000; and Won 2001). If, as is widely believed in Asia, the Asian model of capitalist development was severely wounded by attacks from a range of Western forces, the response should be for Asia to build a firewall around the region to ensure that future raids are repelled. This is the logic of an Asian-only organization, such as the ASEAN Plus Three.

More generally, globalization and the crisis have created a situation of rapid and often unpredictable change that seems out of the control of any planners or policy-makers. For many in Asia, this seems to be an inopportune time to abandon all the comforts and apparent certainties that resulted from the system of controls and government intervention that characterized the "developmentalist state". One result may be, in spite of the influence of globalization, an increase in nationalist sentiment rather than an acceptance of broader regional co-operation. Certainly, economic security and the maintenance of international competitiveness are now key elements of the security agenda in the Asian countries (Van Ness 1999). This makes it doubly difficult to build regional organizations that cover the Asia-Pacific (that is, including the United States), yet it is essential that the United States continue to be involved in the region, at least in certain ways.

Consequences for Asia of the Terrorist Attacks in the United States

It now seems clear that the events of 11 September 2001 will have lasting economic, political, and strategic resonances in Asia. Almost all economies in Asia are heavily dependent on the U.S. market for a large percentage of their exports. Even before the attacks, there had been an alarming slowdown in Asian exports to the United States, especially in key areas such as electronics, and the position will now be much worse. Fears of a new Asian crisis are now being expressed, although this threat may have receded in recent months.

At a more general level, the United States is now asking all nations to give a firm response as to whether "they are with the United States or against it". This is not an easy position for many Asian countries to find themselves in, although there is of course a general denunciation of terrorism. As noted earlier, some ambivalent attitudes towards the United States have been apparent in Asia for many years, but especially since the crisis. The predominantly Islamic nations, such as, Malaysia and Indonesia, have particular problems here, but China is also faced with a series of dilemmas.

As Yuan (2001) has pointed out, China has reacted to the attacks by expressing concern and condemnation. China is, of course, keen to show its credentials as a good global citizen, given its accession to the WTO and the hosting of the Olympic Games in 2008. It has its own concerns with Muslim militants in Xinjiang, and has sought closer relations with the Central Asian Republics to promote anti-terrorism actions. Anti-terrorism was the major focus of the recent meeting of the Shanghai Co-operation Organization, which includes China, Russia, Kazakhstan, Kyrgys, Tajikistan, and Uzbekistan. There is also an opportunity now for a new start in Sino-U.S. relations, which have been very strained. China believes that the attacks in the United States support its argument that missile defence systems are not the way to meet the threats posed by rogue states and terrorist groups. Rather, China believes, the United States should now move away from its tendency to make unilateral foreign policy decisions and instead build broad coalitions. However, China also has concerns about the new situation. It is worried about U.S. military actions, and has laid down several conditions for its support: action must be based on firm evidence, should observe international law, should not hurt civilians, and must be carried out with the support of the United Nations Security Council. China's whole foreign policy approach stresses mutipolarity, a central role for the United Nations, and non-interference in domestic affairs, hence its alarm about many U.S. approaches. China has also been at pains to point out that, in its view, the U.S. foreign policy has made the United States a target for terrorism. China also worries that military action in Afghanistan will result in a permanent increase in U.S. military presence in the region, as happened after the Gulf War. Thus, China and the rest of the region are faced with difficult and important policy decisions that will require careful balancing between competing interests. However, one positive outcome of the current situation may be a willingness, especially by the United States, to participate in a more multilateral approach to regional security.

Managing the New Security Environment in Asia

This section will examine the existing structure of security co-operation in Asia, and evaluate the progress that has been made in managing the myriad of issues already identified. Then the prospects for the further development of effective multilateral organizations in the region will be studied, particularly in the light of the demands on such bodies made by the new global and regional environment which has been discussed earlier. This leads to the central question of the effectiveness of other regional organizations, and the extent to which APEC might be forced to fill the gap left by other ineffective alternative groups.

Attitudes towards Security Architecture and Multilateralism

The clear truth in the Asia of 2001 is that nationalism, which has always been strong in the region, is, if anything, becoming increasingly potent as a force. The reasons and dynamics vary from country to country, but the results are similar, leading some analysts to draw comparisons between Europe in the period just before World War I and the Asia of today. In China, for example, it has been argued that nationalism has been used by the government to reconstruct national identity at home and to counter the "China threat abroad", but the revival of nationalism is also partly reactive:

> More importantly, the West's reaction to China's domestic development led to strong nationalistic responses from China. In this sense, the rise of China's nationalism is not because of China's development, but due to external stimulation. In other words, China's new nationalism is a reaction to a changing international environment. Despite the rise of popular nationalism, the Chinese leadership remains rational. The government does not want China's modernisation to be interrupted by any external developments. Certainly, the regime also faces increasing domestic pressure from popular nationalism. Whether or not China's nationalism will be benign depends on the interplay between China and the West (Yongnian Zheng 1999, p. 159).

One can make similar points about a "new nationalism" in many Asian countries, and in all cases it is the complex interplay between internal forces and the dynamics of globalization that is the driving force. While it is true that Asia is characterized by a great deal of diversity, and may even be regarded as a creation of the Western mind, there is also ample evidence of the emergence of a significant level of Asian identity which transcends historical divisions. This multi-layered process, which some have called the "Asianisation of Asia" is very much a reaction to the West. In part, it reflects a feeling of pride in what Asia has achieved in economic development in such a short period, and hence celebrates the superiority of "Asian values". However, it also expresses a fear of continued or re-established domination by the West, especially since the economic crisis. This is the logic of the "ASEAN plus 3" formula.

Several important consequences flow from this complex interplay of local and international forces. Clearly, the state as an entity of prime importance is showing no signs of decline. There is also a strong sense of realism about relationships both within and outside the region. The stand-off across the Straits of Taiwan in 1996, for example, clearly demonstrated that, in the final analysis, the threat of the use of force can only be successfully faced with a credible threat of sufficient counter-force, and this lesson and others like it have not been lost on the region. This realism is made more critical by the realization that the bipolar rivalry of the Cold War has not been replaced by a simple unipolarity in which the United States stands unchallenged, but by a very complex interplay between the five major powers with a vital interest in the region: China, India, Japan, Russia, and the United States. As Dibb (1995) and others have pointed out, the creation of a stable system of relations between five powers is a difficult and complex task. It is even more challenging if some system of balance of power is being designed. To add a further complication, Asia is also home to a number of important and influential middle powers, which can exert some influence on the security equation. Significantly, there is little experience in Asia with balance of power systems. On the positive side, there are many features of the majority of Asian countries that lend themselves to the development of a workable balance of power. The growing sense of common Asian identity is one factor, and so is the Asian penchant for strong leaders, strong states, and the belief that ideological and human rights issues should not be allowed to hinder relations between states (Dibb 1995). In addition, each of the local powers has some strengths, but also some serious weaknesses, and hence it is unlikely that any one power will be able to become dominant over the others in the near future at least. Thus, while there are significant problems, pressures leading towards a collaborative system are very strong.

> A pentagonal balance of power presupposes a continuous system of diplomacy, providing players with intelligence about all the others and the means to act upon moves that threaten the balance. Such means have to include a sense of regional order comprising a system of collaboration and self-restraint, as well as the restraint of others. The question is whether the security architecture of the region is yet ready for such a sophisticated and intricate concept of order. The answer is that it is not, but that the self-preservation of the great

powers and the anxiety of the middle powers will push events in the next decade or so in the direction of a balance-of-power collaboration. This is because the chief function of a balance-of-power is the preservation of the existing local system of states, for which there is general support in Asia (Dibb 1995, pp. 23–24).

This is, of course, still a long way from the idea of multilateralism in the region. As opposed to the *realist* ideas that are still dominant in most policy debates, a number of *liberal* theorists in international relations have stressed a quite different set of priorities.

While realist positions are based on raw power and the single-minded pursuit of state interest, stressing concepts such as strategic preponderance and regional power balancing, liberals have stressed the need to develop multilateral modes of co-operation. Jervis (1982; 1999) has proposed four preconditions for the formation of security regimes:

- The big powers in the region must all agree.
- There must be some commonality in values and aims among potential members.
- There must be no "deviant" states with an interest in seeking gains at the expense of other members.
- All members must regard conflict as more costly and counter-productive than co-operation.

While these preconditions are not yet present in the Asia-Pacific, a number of authors have argued that there have been some promising movements in these directions, making it worthwhile to pursue new systems involving greater levels of multilateralism (see, for example, Tow 2001). Two different but related forms of multilateralism have been discussed in this context. Some authors have stressed the need to develop *regional security norms and institutions,* building on existing shared values and approaches. Others have proposed the development of *regional interdependence,* consisting of regular dialogues to deal with the causes of regional tensions.

The truth is that there is still insufficient support for such developments, particularly from the major powers. This is especially for China and the United States, both of which have preferred to operate in a bilateral framework, allowing them to take maximum advantage of their size and power relative to those of other players, and minimizing the opportunities for groups of smaller countries to combine against a single power. The limited amount of theoretical work that has been done on multilateralism suggests that it will be some time before Asia is ready for this kind of development in any full sense (Ruggie 1995; and Caporaso 1995). This key issue will be discussed in the following section.

Existing Regional Organizations: Achievements and Shortcomings

This section will evaluate the progress that has been made by each of the major regional organizations that make a contribution to the solution of political and strategic problems in the Asia-Pacific. These are the Association of Southeast Asian Nations (ASEAN), the ASEAN Regional Forum (ARF), and the Council for Security Co-operation in the Asia-Pacific (CSCAP). In the light of this discussion we return to the question of the prospects for multilateralism in the region, an essential precursor to the discussion of the potential role of APEC.

ASEAN. The history of ASEAN goes back to 1967, when a dialogue process was set up by some of the key states of Southeast Asia to co-ordinate responses to the Vietnam War. The long and sometimes turbulent history of ASEAN has generated a large literature (see, for example, Broinowski 1990; Henderson 1999; and Chia & Pacini 1997). It is not appropriate to review all these writings here, but for the purposes of this chapter it is important to list some of the key achievements of ASEAN, some of its problems, and the key method of operation that has become the hallmark of ASEAN and some of its related organizations.

Perhaps the most important achievement of ASEAN is that it has been able to survive for so long in spite of a large number of internal, bilateral, and sub-regional problems. Not only that, but it has been recognized for many years as the voice of Southeast Asia by a large range of players such as the European Union, the United States, and Japan. Not only has it survived, it has become progressively larger as more nations have sought membership. The recent expansion to include all of Indochina, while it has created some real problems, has also been an important step forward. Now ASEAN is able to speak for the entire region. ASEAN, it must be remembered, was also originally established to assist the *rapprochement* between Indonesia and Malaysia following the campaign of confrontation waged by President Soekarno between 1963 and 1967. Since then, it has been able to resolve a number of regional disputes and, more fundamentally, establish a system of dialogue and compromise as the norm in the region. This process culminated in the signing of the Treaty of Amity and Co-operation (TAC) in 1976, and since then, the prospects for armed conflict in the region have seemed very remote. While some of the economic goals that have been envisaged have failed to materialize, the creation of the ASEAN Free Trade Area (AFTA) has been a major advance.

During this period of long and slow development, ASEAN has established a series of principles under which it operates. These are:

- *Non-interference in the internal affairs of members.* This key principle has been under some challenge recently, but it still remains as a distinguishing feature of the organization.
- *Avoidance of complex institutional arrangements.* ASEAN has remained as a relatively loose and informal organization.
- *Absence of a strong secretariat.* Unlike the EU, ASEAN has deliberately avoided setting up a large, powerful and expensive Secretariat. Power still remains very much with the member states.
- *Decision-making by consensus.* With very few exceptions, ASEAN has operated on a consensus model, refusing to accept any decisions that are not supported by all members. The TAC was a treaty in the normal sense, but this is unusual.
- *Voluntary compliance with decisions.* ASEAN operates as an informal and consensual organization rather than being rules-based. Decisions are not binding and are not accompanied by sanctions in case of non-compliance. Peer-group pressure applies, of course, but this takes place in a non-public way.
- *Development at a speed acceptable to all.* No attempt is made to speed up any process in a way that is uncomfortable to any member.

These methods of operation, which have also been accepted by the ARF and APEC, have been hailed by many Asian leaders as a uniquely Asian form of co-operation and decision-making. They are not without their problems, of course. The principle of consensus allows any member a veto over any decision, and this has sometimes been used to the annoyance of most members. The absence of a strong Secretariat means that the effectiveness of debates is often compromised by the lack of any clear and impartial analysis of the issues involved. The lack of an effective central budget also means that many initiatives languish through lack of resources. Since the Asian crisis, these organizational concerns have been overshadowed by a series of important regional problems, but most nations have been too concerned with their own internal difficulties to pay enough attention to regional issues. Moreover, their budgets for such activities have been limited. These internal problems have been most severe in Indonesia, and this has had double impact on ASEAN because, under President Soeharto, Indonesia played an informal leadership role for the entire region. There is now no widely accepted leader or elder-statesman to provide guidance, although it appears that Dr. Mahathir is trying to play such a role. The broadening of ASEAN to include the nations of Indochina is also consuming a great deal of attention as well as human and other resources. These problems of the main ASEAN forum are also a cause for concern because the organization is so important for the vitality of the ARF and APEC.

ARF The origins of the security dialogue that we now know as the ARF can be traced back to the 1986 Vladivostok speech of Mikhail Gorbachev. He called for a Pacific conference along the lines of the Helsinki Conference, to build confidence and reduce the risk of military confrontation in Northeast Asia. This call was taken up by the then Australian Foreign Minister Gareth Evans, who proposed the establishment of a Conference for Security and Co-operation in Asia, based on the European model of the same name. This was followed by similar proposals from South Korea and Canada (Singh 2000). However, these ideas were rejected by the United States. It was not until after the Cold War that attitudes changed enough for the idea to be taken up again. In, particular attitudes within ASEAN were modified. By then Australia had abandoned the CSCE model and instead favoured a simple dialogue process, more in line with ASEAN preferences. ASEAN had concluded that it was necessary to create a forum at a time of great uncertainty, particularly given some doubts about the continued U.S. presence in the region. Southeast Asia no longer felt so separate from Northeast Asia, given the growing levels of economic interdependence, and supported a broad forum for the entire region. In 1991, it was decided that the post-Ministerial Meeting of ASEAN was the appropriate place to discuss such security issues. The United States supported the idea, and the ARF was launched in Singapore in 1993. The first real meeting was held in Bangkok in 1994.

The ARF meets once a year at foreign minister level and is chaired by the Foreign Minister of the ASEAN country hosting the main ASEAN meeting for that year. ASEAN also plays a key role in setting the agenda for the meeting. Importantly, the procedural and decision-making style of ASEAN has been adopted for these meetings.

The first meeting in Bangkok lasted only three hours, but a more substantial discussion took place in the following year in Brunei. A concept paper formulated there proposed that the ARF should adopt a gradual evolutionary approach, which would take place in three stages:

- Stage 1: Promotion of confidence-building measures (CBMs)
- Stage 2: Development of preventive diplomacy mechanisms
- Stage 3: Development of conflict resolution mechanisms

A number of Working Groups was also established. It was agreed that the ARF should operate along two tracks, the official channel and a network of institutes of strategic studies in the region. Membership of the dialogue began with the members of ASEAN plus the dialogue partners, but it has gradually been widened to admit India, Mongolia, and most recently, North Korea. Thus, it includes all of the countries of the region as well as the major powers with an interest in Asia, notably Russia, and the United States. However, because of its large membership (currently twenty-three), it has wide cultural diversity, which can cause problems. The informal ASEAN style has been appropriate at the start but some members feel that at some stage more structures will be needed. A particular problem has been the attitude of China, which has given only lukewarm support to the whole notion of multilateral approaches to security. China has insisted that discussion should be devoted entirely to confidence-building measures (CBMs). Non-ASEAN members have also complained about the lack of consultation by ASEAN. Desmond Ball and others have argued that serious attention should now be given to preventive diplomacy in the region, but this will be difficult to achieve at the moment (Ball and Acharya 1999; and Dupont, 1998).

Preventive diplomacy has the aim of:

•   Preventing severe disputes and conflicts from arising between and within states;
•   Preventing such disputes from escalating into armed conflicts;
•   Limiting the intensity of violence resulting from such conflicts and preventing it from spreading geographically; and
•   Preventing and managing acute humanitarian crises associated with such conflicts (Ball and Acharya 1999, p. 7).

The ARF has organized three seminars on preventive diplomacy, but there seems little prospect for progress, given the opposition of China.

However, there are two more fundamental problems associated with the ARF process. First, ASEAN is at the core of the dialogue, and hence if ASEAN is experiencing severe problems, as was argued above, this has a major impact on the effectiveness of the ARF. At present, ASEAN simply lacks the resources to support such a large undertaking properly. Secondly, the whole process has its core in Southeast Asia, while it is in Northeast Asia that the most intractable security issues are located. The opposition of China to such approaches is particularly worrying (Ball 2000a; and Evans 2000).

Council for Security Co-operation in the Asia-Pacific (CSCAP). This was established as the second-track partner of the ARF, to support the organization in the same way that many saw the Pacific Economic Co-operation Council (PECC) supporting APEC. However, some of the meetings between key institutes of strategic studies, which gave rise to the CSCAP, go back to the 1970s. It now has seventeen members, has held a number of meetings, established a series of working parties, and produced some useful analytical work, but it suffers from some severe problems (Ball 2000). It is not recognized in any way by the ARF as its official partner. Indeed, many members of the ARF have argued that a second-track equivalent is not needed. Still others have suggested that many members of the CSCAP are too close to government to engage in truly independent analysis. The CSCAP also suffers from severe competition in this field. It has been calculated that there are now several hundred second-track forums operating in the region, resulting in severe duplication of effort and lack of co-ordination.

Prospects for the Creation of a Viable Regional Order

The picture that has been painted of the security situation in the Asian region is not a particularly comforting one. The region contains most of the world's serious security problems, including some fifty territorial disputes, and the regional architecture is simply not up to the task of managing the myriad tensions and conflicts. In particular, existing multilateral approaches are poorly developed, even though some progress has been made. Optimists argue that in some ways the post-Cold War situation is more stable than the earlier phase, and the growth of economic independence will ensure that conflicts are handled carefully to avoid the disruption of continued development. There are some serious doubts about both aspects of this proposition. As Paul Bracken (1999) has argued, the very notion of the end of the Cold War may be a Western concept with limited validity in Asia. Bracken says that for powers such as China, what is more important is the concept of the "Post Vasco Da Gama Era". What is desired is a return to the situation before the brief European interlude in Asia, a re-establishment of the dominance of key Asian powers, notably China. This suggests that the future may involve challenge rather than co-operation, and economic rivalry will be a crucial element. If these critics are right, and they may well be, we will need to make much more serious efforts to strengthen multilateral fora in the region. It can also be argued that the middle powers have a particular responsibility to play a greater role (McKay 1996). They have the most to gain from multilateralism, as well as much to lose from increased tension or conflict, and in the past they had been central to the creation of the mechanisms that exist today. A forum such as APEC was partly designed to give greater scope for middle-power initiatives, and these possibilities ought to be developed, but in order to assess the potential for such developments, we need to be realistic about the scope for the emergence of a multilateral regional order.

At the start of his recent analysis of APEC, John Ravenhill (2001) explored the reasons why nations should entertain the idea of co-operation, and concluded that no single set of theories could adequately explain this question. It was similarly difficult to explain under what circumstances nations would prefer regional co-operation rather than wider multilateralism. He concluded that in most instances, economic factors are less important than the broader strategic and political framework, even in the development of economic arrangements:

> Economic motives, however, may be secondary in governments' decisions to construct collaborative economic arrangements on a regional basis. Regional economic collaboration, like other economic regimes, is nested within broader frameworks of military and political power, at both the regional and global level. Arguably, the ultimate goal of regional economic co-operation has always been to reap the positive political and security externalities from the institutionalisation of collaboration. Europe provides a classic example. Similarly, the states of the Association of Southeast Asian Nations (ASEAN) pursued economic cooperation as a medium to build confidence within the region, to defuse inter-state tensions, and to forge a sense of community. The extent to which collaboration has to generate economic benefits in order to promote positive security effects may vary substantially across different regions. ASEAN, for instance, has generated significant benefits in the form of confidence-building activities even though the gains from economic collaboration have been minimal (Ravenhill 2001, p. 27).

He also identified other reasons why regional co-operation might be preferred. These include: the existence of "natural" economic regions; the advantage of smaller numbers of members; the importance of similarities in culture and history; symmetries in economic capacity; and the relative ease of adjustment to liberalization at a regional level.

If these general concepts are correct, what about the implications for regional security co-operation in the Asia-Pacific region? Lake and Morgan (1997) have argued that we are seeing the emergence of a variety of new regional orders, rather than a single world order. After the Cold War, the great powers are less willing to accept the burden of conflict management at a global level, and are searching for alternative ways to share the costs. Thus, they argue, efforts to promote peace, order, and security will increasingly involve arrangements and actions at the regional rather than the global level. Regions are more important as entities since the Cold War, and there are now greater possibilities for more co-operative regional orders. However, regions cannot be viewed as mini-international systems, and local knowledge is needed of their dynamics and special characteristics, and hence the foreign policies of the big powers need to be tailored to the individual circumstances of each region. These ideas have been taken a stage further by Susan Shirk (1997), who has explored emerging regional orders in the Asia–Pacific. She contends that the prospects for achieving stability in the region through a workable form of balance of power are not promising. The bipolarity of the Cold War has been replaced by a complex multipolarity involving at least four major powers — China, Japan, Russia, and the United States (and I would add India). Many theorists (for example, Mearsheimer 2001) have argued that multipolar systems are potentially much more unstable than bipolar ones. In this region, Shirk has suggested, there are several reasons why this should be so. In a region of great complexity, there is a greater risk of miscalculation because of mistaken estimates of relative power and different interpretations of history. Miscalculations can also occur because of confusion about the commitment of coalition partners to deter an aggressive state. Countervailing coalitions usually evolve quite slowly, too late to deter an aggressive state. Coalition building is also inhibited by shifting alliances among partners. Given these problems with any kind of balance of power system, she supports the idea of some form of regional collective security arrangement, and sees evidence that regional leaders are willing to explore the idea. An Asia-Pacific concert of powers, consisting of the four major powers in the region would be more workable than a larger body and would provide significant leadership on a global scale. Even China, she suggests, is showing some interest in the idea. Such a concert would probably emerge on an *ad hoc* basis, be limited in size, and be relatively informal. Decisions would be taken through informal negotiations and the building of a consensus. No enforcement mechanism would be in place to deter an aggressor, but continued co-operation would facilitate the coalition building needed for this purpose. The concert establishes norms of behaviour and encourages co-operation. Above all, the regular interaction that is generated builds a sense of community and of shared values. Such a method of operation, she proposes, is very much in line with Asian norms, and with the operations of existing bodies in the region, but she accepts that there are several obstacles in the way of such an initiative. There are wide variations in ideologies and political systems in the region, and there is no widespread support for the *status quo*.

In a recent article, Khoo and Smith (2002) take a very different position. They advocate that we must not let the events of 11 September 2001, and the subsequent war on terrorism get in the way of the focus on what are still the underlying dynamics of the regional security situation. In particular, the Sino-U.S. relationship remains the most intractable of the great power rivalries in the world. Somewhat provocatively, they argue that the best solution would be a strong but benign American hegemony in the region. They believe that the region is too unstable, has too many difficult problems, and has some exceedingly diverse political systems, and hence any form of concert of powers would be difficult to establish and maintain. What is needed for all concerned is an extended period of stability.

While recognizing the immense problems inherent in establishing a concert of powers in Asia, I find Khoo and Smith's assertions very strange. In the first place, my reading of history suggests that the idea of a benign hegemon is certainly an oxymoron! As Mearsheimer (2001) has shown in great detail, big powers have always behaved in the same ways and with the same motivations, and present-day America is no exception. Using his concept of *offensive realism,* he finds that great powers have always relentlessly sought yet more power, and the real goal of such a state is to be the hegemon in the system. In spite of its current rhetoric, which is based on the promotion of moral and liberal values, the reality of contemporary America, he contends, is no different. There is a wide gap between rhetoric and reality, something which goes largely unnoticed in the United States, but not in the rest of the world. To be blunt, any attempt to increase or even maintain current levels of U.S. predominance in the region would not produce stability, but rather the opposite. To be fair, many commentators and policy-makers in the United States would not support such a notion either. In a new study, Joseph Nye (2002) has warned the United States against hubris and unilateralism in the aftermath of 11 September. In the new information age, he contends, power is a much more complex and diffuse phenomenon than in the past. Raw military capability is not nearly enough, and economic capability and other forms of "soft power" are just as potent. In this context, the United States cannot really be challenged, but it is not strong enough to go it alone. Co-operation, including multilateral approaches to security issues, is essential. Press-Barnathan (2000) also agrees that the United States would in fact welcome some burden sharing in the region, and that regional security co-operation is likely to be more prominent in U.S. policy in the future.

In one critical area, Khoo and Smith are correct in suggesting that a concert of the four major powers in Asia would be unacceptable to the important medium-sized powers in the region, such as Korea or Indonesia. Medium-power action and initiative are an important and potentially constructive force in the region, and medium powers play a very important role in regional organizations. In any kind of multilateral system in the region, such an arrangement is generally desirable although difficult, and membership must not be restricted to the major powers.

So far it has been assumed in the analysis that bilateral and multilateral approaches are mutually exclusive, or, putting it in more theoretical terms, that realist and liberal positions are essentially antagonistic. Some recent analyses suggest that this may not necessarily be so, and that in certain circumstances they may be mutually supportive. In a recent book, Tow (2001) has presented a persuasive case for what he calls *convergent security*. He suggests that while in the present circumstances the bilateral alliance system put in place by the United States is essential to regional stability, it may be supported by multilateral approaches that can gradually transform the region by creating a more complex inclusive architecture. However, in order for this mutually supportive pattern to be established, a number of components need to be put in place. The existing bilateral arrangements need to be gradually modified, moving from "exclusive bilateralism" to more inclusive systems that reassure all regional states rather than threaten them. It is also essential for great power support to be maintained for such convergent strategies. In particular, this means a level of U.S.–China understanding. Adequate incentives for security regime formation need to be in place, and ultimately this involves the acceptance of rules or norms of behaviour. Tow suggests that the best we can hope for in the region in dealing with critical problems such as the Taiwan issue is to "muddle through", hoping that the existing alliances will guarantee stability long enough for more inclusive regional systems to be made effective. This provides a serious challenge at all levels.

Should APEC Play a More Explicit Political and Security Role?

The arguments so far have suggested that the whole concept of "security" is now seen as complex and multi-dimensional, and extends beyond the traditional concerns with just military power. Within the Asia-Pacific region there are enormous problems of security, both of the traditional and new kind. There is a real need for an effective regional security mechanism, but the existing bodies dealing with security issues in the region are singularly ineffective. There are strong arguments in favour of multilateral approaches to security in the region, but the ASEAN Regional

Forum, the body favoured by many to play such a role seems to be particularly impotent. In this situation, should APEC move in to fill the vacuum in this vital area, or at least play a supportive role in the creation of a new sense of dialogue and co-operation in the region? We will review the arguments for and against this idea, and attempt to suggest a constructive way forward for the organization.

Arguments For and Against a Strategic Role for APEC

A number of analysts have presented arguments against any strategic role for APEC, and these have been brought together succinctly by Sopiee (1997):

1. There is strong opposition for such a development among a number of APEC member economies, such as Japan, Australia, China, and the whole of ASEAN. As yet, no country has spoken out strongly in favour of such a development.
2. A number of APEC members, for example, Mexico, Chile, and Peru have no role in Asian security issues.
3. Any development of a security role for APEC would undermine the ASEAN Regional Forum.
4. APEC already has enough work on its plate. A security role would divert it from its designated role in economic co-operation.
5. Any development of this kind would confirm the suspicions of some that there was always a hidden security agenda for APEC.
6. The APEC process has not gone far enough to make security discussions productive. Members are still getting to know each other, and in this situation a simpler agenda is likely to be more productive.
7. Both China and the United States would find themselves in an uncomfortable position.
8. Security dialogue would not contribute to the creation of an Asia-Pacific community, one of the key aims of APEC. Rather, it would introduce more dissent and division.
9. China would not tolerate any security dialogue in an organization which also includes Chinese Taipei.

More recently, in the wake of the Shanghai meetings of APEC, the Canadian APEC Study Centre produced an evaluation of where APEC was heading, and included some speculation about a broader role for the organization (Asia Pacific Foundation of Canada, 2001). It is noted that APEC has already become involved in issues of anti-terrorism and in discussions about some wider aspects of globalization, but it was argued that APEC should not routinely become involved in such complex problems because the organization has no background in this area. Rather, APEC should concentrate on its core business of economic integration.

These are strong arguments, but a number of persuasive arguments can also be made in the opposite direction:

1. APEC is already a *de facto* security dialogue organization. The annual meeting of Leaders is especially valuable as a regular meeting place for the discussion of the pressing problems facing the Asia–Pacific region at any particular time. Indeed, this is a unique forum that plays a special and extremely useful role. The agenda should not be artificially constrained, and certainly, the Leaders themselves would not want it that way. So, in recent meetings, East Timor and global terrorism have been at the top of the agenda. This will not change, and we should be honest about what APEC can do — indeed it gives greater credibility to the group.

2. The broadening of the definition of "security" means that many issues that in the past had not been regarded as serious threats to the stability of the region must now be looked at in a new light. Issues of globalization, environmental security, AIDS, illegal population movements, and so on are crucial to the well-being of the Asia–Pacific community. From the very beginning, APEC has claimed to be involved in the building of this community, and this can only be done if these broader issues, including areas of more traditional security concern, are included in the agenda.

3. Dewi Fortuna Anwar (2000) has suggested that although APEC does not deal directly with political or security issues, the organization is increasingly regarded as an important source of regional stability. Such stability is essential for economic development. In particular, APEC can serve to dampen nationalistic sentiments in the region and create a web of economic interdependency that can transform relations in the long run. However, in order to make this role more effective, APEC needs to move away from the looseness of its present organization and be more proactive. This would counter the view of Buzan and Segal (1994) that APEC can be seen as an attempt to avoid confronting the consequences of the end of the Cold War. APEC, in their view, aims to keep the United States as the guarantor of Asia's security, which in turn "keeps Asians from having to come to terms with each other".

4. In an era of intense global and regional competition, we can no longer regard economic integration as necessarily being a force for stability and peace. In certain circumstances, trade frictions and other economic disputes can be major causes of conflict. As Ball (1996) has argued, there are certain important economic issues with security dimensions that should certainly be discussed by APEC. These include: the implications of economic interdependence for regional security, economic growth and political stability, economic growth and increased defence expenditures in the region, the vulnerability of trade and passage through the key sea lanes in the event of conflict, the conflicts that might result from anti-dumping cases and similar disputes, and the use of development aid to promote regional stability. This might be regarded as the minimum level of security involvement by APEC.

Defining a Way Forward

This detailed review of the relevant literature suggests to me that some kind of constructive way forward, which includes an important although indirect role for APEC in the building of a more stable and peaceful region, ought to be possible to devise. This final section presents a number of ways forward, and couch these in terms of recommendations:

1. *A bridge across the Pacific.* A number of writers have argued that one of the biggest obstacles to co-operation in the region is the wide disparity in the cultures of dialogue and co-operation between the two sides of the Pacific. This is seen as a general problem, but in the security sphere there has been some debate about the different *strategic cultures* in the region (Booth and Trood 1999; and Alagappa 1998). This literature suggests that national attitudes and policies towards the use of force vary quite widely between cultures. Hence, there is a real need to foster greater understanding of different strategic cultures. Beginning with Michael Haas' (1989) seminal work, a number of authors have suggested that there are specific Asian approaches to security issues. These include a longer time horizon, a reliance on bilateral approaches, a strong adherence to principles of non-interference in internal affairs, a preference for informal structures and consensus approaches to decision-making, and a multi-dimensional or comprehensive approach to security. There are, of course, numerous echoes here of the principles under which APEC itself was established. The question of broadening and deepening understanding on both sides of the Pacific is thus not just

a question of security, but covers all fields of exchange. Given the current intensity of APEC's activities, covering a large number of Working Groups and other fora, APEC is already making a big contribution here and needs to consider ways of enhancing this.

2. *Building an Asia-Pacific community.* APEC has often talked about its ultimate aim of creating a more coherent Asia-Pacific community (Hellmann and Pyle 1997; and Morrison, Kajima and Maull 1997). Clearly, it is impossible to build such a community without a reasonable degree of stability and mutual understanding of cultures, aims, and policies. Building a security community is a big task. It has already been achieved to a large extent in Southeast Asia, but there has been no similar success in Northeast Asia, the site of some of the most pressing security issues. While the ARF will continue to grapple with specific security problems, APEC can make a more general and supportive contribution through the intensification of its community building efforts. This will be a slow and gradual task, but one which is essential. A key role is the development of a better understanding between China and the United States. This involves continued encouragement to China to refine its policies and approaches to the region, but it is also concerned with the better integration of the United States into the region. The perception throughout much of Asia that the United States is high-handed and unilateral in its approaches is a major problem in building a stronger, multipolar, and multilateral region. It is difficult to design specific programmes for community building, but this aim ought to be behind many APEC activities.

3. *The crucial role of the Leaders' Meeting.* The annual Leaders' Meeting continues to be by far the most important APEC contribution to political interaction and co-operation in the Asia-Pacific. It is imperative that everything possible be done to continue this forum and enhance its effectiveness. This is best done by allowing the meetings to develop freely, making it possible for Leaders to discuss the most pressing issues of the day. The bilateral and other small group meetings on specific issues, such as the regular dialogues on the Korean Peninsula should also be encouraged. Certainly, APEC should make no attempt to limit discussions to APEC's trade and investment agenda.

4. *Reducing economic frictions.* At several points I have alluded to the ongoing debate about the security implications of economic growth and integration. While this debate is not resolved, APEC can continue to make a major contribution to regional stability through its economic programmes. While Etel Solingen's argument that

economic liberalization by itself will create coalitions for peace is somewhat simplistic, APEC's continued support for economic reform, coupled with its concern for any serious tensions related to trade or access to resources, must be seen as a significant contribution to regional stability. Perhaps APEC needs to go further here. It has had the tendency to concentrate on those topics on which there is agreement, and to avoid areas of potential controversy. This has been defended as necessary in the early stages of the organization's development, but after more than a decade of getting to know one another, it is perhaps time to resolve to meet difficult topics more head-on. Once again, this will not be easy to implement, and there will have to be a slow process of development in this direction.

5. *Dealing with the new security agenda.* The topics covered in the "new security agenda" include many that are squarely within the scope of APEC's established activities. Food security, illegal population movements, international environmental problems, and AIDS are just some examples. Given some of the sensitivities about the individualistic focus of the human security debate, it is perhaps best to couch these concerns within the well-established agendas of comprehensive security. APEC seems best able to tackle these issues, given its concern with economic and technical co-operation. Certainly, it would be hard to fit these broader issues into the programmes of the ARF.

6. *Supporting the ARF in the search for convergent security.* I have argued that the current system of bilateral alliances is probably essential to the stability of the region, at least in the immediate future. Certainly, the United States and its allies see things that way. However, Tow's argument that multilateral approaches can supplement bilateral arrangements rather than conflict with them seems plausible. The encouragement of more "inclusive" bilateral systems is probably best left to the ARF as part of its proposed programme of preventive diplomacy, if this in fact eventuates. However, APEC can make a major contribution through the encouragement of greater regional understanding and co-operation, thus creating the foundations for more comprehensive multilateral approaches to security in the region.

7. *Engaging North Korea.* On a more specific topic, one of the key areas for concern in the region is the Korean question. At various times, both North and South Korea have raised the option of including North Korea in a number of regional institutions, such as the Asian Development Bank (ADB) and APEC. There seems to be some

important advantages in engaging North Korea in a level of dialogue, thus supporting the more progressive elements in that country. At present, APEC has an embargo on expanding its membership, but consideration should be given to involving North Korea in some of its Working Groups.

These are all vital areas for APEC to consider. In the final analysis, however, economic development in the region is dependent upon the creation of peace and stability. At present, we seem to be muddling through, but there are many areas of serious security concern in the region. Thus, the continued impotence of the ARF is a cause for concern. At present, APEC should be seen as supporting rather than duplicating or replacing the ARF, but if the ARF were to fail, it would be essential to search for an alternative security organization, and at that point it would be necessary to reconsider APEC's role.

References

Acharya, Amitav. "Human Security: What Kind for the Asia-Pacific?" In *The Human Face of Security: Asia-Pacific Perspectives*, edited by D. Dickens. Papers on Strategy and Defence No. 144. Canberra: Strategic and Defence Studies Centre, Australian National University, 2002.

Alagappa, Muthiah, ed. *Asian Security Practice: Material and Ideational Influences*. Stanford, California: Stanford University Press, 1998.

Anwar, Dewi Fortuna. "The Role, Significance and Prospects of APEC: Contributions to Regional Security". In *The Security Environment in the Asia-Pacific*, edited by Tien Hung-mao and Cheng, Tun-jen, pp. 129–53. Armonk: M.E. Sharpe, 2000.

Asia Pacific Foundation of Canada. "APEC after Shanghai: Prospects for a Broader Agenda". *Canada Asia Commentary*, no. 21 (2001).

Ball, D. "The Benefits of APEC for Security Co-operation in the Asia-Pacific Region". In *Power and Prosperity: Economics and Security Linkages in Asia-Pacific*, edited by S.L. Shirk, and C.P. Twomey. New Brunswick: Transaction Publishers, 1996.

_____. "Multilateral Security Co-operation in the Asia-Pacific". In *The Security Environment in the Asia-Pacific*, edited by Tien Hung-mao and Cheng, Tun-jen, pp. 129–53. Armonk: M.E. Sharpe, 2000a.

_____. *The Council for Security Co-operation in the Asia Pacific: Its Record and Prospects*. Canberra Papers on Strategy and Defence No. 139. Canberra: Strategic and Defence Studies Centre, Australian National University, 2000b.

Ball, D. and A. Acharya. *The Next Stage: Preventive Diplomacy and Security Co-operation in the Asia-Pacific Region*. Canberra Papers on Strategy and Defence no. 131. Canberra: Australian National University, 1999.

Bergsten, C. Fred. "APEC in 1997: Prospects and Possible Strategies". In *Whither APEC? The Progress to Date and Agenda for the Future,* edited by C. Fred

Bergsten, pp. 3–17. Washington DC: Institute for International Economics, 1997.

Betts, Richard. "Wealth, Power and Instability: East Asia and the United States after the Cold War". *International Security* 18, no. 3 (1993): 34–77.

Booth, Ken and Russell Trood, eds. *Strategic Cultures in the Asia-Pacific.* Houndmills: Macmillan, 1999.

Bracken, Paul. *Fire in the East: The Rise of Asian Military Power and the Second Nuclear Age.* New York: Harper Collins, 1998.

Broinowski, A., ed. *ASEAN in the 1990s.* London: MacMillan, 1990.

Buzan, B. and G. Segal "Rethinking Asian Security". *Survival* 36 (1994): 3–21.

Cai, Kevin. "Is a Free Trade Zone Emerging in Northeast Asia in the Wake of the Asian Financial Crisis". *Pacific Affairs* 74, no. 1 (2001): 7–24.

Caporaso, J.A. "International Relations Theory and Multilateralism: The Search for Foundations". In *Multilateralism Matters: The Theory and Praxis of an Institutional Form*, edited by J.G. Ruggie, pp. 51–90. New York: Columbia University Press, 1995.

Chia Siow Yue and M. Pacini. *ASEAN in the New Asia.* Singapore: Institute of Southeast Asian Studies, 1997.

Dibb, Paul. *Towards a New Balance of Power in Asia.* Adelphi Paper No 295. London: International Institute for Strategic Studies, 1995.

———. "A Trivial Strategic Age". *Quadrant* 14 (July–August 2000): 11–17.

Dupont, Alan. *The Future of the ASEAN Regional Forum: An Australian View.* Working Paper 321. Canberra: Strategic and Defence Studies Centre, Australian National University, 1998.

———. *East Asia Imperilled: Transnational Challenges to Security.* Cambridge: Cambridge University Press, 2001.

Evans, P. "Assessing the ARF and CSCAP". In *The Security Environment in the Asia-Pacific*, edited by Tien Hung-mao and Cheng Tun-jen, pp. 129–53. Armonk: M.E. Sharpe, 2000.

Friedberg, Aaron. "Ripe for Rivalry". *International Security* 18, no. 3 (1993): 5–33.

Haas, Michael. *The Asian Way of Peace: A Study of Regional Cooperation.* New York: Praeger, 1989.

Hellmann, Donald, and Kenneth Pyle. *From APEC to Xanadu: Creating a Viable Community in the Post-Cold War Pacific.* Armonk: M.E. Sharpe, 1997.

Henderson, Jeannie. *Reassessing ASEAN.* Adelphi Paper No. 328. London: Oxford University Press, 1999.

Higgott, R. "The International Relations of the Asian Economic Crisis: A Study in the Politics of Resentment". In *Politics and Markets in the Wake of the Asian Crisis,* edited by R. Robison, M. Beeson, K. Jayasuriya, and Kim Hyuk-Rae, pp. 261–82. London: Routledge, 2000.

Jervis, Robert. "Security Regimes". *International Organization* 36 (1982): 357–58.

———. " Realism, Neoliberalism and Co-operation: Understanding the Debate". *International Security* 24 (1999): 42–63.

Khoo, Nicholas, and Michael Smith. "The Future of American Hegemony in the Asia-Pacific: A Concert of Asia or a Clear Pecking Order". *Australian Journal of International Affairs* 56 (2002): 65–81.

Kissinger, Henry. *Diplomacy.* New York: Simon & Schuster, 1994.

Knutsen, Torbjorn L. *The Rise and Fall of World Orders.* Manchester: Manchester University Press, 1999.

Kwon Youngmin. *Regional Community Building in East Asia.* Seoul: Yonsei University Press, 2002.

Lake, David, and Patrick Morgan. "The New Regionalism in Security Affairs". In *Regional Orders: Building Security in a New World,* edited by David Lake and Patrick Morgan, pp. 3–19. University Park, Pennsylvania: University of Pennsylvania Press, 1997.

Mahbubani, Kishore. *Can Asians Think?* Singapore: Times Books International, 1998.

McKay, John. "Australia as an Asian Middle Power: The Search for a New Role". *Korean Journal of International Studies* 27, no. 1 (1996): 1–28.

McRae, Rob, and Don Hubert. *Human Security and the New Diplomacy: Protecting People, Promoting Peace.* Montreal & Kingston: McGill-Queens University Press, 2001.

Maull, Hanns. "APEC: Its Place in International Relations". In *Asia-Pacific Economic Co-operation (APEC): The First Decade,* edited by J. Ruland, E. Manske, and W. Draghuhn, pp. 16–34. London: Routledge Curzon, 2002.

Mearsheimer, John. *The Tragedy of Great Power Politics.* New York: W.W. Norton, 2001.

Morrison, Charles, Akira Kojima Akira and Hanns Maull. *Community Building with Pacific Asia.* New York, Paris & Tokyo: Trilateral Commission, 1997.

Nye, Joseph. *The Paradox of American Power.* Oxford: Oxford University Press, 2002.

Peng Dajin. "The Changing Nature of East Asia as an Economic Region". *Pacific Affairs* 73, no. 2 (2000): 171–92.

Press-Barnathan, Galia. "The Lure of Regional Security Arrangements: The United States and Regional Security Co-operation in Asia and Europe". *Security Studies* 10 (2000): 49–97.

Ravenhill, John. *APEC and the Construction of Pacific Rim Regionalism.* Cambridge: Cambridge University Press, 2001.

Richardson, James. "The Declining Probability of War Thesis: How Relevant for the Asia-Pacific?" In *Asia-Pacific Security: The Economics-Politics Nexus,* edited by S. Harris, and A. Mack, pp. 81–100. Sydney: Allen & Unwin, 1997.

Ruggie, J.G. "Multilateralism: The Anatomy of an Institution". In *Multilateralism Matters: The Theory and Praxis of an International Forum,* edited by J.G. Ruggie, pp. 3–50. New York: Columbia University Press, 1995.

Shirk, Susan. "Asia-Pacific Regional Security: Balance of Power or Concert of Powers?" In *Regional Orders: Building Security in a New World,* edited by David Lake & Patrick Morgan, pp. 245–70. University Park, Pennsylvania: University of Pennsylvania Press, 1997.

Singh, Daljit. "Evolution of the Security Dialogue Process in the Asia-Pacific". In *Southeast Asian Perspectives on Security,* edited by Derek da Cunha, pp. 35–59. Singapore: Institute of Southeast Asian Studies, 2000.

Singh, Jasjit. *Nuclear India*. New Delhi: Knowledge World & Institute for Defence Studies and Analyses, 1998.

Solingen, Etel. *Regional Orders at Century's Dawn: Global and Domestic Influences on Grand Strategy*. Princeton, NJ: Princeton University Press, 1998.

Sopiee, Noordin. "Should APEC Address Security Issues?" In *Whither APEC? The Progress to Date and Agenda for the Future*, edited by C. Fred Bergsten, pp. 207–9. Washington DC: Institute for International Economics, 1997.

Tow, William. *Asia-Pacific Strategic Relations: Seeking Convergent Security*. Cambridge: Cambridge University Press, 2001.

Tow, William, Ramesh Thakur, and Hyun In-Taek. *Asia's Emerging Regional Order: Reconciling Traditional and Human Security*. Tokyo: United Nations University Press, 2000.

Tow, William T., and Russell Trood. "Linkages between Traditional Security and Human Security". In *Asia's Emerging Regional Order: Reconciling Traditional & Human Security*, edited by William T. Tow, Ramesh Thakur, and Hyun In-Taek, pp. 13–22. Tokyo: United Nations University Press, 2000.

Ungerer, Carl, and Marianne Hanson. *The Politics of Nuclear Non-Proliferation*. Sydney: Allen & Unwin, 2001.

United Nations. *Human Development Report*. New York: United Nations Development Program, 1994.

Van Ness, Peter. "Globalization and Security in East Asia". *Asian Perspective* 23, no. 4 (1999): 315–42.

Won Yong-Kul. "East Asian Economic Integration: A Korean Perspective". *Journal of East Asian Affairs* 15, no. 1 (2001): 72–96.

Yuan Jing-dong. "The War on Terrorism: China's Opportunities and Dilemmas". *Nautilus Special Forum* (#SF-14). Nautilus Institute 2001 (www.nautilus.org/fora/Special-Policy-Forum/14 Yuan.html)

Zheng Yongnian. *Discovering Nationalism in China: Modernization, Identity, and International Relations*. Cambridge: Cambridge University Press, 1999.

Zysman, J., and M. Borrus. "Lines of Fracture, Webs of Cohesion: Economic Interconnections and Security Politics in Asia". In *Power and Prosperity: Economics and Security Linkages in Asia-Pacific*, edited by S.L. Shirk, and C. Twomey, pp. 77–99. New Brunswick: Transaction Publishers, 1996.

INDEX